Let's Go!

Let's Go!

Benjamin Orr and The Cars

Joe Milliken

ROWMAN & LITTLEFIELD
Lanham • Boulder • New York • London

Published by Rowman & Littlefield
An imprint of The Rowman & Littlefield Publishing Group, Inc.
4501 Forbes Boulevard, Suite 200, Lanham, Maryland 20706
www.rowman.com

Unit A, Whitacre Mews, 26-34 Stannary Street, London SE11 4AB

British Library Cataloguing in Publication Information Available

Library of Congress Cataloging-in-Publication Data

Names: Milliken, Joe, 1966– author.
Title: Let's go! : Benjamin Orr and The Cars / Joe Milliken.
Description: Lanham : Rowman & Littlefield, [2018] | Includes bibliographical references and index.
Identifiers: LCCN 2018026463 (print) | LCCN 2018027733 (ebook) | ISBN 9781538118665 (electronic) | ISBN 9781538118658 (cloth : alk. paper)
Subjects: LCSH: Orr, Benjamin. | Cars (Musical group) | Singers—United States—Biography. | Rock musicians—United States—Biography. | Bass guitarists—United States—Biography.
Classification: LCC ML420.O8136 (ebook) | LCC ML420.O8136 M56 2018 (print) | DDC 782.42166092/2 [B]—dc23
LC record available at https://lccn.loc.gov/2018026463

♾™ The paper used in this publication meets the minimum requirements of American National Standard for Information Sciences—Permanence of Paper for Printed Library Materials, ANSI/NISO Z39.48-1992.

Printed in the United States of America

Contents

Foreword

$\mathcal{I}$ grew up a very lucky kid. My dad was a TV producer with a nationally syndicated show called *Upbeat*. From the beginning of the show, I had the job of writing and holding the cue cards for the host, and I also got to hang out with rock stars, from Otis Redding to Simon and Garfunkel.

My journey in music really started on *Upbeat*, moving from cue card kid to associate-producer of the show at age fifteen. I started in radio at eighteen with WNCR, moving over to help launch what became one of the biggest FM stations in the country, WMMS. I moved on to artist management, working with Joe Walsh, Yusuf (Cat Stevens), Dickey Betts from The Allman Brothers, Kenny Loggins, The Michael Stanley Band, and others.

But *Upbeat* also had a house band that would back up these artists as they lip-synced their records. Leslie Gore, Marvin Gaye, Stevie Wonder, and dozens more stood in front of this local band called The Grasshoppers. This band also had a couple of regional hits, like "Who Wears Mod Socks," a takeoff on the old hit "Who Wears Short Shorts," and "Pink Champagne and Red Roses," a ballad sung by a guy named Benny Eleven Letters, so named because no one could pronounce his real name. Benny was the "McCartney" of the Grasshoppers, who had gained enough fame from the TV show to open for The Dave Clark Five. I got to know Benny quite well over the years; I even chose his band to play my bar mitzvah. My friends and I spent most weekends going from club to club to see The Grasshoppers perform. Benny always had me on the guest list, which was a big deal for my pals. I'd always hang out with him between sets because, well . . . yes, he was a good friend, but he also attracted all the girls!

I grew up and became a local disc jockey; we stayed in touch. Benny called me one day to tell me that he had a new band called The Cars and he

Ben visits David Spero at the M105 Studios in Cleveland.
Photo by Bob Ferrell, courtesy of David Spero

was now calling himself Ben Orr. Because of our friendship, I played their record. What I didn't realize was that this was a Hall-of-Fame-caliber band that would change the world. Whenever he came to town, he would come in for an interview on my radio show and we *always* found time to share a meal or two. I always got to eat. Benny basically just signed autographs and had his picture taken.

In many ways, he never left Cleveland, returning to sing on local records to raise money for different causes, *always* giving a shout-out to his hometown and never forgetting where he came from.

I ran into Ben at the grand opening of the Rock & Roll Hall of Fame in 1995, and we shared a table for dinner. We caught up on the years that had passed. The event took place under a giant tent on the Cleveland lakefront. Many of the rock royalty were there; Dylan, Springsteen, Aretha, Lou Reed, The Kinks, Jerry Lee Lewis, and many more. Yet all night long the Clevelanders, among many others, stopped to say hi to Benny. It's funny because I don't remember him even once mentioning that he thought that someday The Cars would be inducted.

The next call I got from him was to tell me that he had pancreatic cancer. I realized this was a call to say good-bye. Benny sounded very weak, but his sense of humor was still intact. We talked about pride in our city, the mark he had made in music, and his love for my father, Herman Spero, and for Joe Mayer. I could hardly breathe when I got off the phone. Though it took a lot out of me emotionally, it meant the world to me that he had called. A few days later he was gone. He was one of my oldest friends, and to die so young and at the top of his game was truly a devastating loss.

I helped put together a celebration of Ben's life at the Rock Hall theater and gave a eulogy that I'm not sure how I got through. Our "Benny Eleven Letters" was gone, but will never be forgotten. And as his life story is told here by music journalist and author Joe Milliken, Ben and The Cars have finally been inducted into the 2018 class of The Rock & Roll Hall of Fame—a fitting tribute to the man that helped make Cleveland "The Rock and Roll City."

David Spero, 2018

Timeline of Bands

1960–1963:   The Cyclones (Ben on drums; Lou Fazio, Phil Oswald, Bob
             Paris, Frank Perry, Bruce Solomon, Jerry Zadar)
1962:   The Del-Fi's (Ben on drums, vocals; Jeff Dickson, Harry
             Harwat)
1964–1965:   The Grasshoppers (Ben on vocals, rhythm guitar, drums; Louis
             Pratile, Sid Turner, Jerry Zadar; managed by Joe Mayer)
             The Grasshoppers #2 (Ben on vocals and rhythm guitar; Rick
             Caon, John Matuska, Wayne Weston; managed by Joe Mayer)
1965–1967:   The Proof Sets/Mixed Emotions (Ben on lead guitar, vocals;
             Johnny Joe Gardina, Chris Kamburoff, Joey Kurilec, Jimmy
             Vince; managed by Joe Mayer)
1967:   The Rush (Ben on vocals, rhythm guitar; John Aleksic, Rick
             Caon, Dan Klawon)
1967:   Colours (Ben on vocals, rhythm guitar; John Matuska,
             Wayne Weston; managed by Bob Bobchuck, Walt Masky,
             Carl Reese)
1969:   ID Nirvana (Ben on vocals; Stephen Dodge, Dan Donovan,
             Joe Donovan, Richard Otcasek, John Wiley)
1970:   Leatherwood (Ben on vocals; Richard Otcasek, Mike Patter-
             son, John Wiley; managed by Al Schwartz)
1972–1973:   Milkwood (Ben on vocals, percussion, bass; Jas Goodkind,
             Richard Otcasek; managed by Al Schwartz)
1974:   Richard and The Rabbits (Ben on vocals, bass; Greg Hawkes,
             Fuzzbee Morse, Richard Otcasek, Ron Riddle; managed by
             Allan Kaufman)
1974–1976:   Ocasek and Orr (Ben on vocals, bass; Allan Kaufman, Rich-
             ard Ocasek; managed by Allan Kaufman)

1975–1976:   Cap'n Swing (Ben on vocals; Glenn Evans, Ric Ocasek, Todd Roberto, Danny Schliftman, Elliot Steinberg; managed by Allan Kaufman)

1976:   The Cars (Ben on vocals, bass; Elliot [Steinberg] Easton, Danny [Schliftman] Louis, Ric Ocasek, David Robinson; managed by Allan Kaufman)

1977–1987:   The Cars #2 (Ben on vocals, bass; Elliot Easton, Greg Hawkes, Ric Ocasek, David Robinson; managed by Fred Lewis, Steve Berkowitz, Elliot Roberts, Lookout Management)

1994:   ORR Band (Ben on vocals, rhythm guitar; John Kalishes, Igor Khoroshev, John Muzzy, Charlie O'Neal, Rick O'Neal; tour manager David Tedeschi)

1995:   ORR Band #2 (Ben on vocals, rhythm guitar; Joe Holaday, John Kalishes, John Muzzy, Bob Squires, Tommy West; tour manager David Tedeschi)

1996–1999:   ORR Band #3 (Ben on vocals, rhythm guitar; Rich Bartlett, Brad Hallen, Tom Hambridge, John Kalishes, Chris Lannon, Ross Ramsay; tour manager David Tedeschi)

1998–1999:   Voices of Classic Rock (Ben on vocals, rhythm guitar; John Cafferty, Bobby Kimball, Mike Reno, Mickey Thomas, Joe Lynn Turner, among others)

1999–2000:   Big People (Ben on vocals, bass; Jeff Carlisi, Liberty DeVitto, Derek St. Holmes, Pat Travers; managed by Bill Johnson and Crossover Entertainment)

GUEST APPEARANCES IN BANDS

1963:   C-Notes

1968:   The Dante's/Outsiders

1995:   The Beacon Hillbillies (Ben on vocals, guitar; Kevin McCarty, John Kalishes)

About the Book

$\mathcal{I}$ was a junior high school kid in 1979 when I first discovered The Cars, hearing songs from their iconic first two albums all over the radio. I'd buy the rock magazines *Circus*, *Hit Parader*, and *Rock Scene* just to learn more about The Cars and all the other cool rock bands of the day.

Originally from Boston, I somehow felt a connection with this new, hip band emerging from Beantown. I bought a "Cars" poster at the record store and started dropping quarters into the jukebox at the local pizza joint, selecting "Let's Go," "Good Times Roll," and "Just What I Needed," over and over again. How ironic that some forty years later "Let's Go" would become the title and rallying cry for my first book.

I actually remember the summer day when I first heard The Cars, while catching a ride to a baseball game with my coach. He inserted an *eight-track* tape of The Cars' debut album into the deck and that very first listen was all it took. Hearing those distinctive "car-horn" synthesizer notes and the techno-sleek drum patterns of "Good Times Roll" had me hooked from the first song! I was instantly drawn to their classic rock sensibilities mixed with this quirky (or dare I say, "new wave") rock-pop sound that left quite an impression on this young rocker. The Cars were just *so* damn cool.

The next day, I went up the street to my buddy Mike's house to tell him about this great new band I had discovered and sure enough, he had already gotten the album! So we cranked it up, shook the walls, and within a couple days I convinced him to let me borrow *The Cars* . . . and that very album still sits in my collection, because I never gave it back. Sorry, Mike.

I never had the pleasure of seeing the band perform live but to this day, The Cars have remained one of my sentimental favorite bands; catchy, yet often transparent lyrics built around unique melodies and hooks that were often uncommon, yet somehow perfect for both rock *and* pop radio. The music featured solid rhythms, precise guitar solos, and innovative keys and synthesizers, all balanced off by the lead-vocal tandem of the mysterious, songwriting Ric Ocasek and the smooth-cool bassist, Benjamin Orr.

The Cars worked hard to create a specific image and really took care of it, as they melded rock, pop, and that sort of (dare I say it, again) "new wave" label into their own unique music brand. The Cars also sounded great through the car speakers (go figure) while cruising around town, and in fact, Ocasek himself once told *Trouser Press* in 1979; "It's fun . . . it is car music. One of the best places to listen to music is in a car. You're in your own world when you're driving around, listening to the radio."

Boston-based author and music journalist Brett Milano, who is interviewed within these pages, put it so well in his own book, *The Sound of Our Town: A History of Boston Rock & Roll*, when he wrote, "For anyone who was around at the time, it's nearly impossible to hear 'Drive' or 'My Best Friend's Girl' without thinking of the clubs you went to, which classes you cut, or whom you were in love with circa 1980. The Cars also looked the part, with a Bowie-esque sense of fashion and sharp outfits. The sound crossed chic European influences (Bowie, Kraftwerk, Roxy Music) with a sense of cheap thrills rock-and-roll."

The Cars, along with other bands of that time, like Talking Heads, The Police, and Blondie, bridged gaps between rock-and-roll attitudes, the so-called "new wave" sound, and the Billboard charts!

Although I wouldn't have foreseen Mr. Orr as the subject of my first book, once I did some research and started learning about Ben's lifelong journey in music, which began behind the drums at age eleven, it was "all systems go" and the project became a labor of love and a great learning experience. I truly feel privileged and lucky to tell Ben's story and confirm once and for all that he really was even cooler than we thought!

While the band that made Ben famous is (obviously) very prominently featured throughout, this is not meant to be a *Cars* book. Rather, it's the life story of a musician who grew up as a teen star out of the suburbs of Cleveland, long before his partnership with Ric Ocasek and the formation of the band that would ultimately make him world famous.

The book also offers up various tidbits regarding the city of Cleveland's rich music history as it relates to Ben, and in fact, the Cleveland aspect throughout is a tip of the cap to him, for Ben was *very* loyal to the city and the people and musicians he grew up with. I believe Ben would appreciate that I have slightly expanded upon his story to shed some light on just a few of the many talented Cleveland-area musicians who, perhaps, never got that big break or the attention they deserved. As you will read, throughout his life Ben was *all about* encouraging others around him to make music and perform.

There is also a lot of "Cars history" in the book, as many who are interviewed talk not only about their fond memories of Ben, but also about some of their memories and interactions with the band. In that context, the book also sheds a bit of light on the eclectic Boston music scene during The Cars' era as well.

Furthermore, this book is not a "tell-all" tale of rock-and-roll excess, but rather a respectful account of an often-private man who also had *a lot* of fun. A serious, hardworking entertainer who, like all of us, certainly had his ups and downs along the way but *never* gave up his dream of being in a successful national band.

This book has been an eleven-year journey of writing, researching, investigating, interviewing, photo gathering, and following a very long trail of leads. One really has *no idea* (I know I didn't) how many people a rock star can know and associate with, and truth be told, I could have gone on with interviews seemingly forever. However, I did interview well over one hundred friends, family members, and music associates spanning Ben's entire life and, hopefully, have crafted a unique perspective on a ridiculously talented and mysterious figure who is described in these pages by a childhood friend as the "Elvis of Cleveland."

One final aspect of the book that requires mentioning involves all the different monikers people use in referring to Orr throughout the book (as well as Ric). In his younger, Cleveland, days, many friends and family affectionately called him "Benny" or "Benny Eleven Letters," while Cars fans and the music press over the years have referred to him as both "Benjamin" and simply "Ben." Within the interview quotes throughout the book, whatever name someone referred to the man as is what you get. However, let it also be known that Ben once told a fellow musician (as quoted in these pages) that "It's just Ben."

So, without further ado, our story begins with the aforementioned music journalist and author, Brett Milano, who had the privilege of interviewing the band in 1999 during their last public appearance together as The Cars. The press conference and interview took place just days before Orr's untimely passing.

Prologue:
Full Circle Cars

The scene was Atlanta's Turner Studios, at a press conference to announce a Rhino Home Video DVD release from The Cars titled *The Cars Live: Recorded Live on Musikladen 1979*. The DVD chronicled a rare concert recorded at Radio Bremen Studios for the longtime German television music show, during The Cars' first (and, surprisingly, only) European tour in 1978.

The day also marked the first time that all five original members—bassist and vocalist Benjamin Orr; songwriter, guitarist, and vocalist Ric Ocasek; multi-instrumentalist Greg Hawkes; drummer David Robinson; and guitarist Elliot Easton—had appeared together publicly in nearly thirteen years. The reunion was surely a welcome sight for loyal Cars fans, but there was also a sense of uneasy urgency in the air as well, for Orr had recently been diagnosed with pancreatic cancer, a sad and seemingly unfair fate for this charismatic entertainer.

The Cars did an exclusive interview that day, with Milano reminiscing about the *Musikladen* concert as well as their historic careers, and the complete uncut interview is included on the official DVD release. Milano was already very familiar with the band, having previously done interviews with individual members, as well as some public relations work for Elliot Easton.

Brett Milano: "Rhino Records had set me up with the interview on short notice and had flown me to Atlanta. By then, all the Cars knew me somewhat; I had interviewed Ric and had some friendly encounters with the other band members as well. I originally met Elliot when I was writing for *Boston Rock* magazine and he had just released his solo album.

"I had also been brought in to write liner notes for The Cars' two-disc anthology, as well as the expanded version of the debut album. I imagine the whole band gave me the okay to conduct the interview, plus, I think they simply liked the idea of using a Boston-based writer."

The event certainly was a historic occasion for The Cars and their fans, for what had essentially ended in a split between Orr and Ocasek in 1988 had now come full circle, reuniting the band's heart-and-soul duo after being apart for over a decade. Yes, this reunion was (using a play on Ocasek's lyric) "just what they needed," at a time when the guys needed to rally around their friend and bandmate.

Brett Milano: "Without a doubt, it was apparent that Ric was very supportive of Ben during the interview and praised his singing to the point of denigrating his own voice. He made a couple references to Ben being the star of the band, which can be viewed on the DVD interview because they didn't edit anything from it. I don't really know what happened leading up to the interview, but I think the DVD reunion was their chance to, once again, do something really good together as The Cars.

"I think the band had already gone through whatever personal reconciliation happened well before I turned up for the interview in the early afternoon. Obviously, there was some distress over Ben's condition, and it certainly was a concerning situation.

"My impression of Ben that day was that he was friendly and humbled. You could see him sort of shrugging off the idea of his being the band's sex symbol. Yet, even with his health failing, you could still see him summoning the charisma he'd always had onstage.

"As a person, I wish I'd gotten to know him better. As a musician, he was simply impeccable. To me, The Cars always walked the line between rock music and high-tech, with Ben's bass playing really holding the two factions together. But most of all, it was that voice. Maybe someone can name a more nuanced, more emotive vocal performance from the 80s than 'Drive,' but I sure can't.

"That whole event was really dramatic for me as a fan. On one hand, I was seeing The Cars back together and getting to be a part of that history; on the other hand, however, I had to absorb that Ben wasn't well. It was extremely bittersweet."

For that one day and despite looking thin and fragile from the illness, Ben Orr once again flashed that trademark persona that, for over a decade, captured the imagination of Cars fans worldwide. However, this long overdue reunion would also mark the band's last get-together, because of the unfortunate passing of Ben a very short time later.

The day would mark the end of an era, a long road that ironically enough did not begin for Orr in Boston with The Cars, but in Cleveland, the home of the Rock & Roll Hall of Fame. Affectionately known by many early on as "Benny," or "Benny Eleven Letters," he was a Cleveland icon from the suburb of Parma Heights and a rock-and-roller from the start!

The Early Years

A CAR IS BORN

$\mathcal{B}$enjamin Orzechowski (no middle name) was born on September 8, 1947, in Lakewood, Ohio, the son of devout, Russian-Orthodox parents Charles and Betty. The Orzechowskis had migrated from Russia and Czechoslovakia and settled in Ohio. Their first home was located on West 49th Street in Cleveland before they moved to the suburb of Parma Heights. After living in a house on Commonwealth Boulevard, they finally settled into a modest ranch-style home at 6909 Maplewood Avenue. Charles worked as a security guard at the White Sewing Machine Company for more than thirty years, and he and Betty, a homemaker, were both singers and dancers and very much enjoyed music and entertainment.

As European immigrants, the Orzechowskis were certainly old-fashioned, overprotective, and very much devoted to their only child, Benjamin. In fact, and although he was quite athletic, their son was not allowed to play sports for fear of injury, and later when he bought his first car, his mother would not allow the vehicle to leave the driveway until it had been properly blessed by the local priest. By age eleven, "Benny" was already discovering music and would entertain his parents and their friends by mimicking Elvis songs in their living room. "I always knew I had something special," Ben once told *Rolling Stone* magazine.

Ben started taking drum lessons and became a hard-core Beatles fan, right down to the Beatle boots and mop-top haircut, a cut that actually created one of Ben's first tastes of the spotlight when a few years later, he was featured in a popular *Life* magazine photo spread about music and the "mop-top craze."

Ben's childhood home at 6909 Maplewood Avenue, Parma Heights, Ohio.
Photo by Chris Kamburoff

Infant Ben.
Courtesy of Diane Kokai-Akins

Ironically, this very article was read by his far-in-the-future Cars band-mate, drummer David Robinson, who had actually ingrained that very article into his young and impressionable mind.

David Robinson: "When I was a kid, that was prime reading for me. *Life* magazine would come in the mail, and I remember reading that article and literally memorizing every photo and thinking, 'Wow! Look at that long hair!' I probably ruined the magazine from flipping through it so much, and of course, Ben had never mentioned the article . . . *ever*.

"But one time, somebody else brought up the article to Ben and I overheard what they were saying and of course, it wasn't even Ben who had brought it up.

"I said 'Ben, you were in *Life* magazine?'

"He just played it off and replied 'Oh, yeah-yeah, kind of.'

"Then the other person said 'Yes, Ben was in this *Life* magazine article about Beatle haircuts.'

"I couldn't believe it! 'Ben, you were the kid with the hairnet on your head in that article?' And he just played it off like it was nothing, not even explaining anything about it while I was jumping up and down and telling him how much that photo had become a part of my psyche and that I knew it so well! But that was Ben, so unassuming and always playing it cool."

Ben started playing the drums and took lessons early on. "I always wanted to make music and sing," Ben told *The Plain Dealer*'s Tracy St. John in 1985. "I had a lot of encouragement from my parents. They started me with drum lessons, and I had 13 years of formal lessons."

Once he began participating in bands, Ben started learning other instruments as well, quite a talent to have at such a young age. His parents were very supportive of his musical endeavors, despite the otherwise reserved and protective environment they provided him. Wayne Weston was a local drummer, a bandmate, and Ben's close friend for many years.

Wayne Weston: "Benny's mom was always great to us in the early days. She was an old-fashioned woman who spoke with a thick European accent. We used to rehearse in Benny's basement or in the garage and she would always be asking us if we wanted something to eat or drink. Benny would usually say no, but she would cook stuff up for us anyway. She also kept an impeccable household. . . . I mean, you could eat off the floor in the garage!

"When the weather was nice, we would open up the garage doors to practice and kids would gather in the driveway like it was a teen dance or some kind of mini concert. We'd be rehearsing, trying to learn new songs, and it would sometimes be hard to concentrate with all the kids around. After a while, too many kids would show up to watch us play, so the police would come around and break up the rehearsals because kids were spilling into the street and causing a safety issue."

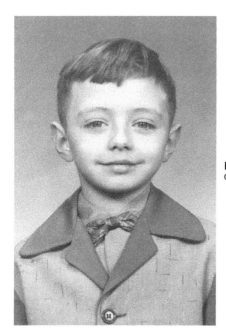

Elementary school photo.
Courtesy of Diane Kokai-Akins

Ben's eighteenth birthday, at home with his mother, Betty. Joe Kurilec also sitting.
Courtesy of Diane Kokai-Akins

Ohio native Kristina Orr was Ben's first wife and had over a decade-long relationship with him.

Kris Orr: "Ben told me that when he was little, whenever he got punished, his mom would make him go into the basement. So he would just go down there and practice 'rhythms' on a block of wood with rubber on top. He loved it because no one would disturb him and he could practice."

CYCLONES AND THE DEL-FI'S

At age thirteen in 1960, Ben officially joined his first band, an "all-instrumental" group called The Starlighters, which would become The Cyclones shortly thereafter. The original lineup featured Frank Perry on guitar, Lou Fazio on piano, and Dennis Vargo on drums. Shortly thereafter, Phil Oswald joined on saxophone, Bruce Solomon on guitar, and Ben on drums. Bob Paris, Jerry Zadar, Terry Veal, and Gary Droste would also spend time in the band.

Frank Perry: "I formed The Cyclones, and there was a singer who went by the name of Johnny Cardinal, and he wanted our group to be his backup band. Dennis Vargo was our drummer, but he was going off to college in the

Ben's first band at age thirteen, The Cyclones.
Courtesy of Chris Kamburoff

fall, so Johnny took us over to Benny's house for an audition, and we all hit it off with him right from the start.

"We were actually first called The Starlighters, but the band really didn't get off the ground until Phil Oswald and then Bruce Solomon joined, and we changed our name to The Cyclones. We had a 'Johnny and The Hurricanes' style of music, so we thought 'Cyclones' would be an appropriate name."

Lou Fazio: "I started seeing this girl named Sue, and she was Frank Perry's sister. They had a piano at their house and we used to fool around playing it. One day, Frank said that we should start a band, and that's how The Cyclones got started, and I was a part of the band for a couple years or so.

"Benny was a little younger than the rest of us, but he was a good guy and was already a really good drummer. After leaving the band, I never ran into him again, and actually, I never knew that he was such a talented guy [who became famous] until recently.

"After having pancreatic surgery, myself, in 2015, another friend of ours from school mentioned that Benny Orzechowski had died from pancreatic cancer. I guess, because he had changed his name early on and we were busy raising our families, we never realized his fame. We really wish now that we would have known while he was still alive."

Frank Perry: "Benny's parents were strict and wouldn't let him go with us to play at some places [namely, bars]. So, we had an alternative drummer, Terry Veal, from a band called The Firelords. Also, Bruce Solomon left the band for a while, so we picked up a guitarist named Gary Droste, and then after he left, guitarist Bob Paris joined. Bruce came back and sometime later, Bob's school friend Jerry Zadar joined. Jerry brought his Fender six-string bass that we all thought was very cool, so we decided to keep him in the band. It turned out to be a very good decision.

"Benny was really good, and I *did* think he was going to go places, even back then. At such a young age, he was already really good and devoted to music, *and* the girls."

Bob Paris had joined the lineup after his mother made a connection with Benny's father, and they had decided their musical sons should connect and play together.

Bob Paris: "My mom worked at a restaurant/bar on Pearl Road in Parma and got to know Benny's father, who frequented the establishment. They thought Benny and I should team up, and although I was not playing in a band at that time, I joined The Cyclones and ended up staying in the band for a couple years.

"At some point after I joined, Frank Perry left the band and I sort of took over the duties of arranging things and booking shows. I had Cyclones business cards made up, but they didn't have Benny's name on them because he was still too young, don't you know. The card had my name and Phil Oswald's on it."

Original Cyclones guitarist Bruce Solomon declined to be interviewed. However, his younger brother, Roland, remembers The Cyclones practicing in the Solomon's house. A keyboard player, Roland would also go on to play a role in the Cleveland music scene.

Roland Solomon: "I was only around eight years old, but I can remember The Cyclones practicing in our house. We lived right down the street from Benny, and my mom was friends with his mother. Even at a young age, I distinctly remember Benny as being very cool.

"One time when the band was setting up to practice I sat down at Benny's drum kit and started hitting, but when my older brother told me to 'get out of here,' Benny just said, 'It's okay, man, let him play.'"

Jerry Zadar: "When I first started playing in The Cyclones I played rhythm guitar, and it must have been during a time when the original band lineup was making some changes. Perhaps Bruce Solomon was leaving the band, but Bob Paris wanted to add a bass player so I switched to the bass. But I also remember playing both rhythm guitar and bass with Bob, Phil Oswald, and Bruce. As I recall, all these players would change from time to time."

It was also around this time, 1962, that Bob Paris would first expose Ben to playing a guitar.

Bob Paris: "I was also a music teacher and had a basement studio in my house, with a separate entrance, called Music Manor. I had a Fender Jazzmaster guitar and I showed Benny some chords on it. I also bought him his very first guitar, a 1962 Kay Arch-top."

The Cyclones would play in the WKYW Traveling Road Show in the early sixties, and a young Ben was already playing the part of a rock star: longer hair, hip clothes, and those heavy-lidded blue eyes, the very persona that would one day make him famous.

Frank Perry: "The Traveling Road Show was started by KYW's Arlene Blank and we were the top group among several. The program did free concerts for hospitals and schools that were doing fundraisers, and it not only featured bands, but also singers [and] magic acts, and they even had a clown as part of the show. It didn't necessarily get us a whole lot of exposure, but it was still a lot of fun to play live!"

Along with The Cyclones, in 1962 at age fifteen, Ben was briefly in another band called The Del-Fi's, a trio featuring Ben on drums and vocals, Jeff Dickson on guitar, and Harry Harwat on accordion. Ben would play mostly polkas in The Del-Fi's through the summer months of that year, but also remained a member of The Cyclones until 1963.

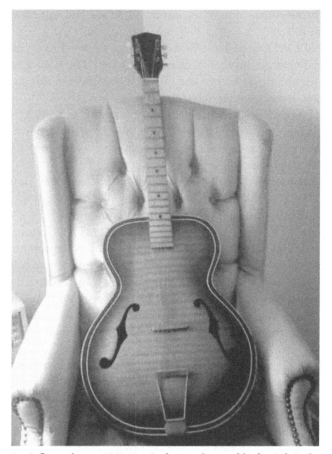

Ben's first guitar, a 1962 Kay Arch-top, given to him by Bob Paris.
Courtesy of Bob Paris

Ben came to join The Del-Fi's when his father and Harry's dad, who were friends from church, decided the boys should get a group together to play at the Lemko Club that the men frequented, which was located on the south side of Cleveland and would much later gain fame when featured in the 1977 film *The Deer Hunter*.

Harry Harwat: "My father, who *made* me play the accordion, got to know Benny's dad through church. They used to go to the Lemko Club, along with a couple other bars, and they became friends.

"So our dads were at the Lemko Club and the management mentioned that they were looking for a band to play. So, my father says, 'Well, my son plays the accordion.' Then Mr. Orzechowski says, 'And my son plays the drums.' So I come home one night and there's Benny and his dad in my house with his drums all set up and they say, 'We're gonna start a band, so let's practice!'"

Jeff Dickson: "After track practice at James Ford Rhodes High School, Harry told me that I had to get a guitar because we had a job on Saturday night. When I asked my parents about the guitar, they asked, 'Do you have a job?' And when I said 'Yes, we're going to make five dollars each,' we went to Sears.

"I didn't know a thing about guitars, and after four days of intense practice my soft fingertips were bleeding, but I had learned a handful of chords."

The Lemko Club was an old-fashioned bar in an old brick building on the corner. Many of the customers were of Polish and Ukraine descent, and the club had strong ties to the church, which is how Harry had gotten the gig. The bar was empty when they began to play, Jeff's fingers began to bleed again, and as they continued to play their polkas, the bar and the dance floor began to fill up.

Jeff Dickson: "As the night got later, louder, and happier after every vodka, a waving arm slapped the microphone into my mouth. These were those big, Elvis Presley microphones and my lip began to bleed. At the end of the night, Harry, Benny, and I took our five dollars each and vowed to practice."

The Del-Fi's practiced at the Orzechowski house as they got ready for their next gig, an Italian wedding reception, and they also worked a couple of Buddy Holly covers into their set of polkas. They lined up gigs throughout the summer months of that year, but the momentum ended in the fall when Harwat graduated from high school and went to Kent State University, while Dickson went to Ohio University.

Bob Paris: "After The Cyclones, I was in a band called the C-Notes. One time, after our drummer quit, I told the band that I knew this little guy who was a good drummer, and after I cleared it with his mom, I brought Benny to this bar in Cleveland. It was Diane's Lounge on Lorain Avenue, and he sat in with the band and just played great!

"Then, when we asked him if he wanted to sing, Benny just stood up and while still playing the kick-drum and cymbal, sang 'Whole Lotta Shakin' Goin' On' and everyone just loved it!

"I had a good relationship with Benny's parents, and I remained friends with his mom for many years. I would pick Benny up and bring him home after Cyclones shows, and I also gave him a few informal guitar lessons in my studio. I also remember bringing my car, a 1960 Chevy Impala convertible, over to Benny's house and we'd wash the car in the driveway because my water at home had too many minerals in it and would spot the paint. We certainly had some great times and remained friends for many years.

"Sometime in the nineties my wife and I visited his mother at her house and she brought us into Benny's bedroom growing up. The room was left like it was when he was young, including some of his clothes in the closet and she also showed us his military uniform. She then showed me a guitar in the closet. When I told her that it was Benny's first guitar and the one I had given to him, she was gracious enough to let me take it home, and I have it to this day."

Paris went into the service in late 1963, while Ben continued playing in The Cyclones and started wearing leather pants and loving rock-and-roll. Then his Cyclones bandmate Jerry Zadar arranged for Ben to audition for another band that he [Jerry] was now a member of.

GRASSHOPPERS

In the fall of 1964, after just turning seventeen, Ben was asked to audition (as a rhythm guitarist and singer) for The Grasshoppers, one of the most popular bands in Cleveland. It was the beginning of the Beatles and the "British Invasion" in America, and all of a sudden, everything was about the British bands throughout the club scene.

In a 1987 interview, Ben recounted, "I guess my biggest break was when I was about 17. A disc jockey in Ohio was looking to put together a band and they needed a rhythm guitar player. At the time I was playing drums. I said, 'sure.' I knew about three chords at the time, like E, A, and B, and that was it. C sharp minor came a little later, you know, for the slow song (laughing)."

At the time, the legal drinking age in Ohio was only eighteen, which was important because any number of bars and clubs had local bands playing every single night throughout the week. Cleveland bands were now changing their set lists from pop and Motown songs to playing the British Invasion music of The Beatles, The Rolling Stones, The Kinks, and Paul Revere and The Raiders.

One such band was The Grasshoppers, which originally featured front man Dante Rossi on rhythm guitar and vocals, Louie Pratile on lead guitar and vocals, Jerry Zadar on bass, and Sid Turner on drums. The band's moniker stemmed from the members' tendency to "leap around a lot" onstage.

When Rossi started the band, he already had a manager in place, Cleveland's WHKW radio personality, Joe "The Emperor" Mayer. Rossi also had a recording contract lined up before he even had the band members in place.

However, Rossi was already friends with Pratile, who then invited Zadar to join the new band.

Jerry Zadar: "Dante already had a manager (Mayer) who was going to finance setting up the band. A contract was drawn up and signed by everyone but me, because there was a clause in the contract that would have jeopardized the income of my full-time job."

Despite the snag, it would get worked out for Zadar to be in the band and The Grasshoppers would quickly become very popular throughout Cleveland. However, Rossi eventually decided to leave the band and form another group, opening the door for Ben to join The Grasshoppers.

Dante Rossi: "The Grasshoppers were a great band and we all had fun and got along great, but the guys were content playing locally as a covers band, and I really wanted to progress as a musician and create original music. So, I decided to move on and form my own band, but I left the Grasshoppers on good terms, and I was really glad that Benny joined them."

Rossi's new band first call themselves The Dante's, then changed their name to The Tulu Babies. Their manager, WHKW radio DJ, "King Bee" Ron Britain, used the catch phrase "It's a tulu baby!" on his radio show. Eventually, they settled on the name Baskerville Hounds and would go on to enjoy regional and some national success with the hits "Debbie" and "Space Rock Parts I & II," which reached #99 and #60 on the *Billboard* "Hot 100" singles chart, respectively.

"Space Rock" would become the theme song for the popular Friday-night television show *Ghoulardi*, and Dante's band would open up for The Rolling Stones at Cleveland's Public Hall in 1965. Rossi would remain close to Ben long after Ben became famous, and in fact, Rossi owned a hair salon just a mile from the Parma Heights house Ben grew up in and cut the rock star's hair for many years.

Dante Rossi: "Benny always liked to look sharp, from the car he drove to his clothes and hair. He had style and really enjoyed looking unique and different."

Jerry Zadar: "I already knew Benny before I met Dante, having played with him in The Cyclones. Benny was very young at the time of The Cyclones and Grasshoppers, and the band had a hard time getting him out of the house so that he could play shows. I got to know his parents well, and I was, many times, responsible for picking Benny up and bringing him home after shows because he didn't drive or have a car yet.

"I set up the audition for Benny with The Grasshoppers, not to play drums but to be the singer and play guitar, as he was just learning to play some chords. He picked up playing the guitar really fast and was good right away.

"We all knew that Benny's good looks and singing capability would be a great asset to the band, and he fit in well with everyone. After we signed a contract, Joe Mayer set up a recording deal with Cleveland record producer Carl Maduri.

"I began altering the pickups on the guitar so that it produced more of a stereo-type sound, and I used two separate amplifiers and speakers, adjusted at different settings and placed at opposite sides of the band. This gave us a more full background sound and during Grasshopper shows, Benny would stand next to Sid, side by side, for an energized drum duet. This was *very* cool and the audiences loved it! Separating the amps and speakers was especially useful when Sid and Benny were playing their dueling-drums routine."

Chris Kamburoff was another young guitarist who joined The Cyclones, who were now called The Chancellors, after Benny left the band, and was also a lifelong friend.

Chris Kamburoff: "I did not yet know Benny when he had left The Cyclones and I joined them, I had only heard the mention of his name from bandmates. I then joined Jimmy Vince and The Proof Sets and at that time, the lineup was Jimmy on lead vocals, Joey Kurilec on drums, me on rhythm

Ben and Sid Turner performing their duet drum solo with The Grasshoppers.
Courtesy of Diane Kokai-Akins

guitar, and David Gardina on bass. Not long after, Benny briefly joined the band as well.

"The Grasshoppers had some really cool traits, such as wearing green Beatle boots and Benny played a white Fender Jazzmaster, Jerry played a white Fender six-string bass, Louie played a white Fender Jaguar, and Sid played a green-sparkle set of Rogers drums, usually standing up. Benny and Sid would occasionally do these cool, dual-drum solos on Sid's kit."

"Sure, we had green shoes," Ben told the late Cleveland music journalist, Jane Scott, an influential rock critic at *The Plain Dealer* in 1978. "We bought them and then dyed them . . . and we sure shook up the travelers at the Greyhound bus station!"

UPBEAT AND THE GENE CARROLL SHOW

In the summer of 1964, "The Emperor" Joe Mayer landed The Grasshoppers a gig as a house band on Cleveland television's *Big 5 Show* (WEWS-TV channel 5), a music television show that would later be called *Upbeat*. The Grasshoppers would appear on the *Big 5 Show* dozens of times from August through October, before opening two shows in November for The Beach Boys at The Arena in downtown Cleveland. They were also the opening act for The Dave Clark Five in December at Cleveland's Public Hall.

The *Big 5 Show* was hosted by Canadian-born television personality Don Webster and was originally produced by the late Herman Spero. Spero was an independent television producer specializing in music-related programming, while Webster had previously hosted an *American Bandstand*–type show in Hamilton, Ontario. Webster had also been a radio DJ in Hamilton and Montreal.

Don Webster: "The general manager of WEWS-TV in Cleveland, Don Perris, was vacationing in Erie, Pennsylvania, and his fourteen-year-old daughter was watching TV. The signal from Canada skipped across Lake Erie, and she said to her dad, 'Hey this could be the guy you're looking for to host the new show you're planning.' They called me."

Herman's son, David Spero, who would go on to become a prominent Cleveland radio DJ and manager for Cleveland music greats such as Joe Walsh, Cat Stevens, and Michael Stanley, practically grew up on the set of *Upbeat* and knew Ben well.

David Spero: "I first met Benny on the set of *Upbeat*, as The Grasshoppers were one of the first house bands on the show, and because my dad was the producer, they had to be nice to me. I also passed out the checks every show.

"The Grasshoppers were also one of the bands at my bar mitzvah, which totally impressed my friends, and when The Grasshoppers opened for The Dave Clark Five, Benny let me come backstage with him. Much later, when he joined The Cars, I was a disc jockey on M105 radio in Cleveland and was *so* proud to play his music.

"I have fond memories of Ben coming to visit me at the radio station after The Cars' debut album hit it big, as well as hanging in the studio with him while he was recording the Cleveland version of 'We Are the World' with Michael Stanley and all the other Cleveland music legends. We hadn't seen each other in years, but it seemed like just yesterday, as it was so great to catch up with him. Benny was always kind to everyone and we stayed in touch long past the *Upbeat* days."

Upbeat ran from 1964 to 1971 and featured many of the biggest rock bands of the time, including The Who, The Rolling Stones, The Yardbirds, Jefferson Airplane, The Velvet Underground, B. B. King, The Dave Clark Five, Paul Revere and The Raiders, and Otis Redding. Tragically, Redding died in a plane crash the day after his *Upbeat* performance.

At its peak, *Upbeat* was syndicated in 110 television markets throughout the country. What truly made the show unique, however, was that various local bands around the Cleveland area were chosen to be revolving "house bands" on the show. This allowed local groups to perform behind these amazing national acts and to receive the national television exposure that went along with it.

Don Webster: "I ended up in Cleveland in September of 1964 to host what originally was called the *Big 5 Show*. At first, I hosted the show along with a different DJ from WHK radio each week. They originally used the DJs because they weren't sure if the 'kid from Canada' could handle it himself. When we syndicated about a year later, the name was changed to *Upbeat*, and we ceased using any of the WHK radio jocks."

The Grasshoppers were one of several local acts that got the opportunity to perform on *Upbeat* and originally had a thirteen-week run as the on-air house band. The first *Upbeat* house band was Tom King and The Starfires, which would later become The Outsiders. Other local bands appearing on the show included The GTO's, Baskerville Hounds, Terry Knight and The Pack (later to become Grand Funk Railroad), Mitch Ryder and The Detroit Wheels, and The Bob Seger System (yes, *that* Bob Seger).

Diane Kokai-Akins was a family friend of Ben's and of Sid Turner, and knew them both from a very young age.

Diane Kokai-Akins: "Before I knew Ben, I knew The Grasshoppers' drummer, Sid Turner, as our grandparents were friends and also our moms. Sid had told me about his band and about a big concert they were doing at the old Cleveland Arena, so my mom and I got tickets and went to the show.

The Grasshoppers, clockwise from left: Manager Joe Mayer, Sid Turner, Jerry Zadar, Lou Pratile, Ben.
Courtesy of Diane Kokai-Akins

We saw Sid while we were looking for our seats and he introduced us to Ben. From then on, Ben became really close with my family and he was over to the house all the time in the early days.

"On Saturday mornings, Ben would take me to the WEWS-TV studio where they taped the *Big 5 Show* and where the Grasshoppers were the house band for a while. They would tape the show all day long and then we would rush home to watch the show on TV at 5:00."

Marilyn Dudas-Stolz was eighteen years old when she went to the Park Lane Lounge with friends to celebrate graduating from high school and met Sid Turner and Ben Orzechowski of The Grasshoppers for the first time. Shortly thereafter, Marilyn and Ben started dating, and that courtship would become a lifelong friendship. Charlotte (Charlie) Tharp-Streeter was another member of this little group that would become very close to the Mayers.

Marilyn Dudas-Stolz: "It was at the Park Lane Lounge that I first met Sid and Ben, who were playing in The Grasshoppers. It was through that encounter that I met the Cleveland radio DJ and Grasshoppers' manager, Joe Mayer, and his wife, Ginny. The four of us (Ben, Sid, Marilyn, and Charlie) became Joe and Ginny's surrogate 'children.'

"Over the next thirty-five years, our lives took different paths, but also intersected often. Joe and Ginny were always there for us and Ben felt that the Mayers were among the most important people in his life. When Ben realized the cycle of life was nearing its completion, he reached back through time to bring his extended Cleveland family close to him."

Steve Dudas (no relation to Marilyn Dudas-Stolz) was a longtime friend of Ben and had become a roadie or "band boy" for The Grasshoppers. By this time, Benny Orzechowski was also becoming affectionately known as "Benny Eleven Letters," for obvious reasons. He was also becoming more well known around the city as an up-and-coming performer.

Steve Dudas: "Onstage, Ben epitomized coolness without even trying. He was just so natural, singing and playing like he was born for it. Ben carried The Grasshoppers with his good looks and stage presence and he had that voice! He had great range, excellent tonal control, and perfect timing.

"A short list of music stars of the time that we got to meet included The McCoys (featuring Rick Derringer), Terry Knight and The Pack, Paul Revere and The Raiders, Sonny and Cher, Eric Carmen, Paul Anka, and Chad and Jeremy. Many of these artists would also comment positively on the band and Ben's performance! Yes, those were very heady times."

Another Cleveland manager and promoter, Walt Masky, joined the *Upbeat* team as talent coordinator when Herman Spero became executive producer and David Spero associate producer.

Walt Masky: "I promoted a lot of dances and shows on both the west and east sides of Cleveland and hired The Grasshoppers to play at many of these dances. Benny grew up in Parma Heights, and I grew up in nearby Parma, and we became friends in the early sixties. I joined the *Upbeat* television show as its talent coordinator and eventually became producer of the show. Later, I became the manager of the Capitol Records recording group The Outsiders and also became friends with Joe and Ginny Mayer."

"We were just amazed watching Benny," Ginny Mayer, the widow of Grasshopper manager, Joe Mayer, told *Rolling Stone* magazine after Orr's death in 2000. "He could play any instrument and he could really sing. He was so smooth and well-dressed. Honest to God, he was just beautiful . . . it was stunning."

David Robinson: "I remember seeing some photos of Ben in his younger days, and it was amazing. You could see that he already had it down, completely formed as a rock star at the age of like fourteen or fifteen."

Steve Dudas: "There was no doubt in anyone's mind that Ben had star qualities from the get-go. Central casting could not have produced a better rock-and-roll persona, he was just so fluid with everything he did onstage, and it all seemed to come so naturally to him and without a lot of effort."

Don Webster: "I remember Benny as being a bright and talented young kid, and I think he was only sixteen or seventeen when he joined The Grasshoppers as lead singer and guitarist. However, many knew him as 'Benny Eleven Letters' because nobody could remember how to pronounce his last name.

"The band released a couple songs in 1965, and had they not broken up, I think they would have done well nationally. They were appearing on *Upbeat* in one hundred cities across the country every week. After Joe Mayer passed away some years later, Benny and Ginny remained close up to the time of his death."

Walt Masky: "Joe and Ginny became Benny's surrogate mom and dad. On many Sundays Benny and I spent time at the Mayer house in Fairview Park, Ohio. Their house was formerly an old store on Lorain Avenue that had been remodeled into a very nice home. I remember Joe's excitement when years later, he told me that Ben had broken out nationally after joining a Boston group called The Cars.

"In the late sixties, I had a small recording studio in my home, and I remember one evening Benny coming over and recording demos of six songs he had written. What I remember most about Benny was that he was very quiet most of the time, very sincere, and he was also very determined to be in a successful, national group."

The Grasshoppers worked hard and built up quite a local following, playing various events and clubs throughout the metro-Cleveland area, including a soapbox derby event, a stadium party before a Cleveland Indians baseball game, and shows at various clubs such as Cleveland's Silver Dollar Lounge, Lakewood's Chateau Supper Club, Mentor's The Torchlight, and Brookpark's Vanguard Lounge.

This, along with several appearances on WKYW Radio's "Sound Surveys," Vancouver's C-FUN Radio's "C-Funtastic Fifty Surveys," and in many *Plain Dealer* newspaper articles, had The Grasshoppers in the forefront of the Cleveland-area music scene.

Steve Dudas: "One of my favorite clubs, Diane's Lounge on Lorain Avenue in Cleveland, was a spot that The Grasshoppers played frequently. They were fun to listen to, played the current popular music and played a lot of Beatles' covers too. I made it a point of going up there on the nights that they played, and after a while, I got formally introduced to Ben.

"Something that stands out from those Diane's Lounge shows was when they performed an instrumental version of the song 'Ghost Riders in the Sky.' Ben and the drummer Sid would place two floor-toms at the front of the stage and do a sort of dueling drum solo while Jerry and Louis played 'Ghost Riders' behind them. It was very well done, with Ben and Sid facing each other, beating the drums in sync while they did this limbo thing, leaning back away from each other without missing a beat. It was always a crowd favorite, and it really got the 'house rocking,' as they used to say.

"Another club I frequented in Parma, the Pearl Ridge Tavern, featured a band called Leon and The Stormers, who put out some wild rock music. I got to know the guys in the band pretty well, including lead guitarist Rick Caon and bassist John Matuska. I became their unofficial 'band boy'. . . they didn't call them roadies back then. I didn't get paid, and everything fit nicely into Rick's 1956 Chevy station wagon.

"Then, when Louie and Jerry left The Grasshoppers and Rick and John joined, I was asked to come along as their band boy. The whole Grasshoppers experience was quite exhilarating for us young guys, to say the least, doing television appearances, working with already famous music acts and traveling to other towns to play. I also remember Ben spending *a lot* of time practicing in the early days. He seemed to be a perfectionist in his vocals and with his presentation. Ben was a very likable guy and in fact, I was actually a little bit in awe of him.

"He was just an easy-going sort of person, one you felt comfortable around. He had a great sense of humor, and his temperament was almost always perfectly level. I never saw him get angry, lose his temper, raise his voice, or chastise anyone around him. I don't remember Ben *ever* saying anything bad about anyone. He actually put up with a lot of teasing from Rick Caon and actually, all of us in a good-natured way, for never showing any aggressiveness or hostility towards anyone. Back then, Ben had a certain maturity that belied his age."

The Grasshoppers continued appearing on bills with national acts that were playing in Cleveland, such as James Gang, The Dave Clark Five, Mamas and Papas, and Peter and Gordon, and were one of the opening acts for The Beach Boys in November of 1964 at the Cleveland Arena.

The Grasshoppers also appeared on the aforementioned *Gene Carroll Show*, another popular WEWS-TV program that showcased a wide range of Cleveland-area talent. The variety show, originally called the *Giant Tiger Amateur Hour*, featured everything from tap-dancing children and baton-twirling majorettes, to accordion players and yes, local Cleveland rock bands.

Hosted by the former Cleveland WTAM radio personality, Gene Carroll, the variety/talent show aired Sundays at noon and ran from 1948 through the 1970s, and in fact, *Upbeat* host Don Webster took over as host of the show in the early seventies.

Other notable musicians who appeared on *The Gene Carroll Show* included Chrissie Hynde's pre-Pretenders band called Jack Rabbit, The Womack Brothers (featuring Bobby Womack), Canadian vocal quartet The Crew Cuts and well-known songwriter Jill Colucci, who has written hits for Travis Tritt, Wynonna Judd, and Michelle Wright. Colucci, who won a contest on the show at the tender age of seven, would also go on to sing movie scores and television and video promo campaigns for ABC-TV.

CAREER CHOICES

Don Burge was a classmate of Ben's from seventh grade at Pleasant Valley Junior High School in Parma through the tenth grade at Valley Forge High School.

Don Burge: "I first met Benny in seventh grade and we used to walk home from school a lot. We were classmates until the tenth grade at Valley Forge High. We had homeroom, auto shop, and shop class together, but he had little interest in shop classes and school in general because his real interest was music! Benny lived three streets over from me on Maplewood Avenue, and he had the whole basement set up like a stage with his drums and guitars.

"Benny was a quiet kid, and he was never in trouble or gave anyone a hard time. However, on the first day of ninth grade he was sent to the office as soon as he sat down in homeroom. He didn't come back that day, and in fact, he didn't come back to school for four days.

"But when he did finally come back and I asked him what the hell happened, Benny said that the school told him not to come back until his hair was cut to school standards. So he had to have his manager come in and tell the school about his band The Grasshoppers and that he needed to have that hairstyle. I didn't even know that he had a manager, but thanks to Benny, we all could have longer hair at school! We sort of lost touch after he left school, but I always followed Benny and his music thereafter. I had heard that he fell ill while in Atlanta, and it is sad that he left us too soon."

Chris Kamburoff: "We all had trouble in school because of our hair and the clothes we wore. We started wearing it long and tried to disguise it by using gel and combing it back. Sometimes it worked, and sometimes not, but Benny simply refused to cut his hair!"

Tom Gahan also attended junior high school with Ben and remembers him as a budding musician.

Tom Gahan: "Benny was a great musician even back then. We were sharing a class on the day President Kennedy was assassinated and when we heard the terrible news Benny left the room, got his guitar and sang ballads for the rest of the period."

It was also around this time that with his newfound advancement in the Cleveland music scene, as well as the blessing from his parents, Ben made the decision to officially drop out of Valley Forge High School in the tenth grade to pursue his music full time. As alarming as that might sound by today's standards, he had already been seriously thinking about music as a profession, and this was a natural progression for him. Yes, "Benny Eleven Letters" was quickly becoming more proficient as a working musician and building a name for himself in the thriving Cleveland music scene.

Chris Kamburoff: "When he decided to leave school, it was certainly not a stretch or surprise that he decided to do this, by any means. Benny, pretty much, was already a full-time musician before he even left school anyway, playing the clubs at night while still going to school. Yes, he really played the part from day-one. He always had that attitude, the mind-set of a rock star and to be in a band."

Louis Pratile was a guitarist and original member of The Grasshoppers:

"Benny was very young when he joined The Grasshoppers, and I was actually very concerned for him. We tried to watch over him, but the night-life at the time sort of overcame all of us. Benny was a wonderful man, and I truly liked him, and he had the kind of talent that was capable of being in Hollywood. I also remember Benny taking up having a British accent, and he got really good at it."

Yes, it was becoming clear to those around him that this was only the beginning for this up-and-coming musician, who by the age of eighteen, was the main attraction in a very popular Cleveland rock band, appearing regularly on television, and now drawing a lot of attention of people around him.

• 2 •

Moving Forward

MOD SOCKS AND PINK CHAMPAGNE

In February 1965, The Grasshoppers released two singles on the Sunburst label. "Mod Socks" was written by Carl Maduri and Louis Pratile, while the other was titled "Pink Champagne (And Red Roses)" and written by Ben. The songs were recorded at Cleveland Recording Co. under the direction of producer Carl Maduri and engineer Ken Hamann. The flip sides of "Mod Socks" and "Pink Champagne" were instrumentals titled "Twin Beat" and "The Wasp," respectively.

The Cleveland Recording Co. was founded by Cleveland radio pioneer Frederick Wolf in the 1930s and was the first professional recording studio in the city. In 1956, Wolf hired a young Navy veteran named Ken Hamann as an assistant engineer for the recording studio.

The late Hamann became chief engineer and would play a major role in building the studio into a state-of-the-art recording facility utilized by many regional and national artists over the years, including Joe Walsh's James Gang, Grand Funk Railroad, The Outsiders, The Lemon Pipers, and many others.

Maduri would also go on to work with national artists such as Wild Cherry, including the #1 hit "Play That Funky Music," Maureen McGovern (#1 hit "Morning After"), Donnie Iris ("Ah, Leah," "Love Is Like a Rock"), and Gary Lewis and The Playboys.

Carl Maduri: "I was working as a promotion-man for Mercury and Warner Bros. Records and doing my rounds at various radio stations when I met Joe Mayer. Joe knew that I had a label, Sunburst Records, and was doing some production work. He told me that he managed a group called The Grasshoppers, and that's how I got to know 'Benny Eleven Letters.'

21

"We produced two Grasshoppers' singles on Sunburst and then made a deal with Warner Bros. with the song 'Mod Socks.' Benny and the band were always very willing to do what you needed them to do. He was a very nice, well-structured young man and easy to work with, as were all of the band and Joe Mayer as well."

The first Grasshoppers recording session featured Ben on guitar and vocals, Louie Pratile on lead guitar, Jerry Zadar on bass, and Sid Turner on drums. Although neither single went too far, the *Upbeat* television exposure did help "Mod Socks" receive some national attention.

Jerry Zadar: "The recording of 'Mod Socks' and 'Pink Champagne' was a new experience for all of us. We had played out the night before and none of us had gotten much sleep. I can remember the drive to the studio; I had Benny and his drum set with me. We got stopped by the police and almost got a ticket, but talked our way out of it and got to the studio in time.

"Benny had written 'Pink Champagne' and we were ready to record it, and we had worked on a couple instrumentals that were used as the B-side. We were working with two drummers and had a basic idea for "Mod Socks."

"The final arrangement was done on the spot and Carl Maduri brought in a female singer to add highlights to 'Pink Champagne.' However, we were not accustomed to the way they recorded and mixed the songs, as we played the background music first and the vocals were mixed in afterwards."

Carl Maduri: "The Grasshoppers attended my daughter's baptism and celebrated and performed at our home in Northfield, Ohio. This was in 1965, an exciting time for Benny and the Grasshoppers, as 'Mod Socks' was being played on the radio and they had made a deal with Warner Bros.

"Yes, those were the very early days in Benny Orr's career, and I can't express enough how happy and proud I was to know and work with him, as I watched his career climb to great heights. Benny did express in an interview some years ago, about working with us in those early days and I was always appreciative of that."

Musician Chris Butler is the former leader of the new-wave rock band The Waitresses and from nearby Akron, Ohio.

Chris Butler: "It was the 'greaser era' and before the British Invasion hit . . . or at least [was] only slowly oozing into the Cleveland teenage culture with its tradition of hot rod bands, pompadours, and ethnic pride all over the city.

"Benny was a constant presence on the *Big Five Show* and *Upbeat*, and I have images of his cool haircut changing over time, until it settled into a deep, banged swoop that he was prone to set in motion with a toss of his head. Sort of a Buckeye Polack equivalent of the mop-top shake. I think my high school band tried to learn 'Mod Socks,' but then we just went back to playing Link Wray . . . the song wasn't 'hood' enough, probably."

In July, Ben's mop-top shake would land his photo in the *Life* magazine article about the mop-top craze titled "Big Sprout-Out of Male Mop-Tops." The magazine spread featured a shot of Ben jokingly wearing a hair net over his head and face while paying a visit to "Frank the Razor," who owned a men's hair salon in downtown Cleveland and cut all the local rockers' hair.

Longtime Cleveland musician Michael Stanley, who would later work on a couple music projects with Ben as well as emcee Ben's memorial service after his death, remembers Ben's early rockin' days quite well.

Michael Stanley: "I first saw 'Benny Eleven Letters' when he was *the* Cleveland rock star with his group The Grasshoppers, who had the local hits 'Mod Socks' and 'Pink Champagne.' I first saw them play at a VFW post in Brookpark, and they were incredible; they looked like rock stars, they had *real* equipment and the girls were going crazy. It was both impressive and inspiring to say the least!

"Add to that the fact that they made regular appearances on the syndicated *Upbeat* TV show that was based here in Cleveland and you had a guy who gave all of us 'be-in-a-band' wannabes someone to look up to and emulate."

With the exposure received from the *Upbeat* show, "Mod Socks" would just miss cracking the *Billboard* "Top 100" singles chart, peaking at #104. Unfortunately, not long after those first Grasshopper recording sessions the band would dissolve, leaving some misconceptions as to why this up-and-coming group would disband just as they were starting to hit their stride.

Over the years, multiple sources have indicated that The Grasshoppers broke up because two members of the band, Zadar and Pratile, had been drafted into the Vietnam War, but as it turns out, this was not the case at all. It was Ben's choice, in early 1965, to move in another direction with his music career.

Jerry Zadar: "I don't know where that story came from, about The Grasshoppers breaking up because I was drafted. I was married and had a family, which at the time, made me ineligible for the draft. I had a full-time job, Louis [Pratile] also had a family and a full-time job, and Sid was going to get married. The truth is that Benny simply wanted to move forward with his career in music while the rest of us, I believe, were content with simply playing in a local band."

Lou Pratile: "Jerry and I were both married and worked full-time, so we were mostly limited to playing in the Cleveland area, but we all got along great and never had any arguments. Only once can I remember a dispute, and that was when our agent wanted us to shave our heads and change our name from the Grasshoppers to the One Cell Amoebas [laughs]! We all said 'no way!' And, of course, Benny liked having his hair long like the Beatles!

"We had a great time playing with many famous bands of that era, and after our sets, Benny would sometimes say to me and the rest of the group; 'Let's go out among the crowd and see if they recognize us'. . . and they sure did, because we'd almost get trampled! Benny always loved his fans. In the end, our breakup really was just a peaceful split, a mutual agreement among friends."

Jerry Zadar: "We used to each get $15 cash for four hours of playing, with breaks and free drinks. In those days, you could buy groceries for a whole week for that amount of money! Comparing that to the $1.65 an hour at my full-time job, it was just a great part-time gig. It was all a fun experience, doing something you really enjoyed and making good money while doing it.

"The Grasshoppers utilizing two drummers was a big hit in the places that we played. We had a steady gig at a bar called the Park Lane Lounge, which was also known as 'The Home of The Grasshoppers.'

"Benny was a very talented artist, and we had a lot of good times together. He was an excellent drummer and singer and he picked up the rhythm guitar very fast as well. Benny loved the attention of being the lead singer and was always popular with the girls. Even before he joined The Grasshoppers, his goal was to be a rock star.

"Benny and I were very close at the beginning of his band-playing days, although we drifted apart and lost contact once he left The Grasshoppers and progressed on his road to stardom. In fact, I only saw Benny once after he became famous in The Cars, when the band came through the Cleveland Airport where I worked. The whole experience with The Grasshoppers was an exciting time in my life and things progressed very fast and just fell into place. From forming the group, changing the front man, the recording contract and television shows, to the bars and concerts we played and watching Benny achieve his ultimate goal in life, I am really *very* happy to have been a part of all that."

PRIVATE CAR

Outside of his growing local celebrity and even though he was very in-tune with it, Ben was always very quiet and reserved about his popularity and especially about his private life. He only revealed family matters to a few of his closest friends, and sometimes, not even to them. In fact, after losing his father in his early twenties, Ben was so quiet about personal matters that today, not many people can even recall the event of his father's passing.

Later in life, Ben would learn that he had an older half-brother named Charles, who lived in nearby Madison, Ohio. He would eventually make a connection with his brother, taking him black bear hunting in Canada. Chuck would pass away a few years before Ben.

David Robinson: "Ben would always introduce us [his bandmates] or friends as 'his brother' . . . you know, 'Hey, this is my brother, David.' Well, as it turns out, it wasn't until years later that we even knew that Ben, indeed, had a half-brother.

"I can remember being the only guy in the band who even questioned this notion by saying, 'What does he mean by that?' But Elliot and Ric would just say, 'Nah, he doesn't have a brother.' But sure enough, he did, and for many years we didn't even know it."

Indeed, records show that Benjamin had a total of five half-siblings, but he kept his private life to himself.

GRASSHOPPERS PART II

After the original Grasshoppers had broken up, Ben was now in search of new musicians for his band. He saw potential in the Castles, after having seen them perform in a local "battle of the bands" contest at his former Valley Forge High School in the spring of 1965.

Wayne Weston: "The first time I met Benny was after we [Castles] had just played our set at a 'battle of the bands' contest at Valley Forge High School. We were one of six or eight bands that played that night and Benny had come to check out the different groups.

"We saw Benny come in the side door to watch us play, and I remember that we all thought that was very cool. I mean, Benny was already a rock star to us and there he was, checking out *our* band!

"After we played, Benny asked who the leader of the band was, which I was. He told me he really liked our sound and that he would be in touch. I remember that really flipped me out because not only did he say he liked the band, but that he would *be in touch with us*?

"A couple weeks later I got a phone call from Benny asking me about our guitarist [the late] Rick Caon and bass player [the late] John Matuska. Of course, I didn't want to lose our guys, but I told Benny I wouldn't hold them back from joining his band, which they did.

"However, Benny also told me 'not to worry about it and that everything would work out.' Well, sure enough, a couple of weeks after that, Benny called me back again and asked me if I wanted to play drums in his band. *Are you kidding me?*

"Of course, he had said it jokingly because the answer was obvious. To be honest, I nearly pissed my pants when Benny asked me to join The Grasshoppers!

Ben and Wayne Weston, Parma Heights, Ohio.
Courtesy of Wayne Weston

It was just about the most exciting day of my entire life. Imagine, a sixteen-year-old kid and his garage band are all of a sudden, *The Grasshoppers*? It was like a dream come true for us."

The new Grasshopper lineup, which was still being managed by Joe and Ginny Mayer, now consisted of Ben on rhythm guitar and vocals, Rick Caon on guitar, John Matuska on bass, and Wayne Weston on drums.

John Matuska: "I can't remember an actual audition to join The Grasshoppers, but if there was one, it would have happened at the old Park Lane Lounge on Brookpark Road, where we became the house band. I don't really think they needed an audition from me, because they had heard me playing previously with a group called Leon and The Stormers.

"We had been the house band at a place called the Pearl Ridge Tavern, more affectionately known as 'Dirty Louie's,' and we were one of four or five bands playing the area clubs in the early sixties. I was all of fourteen years old, with a phony draft card, which was the accepted form of ID at that time. This was all *before* the British Invasion hit, because after that, there would be *hundreds* of bands playing in northern Ohio. All of a sudden, the competition for gigs got much more intense.

"But let me tell you, Ben had Elvis-like good looks that sort of defy being classified as masculine or feminine, like those Michelangelo statues where 'David' and 'Venus' are facially without gender. Remember now, it would be years before glitter/glam rock would come to be, you know, that David Bowie type of androgyny that would become so popular. Ben had that appeal *long* before glam rock ever hit the scene.

"One time, The Grasshoppers were checking into a mom-and-pop motel and when we asked for adjoining rooms, the desk clerk pointed at Ben and said, 'But what about her?' Of course, we all had unusually long hair at the time and this guy was ready to kick us out even *after* we showed him Ben's ID, because he thought it was phony. Of course, this kind of thing wouldn't happen today, but back then, the moral fiber of society was wound much tighter.

"Music was Ben's life, and as with most serious, purist musicians, it's not a social life, not a career, nor a form of expression, it's all three wrapped into life itself! We never really thought of actually being friends at the time, just fellow artists. Looking back today, yes, we were friends, I just never really considered it at the time. Ben was just an incredible artist and great person."

This new version of The Grasshoppers would continue to rehearse and play various area teen dances and parties, until a very strange incident actually led to the final breakup of the band.

Wayne Weston: "We used to rehearse at this local place in Parma called the UAW Hall, and there were always people hanging out with us. So, one night we're there practicing, with some girls and people partying, and it turned out that someone stepped on the neck of John's bass guitar, and when no one owned up to it, he left right there and quit the band. However, by that time, it seemed that the band had pretty much run its course anyway.

"But, Benny . . . he was different. He always had something special and I already knew this before I even met him or was in a band with him. He had a unique, powerful presence and such an incredible voice!

"We would be rehearsing and he would go into the Beatles' song 'I'm Down' with that rockin', Paul McCartney–style voice, and it would sound so good that we'd just flip out [laughs]! I'd be behind him playing the drums and would almost lose the beat of the song just listening to him, because he was just *that* good.

"Other aspects that always amazed me about Benny [were] that whenever we started learning a new cover song for our set, he would retain the lyrics the first time he saw them and never wrote anything down! He just remembered the lyrics to all these songs, and *never once* did I see him write anything down. Also, going all the way back to when we were kids in the early sixties, he always wore his seat belt in the car. Nobody wore their seat belts back then; but Benny did.

"Believe me, Benny just had this incredible electricity about him. He would walk into a room and whether they knew him or not, people just felt there was something special about this guy. By the age of seventeen, he couldn't go anywhere around town without girls following him. I swear that in the mid-sixties, Benny was like the 'Elvis Presley of Cleveland.'"

· 3 ·

Changing Directions

THE PROOF SETS AND THE MIXED EMOTIONS

*W*hen The Grasshoppers finally dissolved in the fall of 1965, Benny would briefly join another popular Cleveland band called Jimmy Vince and The Proof Sets, which featured the guitarist who had taken Ben's place in The Cyclones, Chris Kamburoff.

Chris Kamburoff: "I had joined Jimmy Vince and The Proof Sets, and at that time, the band was Jimmy on lead vocals, Joey Kurilec on drums, David Gardina on bass, and me on rhythm guitar. Ben was the last to join on lead guitar, and with him also came 'Emperor' Joe Mayer as manager. We played for about six months under the Proof Sets name, before changing the name to The Mixed Emotions.

"At that point, David Gardina left the band and his brother Johnny Joe Gardina picked up the bass chores. During this reformation in late 1965, the new lineup hadn't played out yet when Jimmy was contacted by Joe Mayer and told that Benny was looking for a new band.

"When he first showed up to our rehearsal I was really impressed. I said to myself, 'Now here's someone who has got it all. The musical talent, good looks, and the personality.' Well, he was cool with the band and joined right then and there."

The Mixed Emotions played extensively all over Ohio, sharing the stage with the likes of Paul Revere and The Raiders, Terry Knight and The Pack, Peter and Gordon, Bobby Sherman, and Tommy Roe and The Vogues.

The band enjoyed a great deal of local and regional success over a two-year-plus period, playing various covers of popular songs of the day such as "Gloria," "La Bamba," and "Soul and Inspiration." In the spring of 1966,

Ben with The Mixed Emotions. Torchlight Club, Willoughby, Ohio, 1966.
Courtesy of Joe Kurilec

The Mixed Emotions appeared on the *Big 5 Show* in March, opened for Peter and Gordon and The Vogues at Cleveland's Hippodrome in April, played the Cleveland Whiskey A-Go-Go, and opened for The Mamas and The Papas at Cleveland's Music Hall in June, while continuing to play shows at a number of local clubs and special events.

The Mixed Emotions also garnered local press coverage; one time they donated their efforts to help escort a number of Parma orphans for an all-day outing at Euclid Beach Park. They also scored high in the Cleveland Press "Best of the Bands" newspaper poll, in conjunction with the summer "Spirit of '66 Fun 'N' Fashion Festival." Other bands on the bill included Paul Revere and The Raiders and The Saxons. Ballots were published in the *Cleveland Press* newspaper so fans could vote for the various bands that they wanted to see perform at *The Spirit of 66* concert.

Joe Kurilec: "The event was a contest for local bands to be able to play a show with Paul Revere and The Raiders, a band that was a big inspiration to us. We did covers of many of their songs, and in fact, one time we played at The Stable's in Painesville, Ohio, on Halloween night and we rented Raiders' outfits. We even purchased boots that went up to our thighs and we all were very excited about that show.

"We came in second place, and a band called The Saxons came in first, so they must have stuffed the ballot box better than us! Our lead singer, the late Jimmy Vince, had the idea of standing by the stage door as the Raiders left for the stage, for someone to take our picture as we walked beside the Raiders.

"I first started watching Benny when he was in The Grasshoppers, and at that time, I was into a lot of band stuff. An ex-girlfriend's sister was just crazy about him, and once Benny joined The Mixed Emotions, we went over to her house and she almost died over the fact that we were friends and bandmates.

"Ben and I also lived together at my parents' house for a while when I was around nineteen-years-old. I am not sure of the details of why Ben was not at his mother's house at the time, but he was living at someone's house in North Ridgeville, Ohio, as well, and I used to go and pick him up for band practice.

"We were rolling along pretty good with The Mixed Emotions at that time, which came to a peak throughout 1967. During those years we were playing almost every night and did several shows on weekends. Ben was a driving force in the band, and he always added a great deal to our overall sound and look. We were very close during those times and that period was a very great time in my life.

"I remember over the years hearing The Cars and always wishing the best for Ben. We did not really stay in contact, but when his solo album came out, I remember calling the local radio station and asking if Ben could call me, and he did! One bittersweet memory I have was speaking at Ben's

The Mixed Emotions at The Note, UAW Hall, Parma, Ohio, 1966. Left to right: Jimmy Vince, Ben, David Gardina, Chris Kamburoff.
Courtesy of Joe Kurilec

memorial service at the Rock & Roll Hall of Fame, in which I spoke of our time together in The Mixed Emotions. Ben was a very sincere, hardworking musician, and being out front onstage, he always added something special to The Mixed Emotions."

Chris Kamburoff: "We played at The Cleveland Public Auditorium in 1966 with Paul Revere and The Raiders, Chad and Jeremy, Peter Gordon and The King Bees, The Vogues, Billy Jo Royal, The Sun Rays, Terry Knight and The Pack, Bobby Sherman, Bobby Goldsboro, and Tommy Roe, and for some odd reason we went on *after* Tommy Roe. There were 21,000 people there, and what a rush it all was! The stage was set up in the center of the hall and it revolved while the bands were playing. That was very cool for the times.

"While we were in The Mixed Emotions, Ben was looking for a new guitar and wanted a Rickenbacker. We found this old, ethnic music store on Cleveland's West Side called Buday's Music & Accordion Shop, which was a dealer for Rickenbacker guitars. We went in and Ben picked up a semi-acoustic electric 'Rick,' which was really cool. He really loved that axe, because the Beatles, Byrds, and Rolling Stones were all playing them at the time."

Dan McGinty, better known as "Peanuts," is a longtime, Ohio-based music journalist who also worked for the local band The Saxons.

Peanuts: "I first crossed paths with Ben seeing him in The Grasshoppers, and later in The Proof Sets and The Mixed Emotions with Jimmy Vince and Chris Kamburoff.

"The Mixed Emotions were based in Parma, and I was a roadie for The Saxons, based on West 130th Street just across the Parma line. Both bands played similar clubs, teen dances, and high school gigs. However, the only gig the two bands played together was that benefit show in the summer of 1966."

Chris Kamburoff: "The Mixed Emotions would record four songs at Cleveland Recording Co., engineered by Ken Hamann; 'Forever You Have My Heart,' 'I'll Do My Cryin' In the Rain,' 'I Can't Help It,' and 'You Wanna Man Now.'

"Ben and Jimmy sang lead on all four, and Thom Baker was the musical arranger, who also worked with Terry Knight and The Pack and The Out-siders' hit 'Time Won't Let Me,' and he used members from The Cleveland Orchestra for strings, horns, woodwinds, and a harp.

"The Mixed Emotions also did two television appearances on *The Big 5 Show*, as well as several grand openings for *The Hullabaloo Scene* dance clubs in the area."

Joe Kurilec: "At the recording session we used several members from the Cleveland Symphony for overdubs and it had a really great sound. I still feel 'Forever You Have My Heart' could work today! We also would go to Cleveland Recording Co. to watch other bands' sessions such as The Outsiders and The GTO's."

Chris Kamburoff: "When Benny and I were in The Mixed Emotions, after gigs we sometimes would drive around 'till the sun came up, just talking and laughing. In downtown Cleveland at the time, the tallest building was the Terminal Tower. Underneath, there were train terminals and it was very cool.

"There were huge murals on the walls, oak bench seats all over, custom luggage shops, quaint diners, and old fancy bars. We would always go down there and hang out, people watching, and one night this fellow struck up a conversation with us. He was a cross between James Dean and Fonzi, and he seemed okay. Eventually, he asked us for a ride to the other side of town and we complied.

"Benny was driving his lavender Chevy Impala, and I was riding shotgun, and this guy was in the backseat. Then, as he was talking, the guy leaned over the front seat, pulled out a switchblade, held it to my throat and wanted our wallets. I couldn't believe it!

"So, Benny casually talked this guy down a bit and then in one fell swoop, grabbed the guy's arm, disarmed him, and elbowed him in the face. Then he stopped the car in traffic, got out and dragged this guy out of his car and threw him down in the street *and* kept the knife! I was pretty shaken up, but Ben wasn't even fazed! Yes, he was a real and true friend.

"After Benny left The Mixed Emotions, a cool-looking guitar virtuoso named Al Austin joined the band, but we didn't stay together long after that. A few months later, after getting a call from Johnny Joe Gardina, we formed a band called U.S. Male and were managed by WIXY's Cleveland radio man Lou 'King' Kirby. We played all over the state and even recorded a 45-single on Buddah Records, which briefly got to the national charts and landed us on *The Dick Clark Show* on two occasions. Buddah Records changed our name to The Convention when we did the show. At the age of only eighteen, it was a real highlight in my life.

"After the U.S. Male band, I went off to college and eventually formed another band called Moses that played all originals. At the time, there were a lot of teen clubs popping up everywhere, so we were in demand. On a few of those gigs, Ben and Ric would show up to hear the band and discuss the possibility of me playing in their new music endeavor.

"They said that they were moving to Columbus, Ohio, to form a new group. At that time, I was in college, avoiding the draft, and was in a fairly successful all-original band, so I declined the offer. Dumb move on my part, of course, because five or six years later The Cars broke out nationally."

THE RUSH

Also in 1967, Ben would briefly join a band with Dan Klawon (from The Choir), Rick Caon (Castles), and John Aleksic (Raspberries). Aleksic grew up on the East Side in Euclid and was a singer/guitarist in various Cleveland bands such as the Denmarks, The Gang Green, Hobart's Follies, a group called Eve, Target, as well as many others, and briefly, a band featuring Ben called The Rush.

John Aleksic: "Many called him 'Benny Eleven Letters,' but I would pronounce his name correctly, as I also have a Slavic background. I grew up on the eastern-most side of Cuyahoga County and Benny was in Parma Heights on the West Side, which had an extensive Polish population.

"Bands tended to be formed on one side of town or the other, although we would have gigs on either side. I played in my first band [lead guitar and vocals] when I was eleven, called The Denmarks, and we even had a couple of singles that flopped.

"Another band I was in called The Gang Green, became quite popular on the college circuit and even appeared several times on a local, late-night television show hosted by Ernie Anderson. Ernie, who later became a big-time announcer, called himself 'Ghoulardi' and showed really terrible horror flicks.

"Dan Klawon, also an 'East-Sider' from Mentor, played in a band called The Mods, which later became The Choir. After they broke up, I invited Dan to join a working band I was in, Hobart's Follies, and sometime later, we asked Wally to join. However, we lasted only a few months because we had a manager who kept absconding with our money.

"Sometime after that, in 1967, Dan and I formed The Rush. Dan was the person who knew Benny and Rick Caon and brought us all together at my parents' house to jam and party. We liked a lot of the same music, especially Traffic and Steppenwolf, so we started rehearsing. Our problem was, however, we all liked to party a lot.

"Somehow, we hooked up with a female band called The Poor Girls, not as 'girlfriends,' we were just simpatico in the music and partying thing. In fact, I can't remember many gigs, but one was at a 'ski fair' at the Convention Center. I recall this because The Lemon Pipers were also playing there.

"But while we developed an adequate song list, none of us were good managers, and bookings were slim. We stuck it out for several months and had a lot of fun, but didn't work enough to stay at it, so we broke up, with everyone on good terms."

The Choir would eventually morph into the successful national band, The Raspberries, featuring Eric Carmen, Jim Bonfanti, John Aleksic, Wally Bryson, and a little later, Dave Smalley. The Raspberries would have a few major radio hits including "Go All the Way" and "I Wanna Be with You." At that time, Ben also began about a two-year relationship with Wally Bryson's sister, Nancy.

Nancy Bryson Western: "Benny was always kind and thoughtful to my family, especially my brother, Wally. He and Wally always talked about forming a band together, and although that didn't happen, Benny came to Wally's aid during a very difficult time in his life, and Benny said to me later that Wally would only know his full measure of talent and success when he played his own music the way he intended it to be heard.

"Truer words were never spoken, and Wally has always been grateful, as we all are, for Benny's loyalty and help through that troubled time. He truly deserves to be recognized for the joy he brought to many people during his too-short time on earth."

Dan Klawon: "I didn't get to know Benny really well, simply because he was a very private guy and pretty much kept to himself. Yes, he was a sweet and polite person, but what I remember most of all is that voice! I remember watching him on the *Big 5 Show* and he would sing those cool Righteous Brothers songs so well. He was always such an excellent singer.

"I don't remember The Rush playing out very much, but we sure had a lot of fun rehearsing. I remember we did this medley featuring Cream's 'I Feel Free' and the Hendrix classic 'Purple Haze.' We called it 'I Feel Purple' [laughs].

"After our band broke up I didn't see Benny for many years after he became famous, until I saw him at the funeral of our Rush band mate, Rick Caon. After the service, a bunch of us went to a local bar for a drink and we got to catch up on life. Benny remained down to earth and when I told him how happy I was for his success, he told me that it [being famous] isn't always what it appears to be."

John Aleksic: "Benny was a really nice guy, but very quiet and even a bit spooky. He reminds me of Christopher Walken, even in appearance. He was kind of icy, with an almost unemotional demeanor. Ricky played lead guitar, while Benny played rhythm guitar and was the main vocalist in The Rush. He was a great singer and did most of the lead vocals, although I did some as well. However, after this band broke up I never saw Benny or Ricky again, but Dan and I remain friends to this day. Perhaps it was simply an 'East Side-West Side' thing."

COLOURS

Near the end of 1967, and after The Mixed Emotions and then The Rush had parted ways, Ben would get back together with his Grasshopper bandmates

Wayne Weston and John Matuska to form Colours. A much more rockin'
band as compared to The Mixed Emotions, they had thought about calling
themselves The Grasshoppers again, but without the services of Joe Mayer
as manager, they decided to wipe the slate clean and go with the new name.
Colours also had a new manager, a local promoter named Bob Bobchuck.

Joe Kurilec: "I think Benny just wanted to go in a different direction than
The Mixed Emotions, as Colours was a cool, more Beatles-sounding band. I
was at a few of their rehearsals and they did a fantastic cover of 'Sgt. Pepper's
Lonely Hearts Club Band.' After that, however, Benny and I only somewhat
stayed in touch from late 1967 into the early 1970s."

Colours rehearsed at the UAW Hall while playing the Cleveland club
circuit, including regular stops on the West Side. Cleveland musician Jimmy
McCarthy was in a band called The Blackweles, which shared rehearsal space
with Colours and also played some gigs with them.

Jimmy McCarthy: "My band shared rehearsal space with Benny and
Colours at the old UAW Hall on Brook Park Road, which was at that time
called the It's Boss Teen Club. This was before Benny got drafted and they
were working with a guy named Bob Bobchuck and playing the Cleveland
club scene.

"Because we weren't working or going to school at the time, I was able
to spend some one-on-one time with Benny during the daytime. He was very
cool and was more of a teacher than I expected him to be. Benny was friendly,
much more so than he looked and had a great knack for doing Beatles' songs.
He was also the first person to really teach me how different keys give songs
a different sound."

Throughout 1967, Colours stayed busy with gigs, including multiple per-
formances at The Midnight Hour in Cleveland, It's Boss Teen Club in Brook
Park (with James Gang, The Choir, and The Blackweles), The Hullabaloo in
North Ridgeville, and The Village WAH in Middlefield.

Walt Masky from the *Upbeat* days and longtime Cleveland radio personality Carl Reese, who ran Cleveland's Peppermint Lounge with Masky, then
began managing Colours. Masky encouraged the band to cut a single and
funded a session at Cleveland Recording Co. to record "You Came into My
Life," engineered by Ken Hamann.

Walt Masky: "Carl Reese, from WHK radio, and I were partners and
rented halls all over the Cleveland area each weekend. We rented the UAW
Hall every Friday night and had different bands playing there. I remember
Benny rehearsing and playing on many a Friday night, and I also remember
Benny and The Grasshoppers playing the *Upbeat* show. Years later, in the late
seventies, I interviewed Ben on my 'Homegrown' radio show on WMMS in
Cleveland. This was when The Cars were the hottest group in the US."

Wayne Weston: "They told us to cut a record, which we did at Cleveland Recording Co. Walt Masky funded the recording, and he was at the session, along with Carl Reese. Ken Hamann engineered the session, and I remember him complimenting me on a particular drum sound technique I was using. . . . I think I was sixteen years old at the time."

EVERYTHING CHANGES (JUST LIKE THAT)

Wayne Weston: "We recorded 'You Came into My Life' as a single, which we used to practice a lot back at the UAW Hall, and we were jelling pretty well as a band and really gaining momentum. There was some interest in Colours from Roulette Records in Florida. So, Benny, a couple girls, and I rented a convertible and drove to Ft. Lauderdale to meet with them. We had stopped at a store, and I went inside to get some beer, but by the time I came out of the store, things would never really be the same again.

"While in the store I decided to give my mom a call just to let her know how we were doing, and she told me that Benny had to come back home because he had been *drafted*. I couldn't believe what I was hearing!

"I can remember turning around and looking out the store window. It was a beautiful, sunny day, the top was down on the convertible, and there was Benny laughing and just having a great time. To be honest, my heart almost fell right out of my ass! Well, I just couldn't bring myself to tell Benny he had been drafted, so I only told him that I had called my mother and that she said Benny had to call his mom. So Benny went inside, called his mom, and got the news.

"This was on a Saturday afternoon, and Benny couldn't even drive back with us, he had to fly back to Cleveland in order to leave that Monday! Imagine that, one moment you are in an up-and-coming band with a record label interested in your single and the next moment, you are drafted and on your way to boot camp. In that one moment, everything had changed so drastically, just like that."

Ben's mother would go to great lengths in order to get her son out of the service, based on an honorable discharge as being an "only surviving son," including recruiting his old manager, Joe Mayer, to help the cause. Mayer had a connection with the governor of Ohio to help make it happen, but it would be over a year before Ben was able to come home for good. After he had gotten through boot camp, however, Ben did return home for a brief visit and got to see a few friends.

Wayne Weston: "I remember the first time Benny came home from boot camp and we went over to his house to see him. I was excited because

I thought we'd just start our friendship right back up where we left off, but I knew immediately that it wasn't the same.

"I remember walking into Benny's living room and there he was, sitting on the couch in full uniform, right down to his boots. He looked like a completely different person from the guy I saw laughing in that convertible in Miami.

"I could also just tell that the situation had taken a lot out of him, and no one had to say a word; we just knew. I think being in the army in some way switched Benny's brains around because he was now very quiet and reserved. We were still buddies and all, but there was just something different about him after that. It was a situation that he obviously did not want to be in, and you just can't imagine how much of a bummer it all was."

"I got drafted, but luckily, I didn't go to Vietnam," Ben told Jane Scott in Cleveland's *The Plain Dealer* in 1978. "But when I came back, I had mixed emotions about music for a while, and I was disoriented about what I wanted to do."

Ben had remained in the army for a little over a year before finally receiving his hardship discharge in 1969. However, because he had been out of the Cleveland music scene for quite a while (back then, a year was like an eternity without computers or social media), he had to essentially start all over and rebuild his musical identity.

Ben began working at a men's clothing store while contemplating his musical future. This was a little bit of a down period for the former childhood star of Cleveland. However, despite this detour in Ben's long road to success, he never gave up the dream of making music a career. Once he got his feet back on the ground, he became more determined than ever to reestablish his position in the music scene.

Chris Kamburoff: "After Benny had gotten out of the service, I would see him on and off at clubs. He was sort of living out of his car and pretty much just kicking around. He was looking pretty rough, God bless him."

Ben decided he needed to find a band. In the interim, he actually became a member of The Outsiders and The Dante's briefly. Then, old *Upbeat* friend and Colours manager Walt Masky was in dire need of a favor and a guitar player.

Walt Masky: "I had The Outsiders booked by the national William Morris Agency based in New York and Los Angeles. I worked with agent Wally Amos [later to become 'Famous Amos,' the cookie giant], but the agency was not getting many dates for the band, so I started contacting various promoters around the country on my own.

"I also worked with a Texas promoter named Ray Ruff who put together a two-week tour for the band in Texas and Oklahoma. After I already confirmed the dates with Ruff, the Morris Agency called back with a two-week college tour booked for The Outsiders in Oklahoma and New Mexico. Yes, I had double-booked The Outsiders and was in a really bad situation.

"I had previously produced a record by The Dante's for Mainline Records in Cleveland, so I called the group up in Columbus and explained my situation, and they agreed to play the Ray Ruff–booked tour, but I needed to find a lead singer for them. So, I called up Benny and he agreed to join The Dante's and play The Outsiders' dates in Texas. So, one night near the Oklahoma border, the original Outsiders were playing a college about 100 miles away from where Benny and The Dante's were playing at the same time!

"Benny helped complete the tour, and I had no repercussions from either Ray Ruff or the William Morris Agency. Yes, he really helped me get out of a potentially bad situation. What I remember most about Benny during that time was that he was still very sincere, but now reestablishing himself in the music scene and more determined than *ever* to be in a successful group."

· 4 ·

Connecting Cars

ID NIRVANA

$\mathcal{W}$ayne Weston: "After seeing Benny that day when he had come home from boot camp, I didn't see him again for quite a while. When he had finally gotten out of the service, I was in a band called Renaissance Fair and playing nearly every night during the summer months.

"Then one day, I saw Benny sitting on the front porch at his mom's house with this tall, lanky guy. It was the first time I met Ric Ocasek. It wasn't too long after that I saw Benny at a party, the day before he was moving to Columbus."

Over time, there have been varying accounts about the dates and circumstances surrounding their first meeting, but Ben and Ric's musical collaboration certainly began after Ben was discharged from the military.

In the late sixties, Ben met the Baltimore native Richard Otcasek (a.k.a. Ric Ocasek), who was born to a Polish-Catholic family, the son of a NASA computer systems analyst. Richard got his first guitar during his preteen years and started listening to folk artists such as Bob Dylan and Phil Ochs. He started taking guitar lessons, but that didn't last very long.

After his father's work moved the Otcasek family to Ohio, Ric got a broadcaster's license, started building radio transmitters, and also got into photography, developing photo prints in the family basement. He started thinking about his education, but two stints in college were short lived and he came to realize that music was really his calling, so Ric decided to start writing songs, and he has been writing them ever since.

"I thought that was the thing to do," he told *Rolling Stone* in 1979. "I was going to write songs and not do anything else." The young songwriter copyrighted the first song he ever wrote, and thus began a decade-long search for the right combination of songs and musicians to fully realize his musical vision.

From the beginning, Otcasek took control of his bands by handpicking the musicians, yet no particular lineup seemed to take hold. One of these bands was called ID Nirvana. Ric had been struggling as a part-time musician in Columbus and working as a draftsman for Ohio Bell Telephone when he formed ID Nirvana in 1967. The band included fellow draftsman and bassist/ guitarist John Wiley, guitarist Dan Donovan, and Dan's brother, drummer Joe Donovan. Stephen Dodge would also play drums.

John Wiley: "I first met Richard when we were both working for Ohio Bell Telephone Company. I had never spent any time in Cleveland other than going there to see agents or catch a touring act, but Richard and I would go to a place called La Cave to see bands such as Iron Butterfly, The Fugs, and Velvet Underground."

ID Nirvana had been playing the club circuit around the Columbus and Cleveland areas when Richard met Ben for the first time.

"I met Ben in 1968," Ric told *Magnet Magazine* in May of 2016. "I had a band in Columbus called, ID Nirvana, very era appropriate, and he came to see us. He told me he could sing, came to my house, and sang the Beatles' 'Yesterday' in the sweetest voice I ever heard. The next day, he joined that band and every other band I had up to and through The Cars."

In fact, Ric already knew of Ben from his Grasshopper days on the *Upbeat* show. "I remember that Benjamin's band was the best," Ocasek told *Trouser Press* writer Bill Flannigan in 1979. "It was really something to turn on the TV on Saturday and wait for his band to come on."

"We met in Columbus when we were both booking bands, and we formed a booking agency," Ben said in a 1978 interview with Jane Scott of Cleveland's *The Plain Dealer*. "I liked his songs and he liked mine, so we got a band together and started playing in the Ohio State University area. But even there, people didn't always want to hear originals."

Stephen Dodge: "Actually, before ID Nirvana, we first started a band called Hampstead Incident, named after a Donovan song, but I can't quite remember if we actually played a gig under that name.

"I met Ben in Columbus through Rick, after the two of them had hooked up. I had been at Rick's place nearly every night for a couple years while we were putting a band together and bar hopping when Ben started coming around, but I don't recall doing a show with the band that included Ben.

"Rick and Ben became fast friends, had a lot in common, and I eventually faded out of the picture and joined a different band. I do remember seeing a few of their shows with Ben singing beautiful lead vocals, plus some great vocal harmonies from Rick and bassist John Wiley. It was a psychedelic, folk-rock sound that featured some majestic ballads for the ladies. It was very underground and much different from what The Cars would sound like.

"I also remember Ben as a very sensitive and romantic person who was always 100 percent committed to his art, which of course, was proven when he and Rick went on to fame and fortune. Ben's vocal performance on 'Drive' alone is enough to secure his legacy as a fine singer and musician."

John Wiley: "ID Nirvana struggled along for a while, doing gigs around central Ohio. Then one day, Richard returned from Cleveland with this singer and guitar player that basically blew us away with his amazing voice and presence. It was Ben Orr, and right then and there, we realized that ID Nirvana had a legitimate chance of becoming something special."

Ben was asked to join the band and worked on one of Otcasek's demo songs, thus creating the "Otcasek/Orzechowski" duo that would one day make them both world-famous. However, stardom would take a while to materialize for this rock-and-roll odd couple of sorts; the tall and lanky, dark-haired songwriter Otcasek paired with the handsome and charismatic, blond crooner in Orzechowski.

"We got along famously," Ben told *Rolling Stone* in 1979. "It's one of those things where you don't have to say anything and it's just there. We just went on . . . kept going from state to state and doing our thing."

ID Nirvana continued to play around the Columbus area and progress as a band over the next year, opening shows for such Ohio notables as The Bob Seger System, Alice Cooper, The Lemon Pipers, and Strawberry Alarm Clock. To help make ends meet, Ric managed a clothing store called Family Britches and, of course, hired Ben to work in the store as well.

LEATHERWOOD

As 1970 approached, the band's vibe started shifting from a Beatles/Rolling Stones sound of the late sixties, to the more acoustic vibes of the early seventies. Ben and Ric changed their name to Leatherwood and continued to write and rehearse at night, after the day's work at the clothing store.

During this time, Ben met Victoria Simon, a Kentucky-native, who had recently graduated from high school in Columbus and was attending Ohio State University. She was introduced to Ben by Otcasek, who was already a friend.

Victoria Simon: "While attending Ohio State University in 1969, I met Ben when he was working with Rick at Family Britches. I remember them

Leatherwood promotional photo.
Courtesy of John Wiley

playing most every night, and I would go and listen to them practice a lot. Leatherwood played a lot of Crosby, Stills and Nash–type songs, but they were also writing their own material as well. I mostly heard them when they were practicing, wherever they could find a place to play.

"In 1970, they moved to East Lansing to start up a new Family Britches store, and I stayed behind to work and figure out what I wanted to be when I grew up. Music was Ben's first love, as it should have been, but he was also a very romantic and loving man."

John Wiley: "I had to leave at one point to take care of some personal issues, and the band continued working with a talent agency and touring throughout the Midwest. However, they finally broke up in early 1970 and the Otcasek/Orzechowski team moved to Ann Arbor, Michigan, to work at yet another Family Britches store.

"Then, in the spring of 1970, I got back together with the band after Ben got transferred to a store in East Lansing. We hung out in East Lansing, enjoying the college campus atmosphere while Richard continued to write more lyrics, then we decided to take our act to New York City to search for a record deal. When we left, Joe Donovan stayed behind and joined another group."

NEW YORK, NEW YORK

John Wiley: "So the three of us loaded up Ben's car, pooled our money together (which wasn't much), and left East Lansing. We got as far as Toledo and the car broke down, so we found a mechanic and a place to crash for the night and completed our trip to New York City the next day. Rick had met a drummer named Mike 'Spider' Patterson from another band, and when we got to New York City, he called Mike and asked if he wanted to join our group.

"A few days after we arrived in New York City, Rick got hooked up with a guy named Al Schwartz, who was in the business of managing show people and was supposedly Ann-Margret's personal manager."

Indeed, Schwartz worked with the actress, as well as such comedy legends as Jackie Gleason, Milton Berle, and Red Skelton. He would also go on to become a daytime and prime time Emmy Award–winning television producer and director, producing shows such as the *American Music Awards* and the *Golden Globe Awards*. Al's brother, Sherman Schwartz, was the force behind such popular television shows as *The Brady Bunch*, *Petticoat Junction*, and *Gilligan's Island*.

John Wiley: "Schwartz put us up in a room at the Royal Albert Hotel in Greenwich Village, as we were to focus on writing and arranging our material. However, after a couple months he realized that there were simply too many distractions in the city, and made arrangements with the Blooms, a well-off family who owned a small house near their ranch in upstate New York, for us to live there. It was probably too expensive for him to keep us in the city."

Victoria Simon: "After I had moved back to Kentucky with my family and Ben and Rick had moved to New York City, I visited them once, and we all stayed in the Albert Hotel in Greenwich Village . . . and I can remember them still practicing all night long.

"However, back then, we only wrote letters to each other, so our communication wasn't the greatest, but Ben would tell me about the songs that they were working on at the time and the plans they were making to find a record deal."

In a letter written by Ben to Victoria in early 1970, he told her about the band moving to the house in upstate New York, a tiny town about thirty-five miles from Woodstock called Fleischmanns. Ben also wrote about the band rehearsing at the hotel while getting ready to record a demo session at The Record Plant, and that he and John Wiley were writing songs together.

Ben Orr: "This is the most out-of-sight place I've ever seen! John and I are getting started on writing the whole side of an album. It's very even music and pleasant to the ear. Some of the songs are already done, such as 'The Sun as It Leaves,' 'Sleep Nice,' and 'As the Day.' We've got other heavy things in store as well, including an electric violin player from New York City who will be joining us."

Victoria Simon: "I was a very small part of his life, I know, but I think an important one back then. By reading the saved letters he wrote to me, it seemed like we were in love, but very young without lots [of] experience yet. I was very happy when The Cars came to be and I always felt Ben really was the most all-around, talented one of the group. He was my first serious relationship, and he treated me very well."

John Wiley: "We recorded three demos at Vanguard Studios when we were in New York City, but they were done in a hurry and not mixed down, and as a result, were rather rough. Along the way we also recorded some demos while in Columbus, and another one in Cleveland."

However, it wasn't long before Leatherwood's options ran out, and although they stayed connected with Schwartz moving forward, Ben, Ric, and John found themselves back in the Ann Arbor area playing more shows and resetting their path.

They soon connected with famed music promoter (and former White Panther chairman) John Sinclair and opened some shows for such established bands as The Stooges, MC5, Amboy Dukes, and Alice Cooper, all of whom also worked with Sinclair.

This had become a particularly low point for the guys otherwise, however, often playing redneck bars and one-night stands while not making enough money to survive. They would lie to club owners by promising to play songs heard on the radio, only to get the plug pulled on their set for trying to play their own songs. This could be risky in that some club owners would let them do their thing, while others did not appreciate being lied to just to get onstage.

"Once, we got run right out of town by guns," Ocasek told *Rolling Stone* in 1979. "In Alpena, Michigan, we were doing a gig in a deer-hunter's hangout. After we played a few songs a couple of guys with rifles came up and told us to get out."

· 5 ·

False Start

CALL TO BOSTON

*B*en and Rick continued to struggle, in search of the right combination of musicians and songs. By early 1971, Ben had returned to Cleveland to tend to some family matters, including the loss of his father, and contemplate his next move. He also met a pretty, strawberry-blonde named Kristina and they would eventually be married, with a ceremony held at Christ the Savior Church in nearby Parma.

Kris Orr: "I was brought up in Bay Village, Ohio, and met Ben while living in Rocky River, Ohio, in early 1971. Although it's endearing that many people called him 'Benny,' I always just called him 'Ben.' I had met Ric first, however, through a friend of mine named Dan Ramsey.

"To make ends meet at the time, Ric and I both worked at this hip clothing store called JeansWest, and Ben started working there shortly thereafter. One day, I had stopped in the store and Ben had volunteered to fix a flat tire on my car. That was the first time I met him and our relationship grew from there."

While Ben and Kris were dating, Ric had gotten married to his girlfriend, Suzanne, and the two decided to move east to Boston, landing in the suburb of Somerville near Harvard Square. Initially Ben did not want to leave Cleveland again, especially after having recently lost his father, but he did go there for a short time.

"I was sorting out some family affairs, but Rick kept calling me and saying, 'you gotta come to Boston,'" Ben told Cleveland's *The Plain Dealer* in 1985. "I said OK and left, it doesn't take a great deal of energy for me to leave one place and go to another."

He stayed in Boston for three months before returning to Ohio to marry Kris, and then the two settled in Boston with their dog, Shauna.

Kris Orr: "We got married in August 1972, and we were together for ten years. I stayed in Ohio for three months [while Ben had joined Ric] and then moved with Ben to Boston right after our wedding. Milkwood was the band they were developing before we were married, and eventually, Paramount Records signed and locked them in for a couple years."

Ric liked all the culture in Boston and the notion of being so close to the famed Harvard University. What's more, because of the many colleges and the student population throughout the city, Boston was well regarded as not only a hotbed of music, but also a city of great creativity and artistic opportunity.

"The first day I came to Boston in 1972, I remember seeing Jonathan Richman and the Modern Lovers on the Boston Common and thought, 'this is the Velvet Underground all over again,'" Ocasek told *Girlposse.com* in 2005.

He would eventually become friends with Jonathan and the band, whose drummer just so happened to be a musician named David Robinson. Then Ric hooked up with a guitar player from Chicago named "Jas" (Jim) Good-kind, after seeing his ad in the *Boston Phoenix* newspaper looking for a singer.

Ben and Kris. Early 1970s portrait by Jerome Higgins.
Ben Orr Collection

Originally from New York City, Jim moved to Chicago at age fourteen and learned guitar from Harvey Mandel, who would go on to form the band Canned Heat, and also worked with The Rolling Stones and bluesman Charlie Musselwhite. After graduating from college in 1971, Goodkind and a bass player friend hitchhiked to Boston in an attempt to start a band.

Jim Goodkind: "I met Rick after advertising in the *Boston Phoenix* for a singer. He had just moved to Boston with his wife, Suzie. His audition went okay, but as soon as he played me a few of his own things, I scrapped my own band project and Rick and I started Milkwood, playing the Boston coffee house circuit as a duo.

"Then Rick convinced Ben to move from Cleveland and join the band so we could create three-part harmonies. We played as a trio for about a year and opened shows for the likes of John Prine and other like artists coming through Boston. We mostly played in Boston, New York City, Philadelphia, and a few other towns in the Northeast."

MILKWOOD/*HOW'S THE WEATHER*

Milkwood would also make its way back to Ben's hometown of Cleveland, and his old friend, Grasshoppers' drummer Wayne Weston, went to the show.

Wayne Weston: "I remember picking up the newspaper one day and seeing that Benny was back in town with Milkwood and playing a show at a club I would later come to own. They were an acoustic, folk-trio set up with Benny on bass! I can remember thinking 'What in the world is this?'

"You see, I know that Cars fans know him as a bass player, but in Cleveland, Benny was known as a guitar player. So it was really strange to see Benny playing the bass in this folk-style band, and especially because he had *always* liked to play rock-and-roll!"

Kris Orr: "Ben could pretty much play any instrument, although I never saw him play a horn. He started playing bass in Milkwood, and I believe that was the first time he had ever gone onstage with one."

As Milkwood continued to work its way into the Cambridge–Boston music scene, the trio was performing at folk clubs like the Inn-Square and The Idler in Cambridge. It was around this time that eventual A&M recording artist, Peter C. Johnson, was also playing at the same clubs.

Peter C. Johnson: "I first met Ric and Ben when they were Milkwood, and when some guy [Al Schwartz] from out of town had come in to produce them, we were all jealous because at the time, Andy Pratt was the only one of us who had signed a record deal. After that, The Idler's backroom became the place where Ric and Ben [along with many other artists] began to really hone their craft, and they played as a duo at the time.

"When Ric put Cap'n Swing together, he invited me to a bar in Gloucester, Massachusetts, to see the band, and my reaction, being a narrow-minded singer/songwriter type, may have been to look down my nose a bit and express my indifference over their 'pop' leanings. I don't remember, because I was under the influence of both alcohol and cocaine at the time and could be quite an asshole. In any event, I don't recall that Ben ever spoke to me again. In retrospect, I happen to think that 'Best Friend's Girl' is one of the great pop songs of all time, I was just too stuck in my narrow musical framework."

John Gorman was the operations manager at WMMS-FM in Cleveland, but had also come from Boston. "Before I left Boston for Cleveland, Ben and Ric were performing as an acoustic duo. I happened to catch them once in some small joint and then a few years later, someone from Boston sent me a demo of The Cars, which I thought was really good.

"I never played the demo on WMMS and actually misplaced it, something that would've come in handy when The Cars' first album actually came out. I remember the note with the demo tape mentioned that it was a band put together by 'those two guys' [Otcasek and Orzechowski]. It wasn't until *The Cars* album came out, less than a year after I got that demo tape, that I learned that Orr was actually Benny 'Eleven Letters' from Cleveland."

Jim Goodkind: "Ben and I briefly had an apartment together north of Cambridge, while Kris was still living back in Cleveland. Ben was a pretty simple guy with simple tastes. He had such a great voice, was a good bass player, and his musical tastes were the progressive groups of the time like Yes, Emerson Lake and Palmer, and Pink Floyd."

In late 1972, Ben, Ric, and Jas started some late-night rehearsing and demo sessions at Aengus Studio in Fayville, Massachusetts, a local studio financed by musician Andy Pratt and built by Jonathan Cole and the late Bill Riseman. A local recording engineer who enjoyed working with young musicians, Riseman would also go on to own Northern Studios in Maynard, Massachusetts. Aengus Studio was originally launched in a ranch-style house in Winchester, Massachusetts, before relocating to Fayville.

Later on, after The Cars had finally landed their record deal and had hit it big with their debut album, the band would remember Riseman's kindness by returning to Northern Studio to begin work on new songs for their follow-up Cars album, *Candy-O*.

Boston-area singer/songwriter and Harvard University graduate Andy Pratt, who hit the charts in 1973 with his *Billboard* "Hot 100" hit song "Avenging Annie," was an original investor and partner at Aengus Enterprises.

Andy Pratt: "I met Ric and Ben at Aengus and they had a manager with them named Al Schwartz who was talking about how talented they were, and there was a buzz that they were musicians to watch. We all hung out together for a while back then, and we used to go to the Casablanca on Harvard Square a lot."

Ben and Ric had stayed in contact with Schwartz after they left New York City. Schwartz would become Milkwood's manager and subsequently work out a record deal for the trio with Paramount Records in New York City. However, they needed studio time and some additional musicians in order to lay down the tracks that would become their debut release, titled *How's the Weather.*

Enter local session musician, Greg Hawkes, a friend of musician and studio engineer Nick Koumoutseas. Koumoutseas had started sitting in with Ben and Ric during these after-hours studio sessions and worked with them extensively over the next couple of years. Koumoutseas would go on to work in the Washington, D.C., punk rock scene in the 1980s, where he still resides and works as a studio engineer. Nick's brother, John Koumoutseas, was also an engineer at Aengus Studio and assisted on some of Rick and Ben's early recording sessions.

Nick Koumoutseas: "In 1970, I had started working as an audio engineer intern at Aengus when it was located in Winchester, Massachusetts. I met Jonathan Cole, a partner in the Aengus venture and after meeting Bill [Riseman], he offered that I learn by working on small studio improvements and by also helping Andy Pratt from about midnight to dawn for several months in late 1970.

"Then, when Aengus moved to Fayville and I could no longer work for free, Bill offered me the 'foreman' position to help finance my entry into a recording engineering career. After about six months, I was an audio engineer. It was an easy transition with a Tufts engineering education in hand and prior experience.

"Greg Hawkes was part of a band called Waves with Fuzzbee Morse, Ron Riddle, Bill Anstatt, and Larry Porter, and I was the engineer on their session. They dazzled me, and I offered to continue the recording project at my expense, while their band morphed. During the same time period, I was engineering the Milkwood album, and when we tossed about the idea of adding horns, of course, I called Greg."

A Berklee College of Music student, songwriter and multi-instrumentalist Fuzzbee Morse would go on to play, record, and tour with such legendary artists as Frank Zappa, Lou Reed, Bono, Richie Havens, and Jaco Pastorius, to name a few.

Fuzzbee Morse: "Greg Hawkes, Ron Riddle, and I had already been playing together for a few years when we met Ric and Ben. The three of us met at Berklee, got in cahoots very quickly, and ended up moving to a house in Southborough, Massachusetts, together. Our band was called Waves."

Also a Berklee student, Ron Riddle has drummed with such artists as Happy the Man, Blue Oyster Cult, Mick Ronson (David Bowie), and John Sebastian, while also composing music for television and film entities such as CBS, Disney, Discovery, CNN, and Animal Planet.

Ron Riddle: "We would all just hang out and jam on Zappa tunes together. Greg didn't play keyboards at that time but played soprano sax and flute. Later, we all decided to drop out of school and move into a house in the country where we did nothing but jam every day for about a year. It was a truly amazing time!

"Those sessions were life-changing, as the improvisational element of the band was unlike anything I'd experienced before or since. I've always felt that if that band could have stayed together, it would have been a major contender, but unfortunately, the band had no clue how to make a living or how to make money with our music so the end was inevitable."

Fuzzbee Morse: "It was while living in Southborough that we started recording at Aengus, which was right down the road from us, with engineer Nick Koumoutseas. Nick brought Greg in on the Milkwood album and through Nick, we met and joined forces with Ben and Ric. The five of us hit it off right away."

Ron Riddle: "Waves was sort of limping along at that point and there's a number of conflicting versions as to why the band broke up. Perhaps it was bad management or lack of money.

"Immediately after Waves, Greg and I (probably because we didn't know what else to do) started performing as a duo-comedy act, sort of in the vein of *Firesign Theatre*, and were involved with a project at WGBH-TV in Boston called *Video Workshop*. After the end of Waves, Greg, Fuzzbee, and I would later join up with Ric and Ben to try and form another band."

Another of Riseman's associates was Robert "Jesse" Henderson, now a renowned recording engineer and best known for his work at Long View Farm Studio in Brookfield, Massachusetts, with such music legends as The Rolling Stones, Aerosmith, and Stevie Wonder.

Jesse Henderson: "I met Ben when he first came to Boston, along with Ric and his [Ric's] wife Suzanne, as they all shared an apartment in Somerville. My introduction [to them] came from a bandmate at the time who was managing a WEA record distribution branch in Woburn, Massachusetts, where Ben and Ric's wives also happened to work."

Jim Goodkind: "It was Al Schwartz, their former manager with ID Nirvana, who became our manager and got us the deal for the Milkwood album. The deal was a result of Al's relationship with Joe D'Imperio, who had been with RCA Records and was then running Ringling Bros. Barnum & Bailey

Records for Paramount. Joe had also helped develop the careers of Jefferson Airplane, The Youngbloods, and The Monkees.

"Aengus was a pretty new studio at the time and had some great equipment. Andy Pratt was spending a lot of time there, working with John Nagy on the first album, and Jeremy Spencer of Fleetwood Mac was also recording there at the time. The recording of *How's the Weather* was fun, but difficult, since we really hadn't played together in band format before; we were previously more of a folk trio."

"Richard Otcasek" (as it states on the album's back cover) wrote nine of the ten tracks on *How's the Weather* while singing eight, "Benjamin Orzechowski" wrote and sang one track, titled "Lincoln Park," and Jas Goodkind also sang lead on one track. The album was produced by Schwartz and engineered by Nick Koumoutseas, with a "special thanks" to Bill Riseman on the back cover. Although the release failed to chart or create an impact, the recording sessions for this album gave Ben and Rick some valuable experience working in a professional studio setting.

Jesse Henderson: "I remember Ben as a quiet guy. He had a dog named Shauna when I first met him, a white dog with blue eyes and devoted to Ben. At the time, I was the chief engineer at Aengus Studio, although I ended up only playing drums on the Milkwood record and not doing any engineering.

"I engineered a lot of sessions with Jeff Lass at Aengus, and I also worked with musicians David Humphries and John Payne, likewise from Aengus sessions. We had a talented pool of well-regarded musicians including Greg Hawkes, a friend of engineer Nick Koumoutseas. Both Nick and I had been introduced by Bill Riseman, the architect of Aengus Studio.

"Aengus also built analog recording consoles and sold one to Long View Farm Studio, which is how I ended up working there after the demise of Aengus in 1975. Riseman then took over the operations of Northern Studio where I also freelanced for a year or so.

"Bill Riseman was my mentor, and I got to see The Cars for the first time at The Rathskeller on Kenmore Square, before they signed a record deal. I also remember a well-known client of mine telling me at the time that the band *didn't have anything*? Well, the rest, as they say, is history."

Jim Goodkind: "Schwartz also decided to produce the Milkwood record, and he wasn't very good. In fact, we were all very unhappy with the final product. I remember it being a big disappointment, after reaching the high of getting a record deal in the first place.

"While we were in the studio doing the Milkwood album a woman named Niki Aukema, also managed by Schwartz, came in from New York City to record her debut album. She had a great keyboard player named Roy

Bittan, who is now with Bruce Springsteen, and I was hired to play those sessions as well."

Ben and Andy Pratt also appeared on the Aukema album, with Ben playing bass on a song titled "Lucky Lost Sin."

Andy Pratt: "Yes, we did play on that album. Niki was a great singer and friend of mine back in those days. Not long after that, my song 'Avenging Annie' was on the radio, and at one point in 1973, Ric, Ben, Greg Hawkes, and Fuzzbee Morse tried out to be my touring band and although I ended up going in another direction, they were great musicians and we were always friends. In fact, both Ben and Ric came over to my house a few times, separately, and played songs for me they were writing at the time. I really liked their stuff.

"I got busy with my career after that, and then all of a sudden, 'Just What I Needed' was on the radio and they were off and running! I guess they went through a few configurations and then it was [connecting with] Roy Thomas Baker and huge success.

"As for Ben, I remember him as Ric's musical partner, and he seemed very comfortable with that, always being happy and friendly. Ben and Ric always fit together very well with their guitars and singing, and of course, I also really loved Ben's singing on 'Drive.'"

The Milkwood album is listenable but, overall, not a very creative attempt to capitalize on the popularity of folk music at the time. The album cover art also did not help the cause, depicting Otcasek and Orzechowski in fur coats, long hair and mustaches covering their faces. Not exactly a sharp, Cars-style motif. The album was released without any promotion, failed to chart, and faded quickly.

It would seem that the album was not truly indicative of the talent it showcased. A review of Milkwood performing live from June of 1973 stated in part, "Richard Otcasek, Jim Goodkind and Ben Orzechowski are destined for bigger things. Otcasek and Goodkind blend their acoustic guitars to almost delicate perfection, with Goodkind pulling off some lead riffs that belie the capabilities of a wooden ax. When you add Orzechowski's weird but funky bass style to the guitars and tight three-part vocals, you come up with a much impressive group."

Jim Goodkind: "The disappointment that Rick, Ben, and I felt after hearing the finished Milkwood album created a 'down' atmosphere among us. Even though we played out to support the record, we really didn't believe in it, and then, pretty much stopped believing in ourselves as an entity. We split up within six months after the album was released, and I joined Niki Aukema's band with Roy Bittan.

"Rick and Ben had a tough time of it for a while, sometimes playing alone, sometimes together, and sometimes with me. However, it's my opinion that Rick's belief in himself and his music and ambition are the things that ultimately created the conditions for the success of The Cars, and of course, Ben was right there as well, based on the strength of his incredible voice and rock-star presence."

However, despite the failure of the Milkwood album, Ben and Rick not only gained valuable time in the studio, but also created the connection with their future bandmate, Greg Hawkes.

Arguably the most creative song on *How's the Weather* was "Timetrain Wonderwheel," which seems to build energy and resemble some musical groove Ben and Rick were about to go in. The track gives wind arrangements and saxophone credit to the aforementioned Greg Hawkes, the Berklee College of Music student.

Born in October 1952 in the Baltimore area, Greg was drawn to music at an early age (as well as Japanese science-fiction movies) and studied piano in grade school. He played guitar in his first band, The Aardvarks, in addition to playing in a few other bands throughout his high school years.

Greg also learned to play the flute, recorder, and saxophone, but keyboards would eventually become his specialty. The experimental sounds of Frank Zappa and The Mothers of Invention would draw Greg to piano and synthesizers. Hawkes also attended the Berklee School of Music in Boston, studying composition and flute for two years, during which time he began to develop a reputation in the Boston area as a versatile studio musician.

Greg Hawkes: "I first met Ric and Ben when they were recording the Milkwood album. I was introduced to them by Nick Koumoutseas, who was engineering. It was recorded in Aengus Studios around January or February of 1973.

"*How's the Weather* was the first album that I ever played on, and strangely enough, I played saxophone. I just played on one song, 'Timetrain Wonderwheel,' and I still have my vinyl copy on which they spelled my name wrong on the cover. But then again, Ric had not yet dropped the "t" from his name and Ben had not yet shortened his.

"After the album, I stayed in touch with them, and Milkwood soon became simply Ric and Ben performing as a duo. I remember seeing them play at The Idler in Harvard Square and at Jonathan Swift's in Cambridge. One night I even played with Ric as a duo, when Ben had gone back to Cleveland for some reason. But from then on, I played on just about all of their demos, and then joined them in the Richard and The Rabbits band, which was really the first band that I played keyboards in."

Nick Koumoutseas: "I always think of them as 'Ric and Ben,' as if they were one person, but of course, that's not true. In fact, they were very different and very complementary. Ben was no mystery; happy, talented, self-confident, and always dressed well. He was easy to be around and really made you feel like he respected you. They say someone has charisma when they make *you* feel good, and that was Ben.

"As a young engineer, I learned a lot about teamwork while working with Ric, Ben, and Jim, as they worked hard on vocals and arrangements, and it was fun to aid and abet. The album took two or three months at Aengus studios. The three of them would just push and push until they had something beautiful, clever, or whatever. They would pull vocal ideas out of nowhere, and Ric polished it up and *boom*. That process was a lot of fun to me."

After the Milkwood sessions, Hawkes would eventually play a much greater role in Ric and Ben's plans, of course, but not before playing in other bands such as with country-rockers Orphan and Martin Mull's Fabulous Furniture, a musical comedy act in which Greg played a variety of instruments and noisemakers. Hawkes also appeared on the 1976 Mull album *Days of Wine and Neurosis*, playing saxophone, clarinet, and flute.

"Greg had the simplicity concept," Ocasek once told *Rolling Stone* in 1979. "But he also wasn't afraid to do interesting things and I knew he'd be the keyboard player I wanted."

Nick Koumoutseas: "After a while, word got out that Aengus was in trouble because of too much debt and because there was also a natural competition at the studio among the engineers, I felt it was best if I moved on, simply because I had connected with the owner of a bar in nearby Hudson, Massachusetts, and had somewhere to go. Jesse Henderson, a good friend, stuck with it and would become the engineer at Northern Studio and ultimately at Long View Farm and has had an illustrious career."

• 6 •

Richard and The Rabbits

$\mathcal{W}$ith Ben and Ric both married, and Ric a father, there was perhaps more urgency to make something happen with their music careers. After Milkwood dissolved, they formed a new, harder-rocking band called Richard and The Rabbits.

They recruited Hawkes to join the lineup, although he also continued his steadier gigs with Orphan and other session work. Other band members included guitarist Fuzzbee Morse and drummer Ron Riddle from Waves.

The band would hone their chops playing at a local club in Hudson called The Poor Farm. The owner was also installing a recording studio upstairs above the club, and aside from a couple short visits in Cleveland recording studios, this would essentially be the first multitrack recording studio experience for Ben and Rick.

Greg Hawkes: "The band name was given to us by Jonathan Richman of The Modern Lovers, which, ironically, was also the band that a drummer named David Robinson was in. The Rabbits lineup wouldn't last very long. It dissolved after a year or so, then I took the job playing with Martin Mull while also doing other session work."

The band advertised for a soundman and found a young musician named Allan Kaufman. Originally from Long Island, Kaufman not only got the gig, but also happened to be the roommate of a left-handed guitarist named Elliot Steinberg.

Allan Kaufman: "Elliot and I were roommates for a lot of years, and we lived in Jamaica Plain and in Allston. In 1974, I answered an ad in the alternative Boston publication *The Real Paper* for a soundman and it was for Richard and The Rabbits. So, I ran sound for the band and off of that, Ric and I became close. Of course, Ben and Ric had already done the Milkwood record, an acoustic, soft-rock thing that went 'cardboard in Canada.'

"But it's amazing that I still remember some of those songs. I don't remember what I had for lunch yesterday, but I remember Ric's lyrics to songs like 'Beantown, Don't You Let Me Down,' which was a Richard and The Rabbits' staple. I was also close with their wives, Kris and Suzanne, and during and after the time Richard and The Rabbits ceased, there was not a day that went by for a while, that Ben, Ric, and I were not together.

"We did a bunch of gigs, the last of which was at an Atlantic Records album party for the band Foghat, held at a roller skating rink where everyone was skating around and throwing whipped cream pies at each other while the band played!

"I remember *very* vividly, Ben being onstage and getting hit with a pie square in the face! But because he had an ancient soul and a heart like a Fleetwood Cadillac . . . you know, other guys might have been pissed off about something like that, but Ben, he just thought it was a gas!"

Of course, it is in hard times such as these, that having a sense of humor can be vital in a young band's existence of highs and lows, rough gigs, promises, and near-miss record deals.

Ron Riddle: "I remember Richard and The Rabbits had a showcase lined up on Nantucket Island [called The Lamppost, in Oak Bluffs] just outside of Boston. We were told that Elektra Records executives would be there and we'd be playing for them. We wouldn't get paid, but we would get fed. At this point in our careers, we were all dirt poor and we certainly weren't eating a lot of lobster, which was the featured dish on the menu. Hey, for a potential record contract and a lobster dinner, count us in!

"So, we had to take a ferry to get to the island with all our equipment, and when we docked, we found that we were to set up and play in a kind of amphitheater/ball field that was a bit of a walking distance from where the dinner was being served.

"By the time we set up, it was time to start playing, so, poised for success, we ripped through a set of our best originals. However, about halfway through the set, we started to notice that no one in the audience looked anything like a record executive, and in fact, the only people there were a semi-enthusiastic crowd of 'specially challenged' kids on a field trip of some sort.

"Then, it wasn't long before a rainstorm came through and we had to call it quits. So, what happened to the record executives? Turns out, they were all down under the pavilion, dry and out of the rain enjoying their lobster dinners!

"By the time the gear was packed up, we had to take our food 'to go' so we wouldn't miss the ferry going back, and needless to say, the record contract we were hoping to snag was apparently not even on the table. Discouraged and back at the parking lot, I had set my food down as we loaded the last piece of gear into the van. 'Well, at least I got a lobster dinner out of it,' I exclaimed.

"Then, just at that moment, Ben ran over my lobster dinner, crushing it into the pavement with his car! He stopped, as his window automatically rolled down and he looked over at me with this cool grin and said, 'Well—that's show biz!'. . . It was so hilarious and had us all rolling on the ground. I laughed so hard I couldn't breathe! When we got back to the house, Ben shared his lobster dinner with me and we laughed some more."

Jon Macey is the singer and guitarist of the longtime Boston rock band Fox Pass, who played gigs with Richard and The Rabbits.

Jon Macey: "Fox Pass played on Boston's Charles River in 1974 and Richard and The Rabbits opened the show. The other band on the bill was Harlow, which featured Tom Scholz of future Boston [the band] fame.

"I seem to remember Greg being in the lineup that day as well. It was a big outdoor show, run by Bob Gordon, who had organized the 'Cambridge Common Concerts' for years. Finally, that was shut down and Gordon moved it to Herder Park on the Charles."

Fuzzbee Morse [upon meeting Ben]: "The minute he opened his mouth to sing, it was obvious he had a great, natural voice, and my first impression was that Ben had a Paul McCartney–like voice with great range and tone, and he tended to sing the parts above Ric. He was also a solid bassist and used a Rickenbacker while in the Rabbits. Ben wasn't what you'd call a virtuoso bass player, but he was always right in the pocket and very dependable.

"Ben also had a great sense of mischief and a twinkle in his eye a good deal of the time. He always had one eye out for action and was a bit of a bad boy, but never in a malicious way. He also certainly had an eye for the ladies and vice versa. Ben also used to speak to me of his Polish parents and grandmother being very important characters in his life."

Tom Yates is another Boston-area musician who played with Ben, Ric, and Greg during this time period.

Tom Yates: "I actually met Greg Hawkes first, because he was playing in Martin Mull's group with drummer Rich Adelman, and I had also been in a band with Adelman. Rich wound up living in Hudson, Massachusetts, where I am from, and he used to have jam sessions at his house with Greg and others, including Jonathan Edwards and Mull.

"Just around the corner was a club called The Poor Farm, which later would have Richard and The Rabbits as one of their regular bands, and I was in another band that played there regularly called The Estes Boys. Upstairs was a recording studio, also called The Poor Farm and Ric and Ben did some recordings there as Otcasek and Orzechowski. I also did some recording there, with Greg helping out on sax and bass."

Nick Koumoutseas: "Along with my brother and with the help of Steve Crump [from Aengus Studio], we started Poor Farm Recording in Hudson. Steve is also one of the original inventors of the Bose noise-canceling headphones. My brother John is the original Arp tech and is still widely regarded as a go-to man for repairing classic synthesizers.

"Somehow, Tom Scholz found out about the scene and offered to swap the use of his twelve-track in my studio for late-night studio time, as he began working on what was to become the debut Boston album. My brother worked with him and said that Tom told him he used the twelve-track takes done at Poor Farm to make the historic debut Boston record.

"The Poor Farm became a place to mix, mingle, and speculate, and being located right over a bar really helped, as Ric, Ben, and Waves stuck with me in our endeavor to do 'something.'

"I loved Ric's song writing but also wanted to 'rock 'em up,' as I had many little talks with him, trying to prod him into a rock-and-roll posture, and I believe he took it to heart, combining elements of Otcasek and Orzechowski with Waves to become Richard and The Rabbits. Eventually Ron Riddle left the fold and Glenn Evans became the drummer."

After Richard and The Rabbits broke up, Riddle went to Washington, D.C., and then Hollywood to record with the progressive rock band Happy the Man, which was signed to Arista Records and produced by acclaimed producer Ken Scott.

Ron Riddle: "I didn't see any of my former bandmates for a while, until one day Happy the Man was coming down the elevator from a meeting with the record company and as the elevator doors opened and as I stepped out, The Cars were stepping in!

"In the wake of The Cars' huge success and later, with the death of my friend and bandmate, I still smile remembering Ben driving over my lobster dinner with his car, and like a movie star, delivering his cool line.

"However, along with that, my memories of him are very sweet. He was *always* a gentleman to me, and I don't remember him ever getting ruffled or upset with anyone. He had a movie-star persona, kind of like if a young Richard Burton were a rock star . . . and of course, that gorgeous voice that everyone today is so familiar with."

Fuzzbee Morse: "I was involved in all of the Richard and The Rabbits sessions, and I did sessions with Ocasek and Orr at The Poor Farm, with Greg on winds and keyboards and Ron Riddle on drums. I played guitar and keyboards on those sessions.

"We also did sessions with the same group, but with Glenn Evans replacing Ron on drums. The Rabbits also did other sessions at another studio for a bunch of songs, including 'Beantown' and 'Canoe,' and that lineup was myself, Ric, Ben, Greg, and Ron.

"This lineup always felt special to me. Ric was writing lots of good songs, Ben and Ric sang beautifully together, and Greg, Ron, and I were already very close from our previous band and recordings, so the band sounded great both live and in the studio."

Andy Mendelson is a musician and engineer who also worked with Rick and Ben, and much later, along with his brother, Richard, would purchase the Syncro Sound recording studio from The Cars.

Andy Mendelson: "I had just moved to Boston, and first met Rick and Ben when they were in Richard and The Rabbits. My brother was also an engineer at Aengus Studio. However, I got to know them better a few years later when they were Ocasek and Orr, a folk duo playing around town. They recorded some demos at my basement studio in Arlington, and I also played some electric guitar on some of their demos at a studio in Maynard [Northern Studio].

"I also had my own band around that time, and Greg Hawkes played keys and sax in that band. I began recording and touring with Andy Pratt [and] eventually recorded a solo album on Arista Records, and Greg did some work on that as well.

"I remember Ben as a very warm and super-creative guy, with a playful sort of intelligence. I have this image of him at Greg Hawkes's wedding and thought he had transformed into a tremendously charismatic dude, probably much as the world would see him, when The Cars blew up soon thereafter.

"A number of years later, after my brother and I had taken over Syncro Sound, I was working on some song demos for his girlfriend [Diane Grey Page], and my impression then was that Ben had become an extremely private person."

The late Thom Moore was another recording engineer working with this lineup and would end up not only working with The Cars, but also touring around the world with many bands.

"I played in local bands as a teen, but I soon knew I couldn't keep up with the top cats," Moore once stated in a website blog published by former White Zombie guitarist, J. Yuenger, who had also worked with Thom.

"At the time, I attended an art school that had a very primitive sound studio outfitted with a basic, three-channel mixing board and an EMS VCS-3 *Putney* synthesizer . . . and I got hooked. I built a basic lighting system for some friends in a band, and we cut some demos at a local studio [Poor Farm] that the drummer, Glenn Evans, was friendly with.

"I started hanging out at the studio and assisting on some projects, picking up as much knowledge as I could, and one day, Glenn asked if I could go with him to the studio to help set up his kit. The session was for a band made up of Ric Ocasek, Ben Orr, and Greg Hawkes, and everything went well.

"By that time, some friends from MIT [Massachusetts Institute of Technology] had designed and built a sixteen-channel recording/mixing console and we *jumped* at the chance to have an edge on the competition. The console had an early MXR flanger and phase shifter, and I had an Echoplex for delays. One night, Glenn invited Ric and Greg to the club, and they were impressed with the mix and sound quality."

Tom Yates: "I was also in a band with drummer Glenn Evans, who got involved with the Otcasek and Orzechowski project and then recommended me for an upcoming recording session. We rehearsed a couple times and then recorded four songs at Northern Studios: 'Never Gonna Get Over You,' 'Everyday' [a Buddy Holly cover], 'Twilight Superman,' and 'Start It All Again.'

"Ben sang lead on 'Everyday' and played bass on all four songs. I am not positive, but I believe the recording session happened after Richard and The Rabbits had already dissolved."

Allan Kaufman: "So, after Richard and The Rabbits, they started doing the acoustic duo performances and *that* is when they started calling themselves 'Ocasek and Orr.'

"They started a regular gig at The Idler, a little coffeehouse in Harvard Square on Wednesday and Saturday nights, and other places as well, such as the Inn-Square Men's Bar in Cambridge. Now that was an iconic joint; *everyone* played there.

"The owner of the Inn-Square, Marshall Simpkins, was actually the first to realize where Ric and Ben could go when they first arrived in Boston. He had been instrumental in leading them toward recording demos at The Poor Farm, and actually was the first to book live what became Milkwood."

Marshall Simpkins was the co-owner of The Inn-Square Men's Bar from 1974 to 1984, located in Inman Square in Cambridge, one of the first clubs in Boston to book the Ocasek & Orzechowski duo.

Marshall Simpkins: "We opened the bar in 1974, and back then, the drinking age was only eighteen, therefore, we had bands booked every night. We wanted to get away from being a 'men's bar' so we had 'Ladies Invited' added to the marquee, because we didn't want to lose the regular patrons, plus we didn't have the money to change the sign! I started hiring females to work the doors and bartend, as to change the atmosphere.

"We had a lot of big names play at the club including Bonnie Raitt, Patty Larkin, and 'Til Tuesday, and had many of the great local bands as well such as Nervous Eaters. I first started booking Ric and Ben when they were still a duo, and they hosted a Sunday afternoon 'step up to the mic' event, with them playing with and in between the guest appearances.

"I hit it off well with Ric, and Ben was always a really nice guy and talented singer. The Cars were a great band, and it's great to see them finally reach the Rock & Roll Hall of Fame."

Allan Kaufman: "I was kind of the 'and' in Ocasek and Orr because I would play congas with them during these shows. It was really a lot of fun, and we had a great time. However, in the meantime, Ben and Ric were also both getting antsy to be in an electric band again."

In the summer of 1975, Ben participated in a recording session back home in Cleveland for Jim and Marcia Skaggs, who were recording a three-song demo tape in anticipation of the upcoming 1976 bicentennial celebration. The project, recorded at Cleveland's Agency Recording Studio (located

Ben at Cleveland's Agency Recording Studio in 1975, recording a song for Jim and Marcia Scaggs' bicentennial EP, produced by Joe Mayer.
Courtesy of Bob Paris

next door to the famed Agora Ballroom), was being produced by old friend Joe Mayer, and Ben took part on a song called "New Born Love," providing vocals and guitar.

It was around this time that another Berklee College student, a left-handed, Long Island guitarist named Elliot Steinberg (aka Elliot Easton), would come in contact with the band through Kaufman.

Born in December 1953 in Brooklyn, New York, before moving to Massapequa on Long Island, Steinberg was musically influenced by The Beatles and surf-era music in his early teens. Elliot's parents bought him a cheap electric guitar, then he saved up his money washing dishes at a local restaurant in order to buy his first Fender guitar in high school.

Having honed his chops in the Long Island club scene, Steinberg attended Brockport, a state university in Rochester, New York, for a year, before finally heading to Boston in 1972 to study guitar at Berklee.

He played in a country band in Boston's notorious "Combat Zone," and while not exactly his cup of tea, learning a lot of country songs helped to cultivate the finger-picking style Elliot would become known for. He really loved the eclectic Boston music scene, and was determined to not simply play in a covers band, but somehow carve out his own identity.

Greg Hawkes: "I remember one night, Richard and The Rabbits were playing at Jonathan Swifts and this was the first time that I met Elliot, who had come down to see the band with Allan Kaufman."

Allan Kaufman: "Over this period of time Elliot was my roommate and one of my closest friends, and when Ric and Ben said 'Okay, let's do a rock band, who are we going to get on guitar?' I told them the only guitar player you are going to want is Elliot. You gotta hear Elliot!

"He culled his playing by sitting on the couch and playing to all the Steely Dan, Little Feat, and Allen Toussaint–New Orleans records, and he also got the Miles Davis memo that the most important notes are 'the ones you don't play.'

"That's why Elliot's guitar licks are always so tasty and well thought out, because not only does he really know how to play and have great hand-eye coordination, but it's also the way he hears stuff that makes Elliot such a formidable guitarist.

"So, Elliot came down, and the first thing that Ben said to him was 'Okay, amaze me' [laughs], because I guess I may have over-hyped him a little bit. Elliot was a great player, though, and the rest as they say would be Cars history."

• 7 •

Cap'n Swing

During 1975, Ben and Ric shifted back to a rock music format, creating a new band dubbed Cap'n Swing. The lineup featured Ben as front man on vocals, Ocasek on rhythm guitar, Steinberg on lead guitar, Glenn Evans on drums, and newcomers Todd Roberto on bass and Danny Schliftman on keyboards, as Greg Hawkes was touring with Martin Mull's Fabulous Furniture at the time. Cap'n Swing would develop into more of a smooth, jamming band with a jazzy twist, much in the same vein as the aforementioned Steely Dan.

Allan Kaufman: "Elliot and I were listening to a lot of R&B, soul, and 'musician's band' stuff at the time, such as Little Feat and Steely Dan. I initially suggested that Ben just be the lead singer and not play the bass. Ben was not sure at first, but then he thought about the cool chicks he could get if he didn't have an instrument between him and the microphone [laughs] and he said, 'Okay, I'll give it a try.'

"So then we got these great players, a bassist named Todd Roberto and a keyboard player named Danny Schliftman, who now goes by the name Danny Louis and has been in the very successful band Gov't Mule for the last fifteen years. We then auditioned about a hundred drummers and ironically, the one Ric *really* wanted was a jazzier player that was already in another band."

Danny Louis: "Ben was a good friend, and we played a lot of great music together in just a few short years. We were pals. I've only known a few great singers who were pure 'naturals' like Ben. He just opened his mouth to sing and sounded perfect—like a hit record.

"His musicianship was stellar, and he was just a very fun guy to know and hang out with. He was consistently a good and kind fellow, and I'll always miss him and remember fondly all the good times we spent together."

After the auditions, the band went with drummer Glenn Evans, who also had a previous connection with soundman Thom Moore. Before joining Cap'n Swing, Evans had gone to work for the Richard Carr Agency of Rhode Island, and the first band he was asked to join was Moonfast, whom he had been introduced to by the aforementioned Moore. Moore was also Moonfast's soundman before getting into engineering and connecting with Richard and The Rabbits. The Poor Farm engineer, Nick Koumoutseas, also remembered Evans quite fondly.

Nick Koumoutseas: "Glenn is a real friend and was always eager to be part of the team. He basically wrote the drum parts for 'Bye Bye Love,' and was the drummer on most of the Northern Studio sessions with Jesse Henderson as engineer. Later, he worked with national artist Dr. Hook and the Medicine Show and now leads a very cool, Tampa-based surf band called Hodaddys."

Glenn Evans: "It was just a different time back then . . . the drinking age was eighteen and the bars were packed with people every night. So these various agencies would book bars exclusively and have a large roster of bands they basically molded and controlled to create the new FM radio cuts of the time."

However, when the drummer had the opportunity to join Cap'n Swing and took it, he would be temporarily blacklisted by the agency for leaving. Evans had already done some recording with Ric and Ben when he was asked to join the band.

Glenn Evans: "It was time for me to do something original and creative, so I jumped ship on the agency to join Cap'n Swing. Some of the demo tracks I played drums on received drive-time airplay on WBCN radio. Recordings that, I like to think, helped pave the way for The Cars to eventually land a record deal.

"I remember Ben as a very nice guy, always accompanied by his white wolf and driving a purple Impala, jacked up in the back with big tires and chrome reverse wheels. Rick was cool, but aloof, a constant radio button-pusher and he drove a blue VW bug with gray fenders."

Cap'n Swing would gain momentum, playing gigs all over the Boston area, including The Mirage, Paul's Mall, The Club in Cambridge, Little Earl's in Gloucester, Bosco's at Scituate Harbor and later a failed showcase performance at the famed Max's Kansas City in New York City, in which the band was told that their music and visual image was "all over the place." Despite the disappointment of Max's Kansas City, however, the band learned from the experience, knowing they needed to continue developing and tightening up both their sound and visual image.

Steve Berkowitz, who would go on to work closely with The Cars as a tour and studio manager, and band co-manager with Elliot Roberts, also knew members of the band long before they became famous. Berkowitz would also go on to become an A&R executive, and Grammy- and Blues Award–winning producer, having worked with such artists as Bob Dylan, Johnny Cash, Leonard Cohen, Tony Bennett, Robert Glasper, Branford Marsalis, and Jeff Buckley. He has enjoyed a forty-plus-year career in the music business.

Steve Berkowitz: "I knew the guys in the band going back to around 1968 or '69, when David Robinson and I both worked at the same Boston record store called New England Music City. David worked days, and I worked nights at the record store; we were concert buddies, and I also played guitar, so we would get together with his roommates and jam. They would eventually become the band Modern Lovers.

"I used to see the Ocasek and Orr folk duo in the coffeehouses around town, and I also started this 'blues jam' at the Speakeasy in Cambridge called 'Blue Lodge.' That's where I had met this cool, left-handed guitarist named Elliot. I was a friend of Elliot's roommate for a time, Allan Kaufman, who started telling me about this really cool band he was managing called Cap'n Swing."

Allan Kaufman: "Now, Cap'n Swing was already playing out and I wanted to make a big splash. The Mirage was on Commonwealth Aveune and the club was billing themselves as sort of the 'Studio 54 of Boston' kind of thing on Friday, Saturday, and Sunday. So, I went to the owner and said, 'Look, I want to put in this unbelievable *rock* band for you on Tuesday, Wednesday, and Thursday'. . . and they agreed.

"This was big for the band's progression because you can rehearse in a studio or rehearsal hall all you want, but there's nothing like having the feedback from a live audience to build band chemistry.

"By this time, we were all so broke and The Mirage had these industrial-size cartons of Goldfish crackers that Ben, Ric, and I were fucking literally living off of [laughs]! But after a few weeks, we started getting a crowd at the club, and then I started working with a booking agent named Tim Collins, who later worked with Aerosmith.

"We started booking the band in more establishments, and then, I knew someone who was managing The Bell Buoy on Scituate Harbor near Boston and we started doing a once-a-week gig downstairs in the basement, at a place called Bosco's. This is when Ben really started coming into his own as a front man and realizing more and more of his connection to the female fans."

Barbara Rhind was the manager at the Scituate Harbor establishment and booked Cap'n Swing to play Bosco's. She would continue to be friends with Ben after he became famous.

Barbara Rhind: "I was managing both Bosco's and The Bell Buoy, doing everything from bartending and scheduling to inventory and booking the bands. Allan Kaufman came to me, more than once, urging me to come and hear this band called Cap'n Swing. He was so hyped up about these guys that I finally decided to go check them out. It was Allan's persistence that got me to go see the band.

"They played some really obscure tunes, and I remember the first time I saw them, Ben stood out the most, he wore some kind of orange, karate-looking outfit and eye makeup. I just found him interesting at that time. I wasn't just mesmerized by the music, but I was mesmerized by Ben as well!

"I actually went to see them perform three times in a row before I decided to try them out at The Bell Buoy. I was taking a chance and selfishly booked them for my own feelings about the music. I knew it wasn't going to go over big down there, and it was going to take some pushing and prodding. I booked them for five nights straight and they would come and rehearse during the afternoon, so I would sit there and listen to them all day. It worked for me because I loved those guys!

"In their early days, people just didn't 'get it,' which was frustrating for me because I really believed in them and kept booking the band anyway. It's funny, because I still see some of my customers from those days and *now* they say how they loved the band and all, but my question is, where was all the support back then?

"I really did believe in the band after I saw them a couple times and they had me hooked, but I think Allan Kaufman 'got it' right out of the gate because he really believed in that band from the very beginning.

"I remained friends with Ben, off and on, even after Cap'n Swing became The Cars. As a musician and singer, Ben really believed in himself and always knew that he would make it. He was charismatic, romantic, and a very patient person . . . he was a dreamer.

"He was a great singer, and the thing I noticed about him as a bass player was that he just played. Not a lot of movement or romping around onstage, he just stood there and played, and it was his charisma that spoke for him . . . he could mesmerize you with his looks and his voice. It didn't matter if you were male or female; he just had this power!

"The first time The Cars played at Boston Garden, Ben gave me tickets and backstage passes for the show. I sat in the Loge area with all the guys from the Boston Celtics. I took my boss with me because I wanted him to see that this band *did* make it, just like I had told him they would."

Allan Kaufman: "It was at Bosco's where the band, as a whole, really started coming into its own. However, during this whole time you also have to understand that Ric was not necessarily happy with the music, because the kind of stuff Elliot, Danny, Todd Roberto, and I were listening to was jazzy and more R&B-sounding, while Ric was more minimal . . . more like Suicide, New York City punk, Nico, and Velvet Underground.

"When they finally morphed from Cap'n Swing to The Cars, Ric said, 'I want Ben playing bass, because I don't want some monster Berklee-graduate player, I want steady and simplistic.' And yes, Ben was a very good bass player, make no doubt about it.

"They all wrote in Cap'n Swing, but I think there was only one song where anyone else actually got a songwriting credit. They wrote a batch of songs, and some ended up in The Cars' repertoire, not least among them, were 'Bye Bye Love' and 'Just What I Needed.'

"Ric is an amazing and prolific songwriter and that's undeniable, it's not even subjective, that's fact! He wrote a song called 'Strawberry Moonlight,' and if you listen to the changes, that song became 'Best Friend's Girl,' but the only Cap'n Swing song that The Cars truly morphed was 'Bye Bye Love.'"

Ocasek was also contemplating making more changes to Cap'n Swing; however, they were also continuing to shop the existing lineup because they were finally starting to get some attention. In essence, Ric was caught in between the momentum that Cap'n Swing was building, and the desire to tear it down in favor of the more minimalist sound he really wanted.

Allan Kaufman: "Also, we had done some other demos, pressed a bunch of acetates and I booked the band to play the Max's Kansas City show. Ben, Ric, and I made about a dozen trips to New York shopping the band, where I had arranged for Ric and Ben to play the Cap'n Swing songs acoustically for people, such as the president of CBS Records and the head of A&R at Arista Records.

"During that time, Ben and Ric (especially Ben) got really tight with my parents and siblings, and every time we went to New York, we would stay at my house on Long Island. In fact, up until my mom sold the house, she used to call the guest room 'the Cars room' [laughs]. In essence, Ben sort of became like a Jew-by-proxy, you know, hanging out with my family in a predominantly Jewish suburb on Long Island!"

Glenn Evans: "After waiting over a year for the pending record contract to happen, I left Cap'n Swing. My last gig with the band was a three-night stint on Nantucket. I was very late on my van payments and the band's equipment was in my truck as I came off the ferry in Hyannis with Elliot Steinberg in the passenger seat and fifteen dollars in my pocket for three nights' work."

Michael Blackmer is the son of David E. Blackmer, inventor of dbx noise reduction, and is a prolific, Boston-area recording engineer, technician, inventor, and studio designer in his own right. Early on, he worked and did repairs on the band's equipment. Later on, Blackmer's company, Audio Professionals of Boston, would do the technical installation of The Cars' own studio in Boston.

Michael Blackmer: "I met Cap'n Swing back in the mid-1970s through their soundman, Thom Moore. I also did some work for Bill Riseman at

Aengus Studio's original location in Southborough, Massachusetts, and was very much his right-hand technical man, along with a core of other talented engineers.

"During the mid-1970s I was a member of the Dr. Decibel work group in the basement of *Natural Sound* in Framingham, Massachusetts. Along with several other magnificent weirdos who could repair pretty much anything, short of the human heart, I got to know Thom Moore when he, several times, brought Cap'n Swing's equipment into the shop for repair. We hit it off surprisingly well, considering how very different we were in temperament. Thom was *not* at all a hippie.

"As for Ben, I have only great memories and I miss him greatly. He had a fantastic voice, a great sense of humor, and was such a kind-hearted and generous person."

David Robinson: "I can remember seeing Ben's and Ric's names around town as another band, Cap'n Swing, but it wasn't the same places that I was going to at the time, so I hadn't gotten to see them play live.

"Then, a mutual friend of mine and Ric's, Maxanne Sartori, had mentioned them to me, and she thought they were good, so I went and saw Cap'n Swing at Paul's Mall. They were kind of a mish-mash group of people, and when they came out, Ben was wearing these white, satin Karate pajamas and flip-flops!

"I remember thinking 'What kind of a look is this?' Ben only sang and didn't play the bass, but I did notice right away how great his voice was! The music was quirky-pop sounding, and not really coming from a hip place, but more a nerdy place. So, I wasn't overly impressed."

Mark (a.k.a. Cowboy Mach) Bell is a longtime Boston singer, having fronted Boston rockers Thundertrain (which Allan Kaufman would later manage), as well as doing a stint in Aerosmith guitarist Joe Perry's solo band.

Mark Bell: "Thundertrain played a gig in Medway, Massachusetts, at The Hungry Lion, and Cap'n Swing was also on the bill. I had never heard of them and thought they had a weird sounding name. They struck me that night as some sort of Steely Dan music and not really the high-energy stuff that I gravitated to. Plus, they didn't really have a look, just a bunch of dudes and one of them seemed too tall for the rest.

"Not long after, however, I started hearing them on WBCN, and when you didn't have to look at them, the sound fit the airwaves pretty well. The guy who ran sound for Cap'n Swing, Allan Kaufman, would later become Thundertrain's manager.

"The next time we played with them a few months later, they were The Cars. They opened for Thundertrain at a skating arena in Berlin, New Hampshire, and they looked totally different and were really cool. I don't really recall Ben Orr onstage when I saw Cap'n Swing, but in this new lineup, he stood out like a beacon!"

Cap'n Swing would continue to hone their sound and while still in search of a record deal, recorded eleven demo tracks at Bill Riseman's Northern Studio in the summer of 1976, including such tracks as "Crazy Rock and Roll," "Come Back Down," and "Strawberry Moonlight." The latter two songs would get some local radio airplay in Boston. Another track, "Bye Bye Love," would later come back into play in a big way.

Jesse Henderson, the engineer who had played drums on the Milkwood album, was once again involved, only this time behind the mixing board instead of the drums.

Jesse Henderson: "The Northern sessions with Cap'n Swing were recorded during the midnight-to-six-a.m. shift, and recorded live, to two-track stereo. We made it a point to be ready to record within an hour of setting up.

"At Northern, the control room was upstairs, so I had to run up and down a lot during that first hour before a session. We didn't fuss too much, for it was all about content. Also of note, I remember that Ben did *not* play bass on these sessions."

Jeff Lock was the lead guitarist of another Boston-area band called The Atlantics and remembers gigging with both Cap'n Swing and The Cars.

Jeff Lock: "I remember we did a gig with Cap'n Swing at The Armory near BU [Boston University] and later on, we would also do a two-night show with The Cars at the Paradise Rock Club in Boston.

"I can remember talking to Elliot that night at The Rat, after they had just got their record deal. We talked about his Strat and he was very laid back about the whole record deal thing. We [The Atlantics] were also trying to get signed, and I have to say that at age twenty, I would have been bouncing off the walls if I had just gotten signed to a record deal!"

Boby Bear was the drummer for The Atlantics and recalls performing with Cap'n Swing, as well as a certain encounter he had with Ben.

"Between our debut in 1976 and the release of The Cars' first album, The Atlantics crossed paths with Ben Orr and company numerous times. In the summer of '76, we were doing a show with Cap'n Swing at the famous Cambridge Armory. The room was positively massive and the bands were performing on some sort of hi-tech flatbed that served as a mobile stage with built-in lighting and PA systems.

"Cap'n Swing seemed to be one part jazz, one part hippie-granola, one part avant-garde, one part Velvet Underground, and zero part of any of what was taking hold musically or visually at that time. To put it bluntly, no one really knew what to make of them, or what to do with them. At the time Ben was serving as the front-and-center lead vocalist, who was already famous, or even notorious, for his good looks and ever-present castanets. I don't think that people were taking them seriously, but little did anyone know what Ben, Ric, and Elliot were about to do, very soon.

"Ben was the only one who looked like a rock star, otherwise, they were a motley-looking crew. I don't have anything bad to say about Cap'n Swing, but the one thing I *can* say is that no one in the Boston music scene saw The Cars coming.

"The pack of Ball Square, Somerville street hockey players who humped gear for The Atlantics, were unfortunately rather unenlightened when it came to Cap'n Swing. In fact, I heard varying reports about the conduct of one of our roadies that night, who supposedly peed in one of their guitar cases, stole beer from their dressing room, and made some nasty remarks. We banished the kid, but to this day, I don't know the full extent of his poor conduct.

"However, after the show that night I made a personal apology to Ben, and his response is something that I'd look back on in years to come. As we shook hands, he broke out with the dimples and calmly said, 'No problem man . . . no problem at all.' This was far more than the words of a nice guy. This was the look in the eye of a guy who knew that ultimately his band, in whatever form, was going places.

"It was truly one of those 'you had to be there' moments that I never forgot. I only bumped into Ben a few times after The Cars became famous, and he was always just as classy and decent as he was that night at The Armory.

"In my years [1975 to 2006] of performing in Boston, I ran into a lot of interesting people, but few of them were as classy, good-looking, and talented as Ben Orr. I regret that I didn't know him better and he was taken from us far too early. All we can do now is imagine what he would've gone on to do."

In the late summer of 1976, Cap'n Swing played the Newbury Street Music Fair, hosted by WBCN Boston radio DJ Maxanne Sartori, who was also responsible for first playing the Cap'n Swing demos on her afternoon radio show. In fact, she was notorious for searching out and playing local bands on the airwaves, also helping to break nationally another Boston band, Aerosmith, just a few years prior.

Back in those days many radio DJs were allowed to not only choose what songs to play during their radio shows, but also experiment with lesser-known bands and even play demo tapes of unsigned bands. Sartori liked Cap'n Swing, started going to their shows, and would become friendly with the band.

"They married the musicality of Steely Dan, the art of Roxy Music, and the darkness of The Velvet Underground . . . they were amazing," Sartori told *Rolling Stone* in 1979.

The band would also seek advice from Sartori, as she was living with another struggling, soon-to-be-famous musician, Billy Squier. In fact, at one point, they asked Maxanne to consider officially working with Cap'n Swing, but she turned the offer down, feeling she wouldn't be able to develop the platform needed for the band to truly succeed on a national level.

· 8 ·

Creating Cars

A NEW MODEL

*W*hen the Max's Kansas City showcase gig in New York City did not land Cap'n Swing a record deal, Ric indeed changed the band lineup, moving away from the very talented, but jazzier-sounding Schliftman, Roberto, and Evans, while retaining Ben on bass, Elliot on guitar, and also bringing Hawkes back into the fold.

Allan Kaufman: "Of course, Ric already knew Greg Hawkes from the Milkwood sessions and Richard and The Rabbits, and Greg also knew David Robinson from playing with Jonathan Richman and The Modern Lovers, you know, that real minimalistic, more of a new wave-punk sound.

"Danny [who actually wrote the keyboard hook for 'Just What I Needed'] was not happy and rightfully so, and in 1977 and '78, I was managing a Boston band called Sass that played The Rat a lot, and I brought Danny into that band. He went by the name 'Danny Keys.' Sass got a record deal, which was actually the very last record made on the old Roulette Records label.

"Danny is one of the most formidable keyboard players, and can play anything: trumpet, trombone, Hammond B-3, Fender Rhodes, grand piano . . . and he gets to do all of that in his current band, Gov't Mule."

Ric scrapped nearly the entire Cap'n Swing repertoire of songs and instead, opted for a stripped-down, more minimal rock sound with less extended jams and tighter song structures. This style change also lent more to a darker, more opaque writing style that he was now developing.

He also directed Ben away from the front-man role and returned him to playing bass onstage. Just like the early days in Cleveland, Ben was again adapting his role to whatever his band needed.

"We kept Elliot from that band [Cap'n Swing] because he was such a good lead guitar player," Ben told the *The Plain Dealer*'s Jane Scott in 1979. "We also hung on to Greg on keyboards, who at the time, was also playing with Martin Mull."

The last significant move was to bring in former Modern Lovers drummer David Robinson. Yes, the very drummer Ric had seen play on the first day he had come to Boston.

Robinson was born in April 1949 in Woburn, Massachusetts, and was the only Massachusetts-native in The Cars. In 1970, he became drummer for The Modern Lovers, a highly influential band that helped bridge the gap between late-1960s garage-rock and the newer punk sounds of the 1970s. He also played in the Los Angeles punk band The Pop! before joining Boston garage-punk rockers DMZ in 1976.

Ric saw DMZ perform at The Rat, and not only liked Robinson's drumming, but also his visual style. After Ric played him some rough demos, David decided to join the band. "I figured it was all worth a try because it was going to be my last band anyway," Robinson told *Rolling Stone* in 1979.

David Robinson: "There was a band in Boston called Reddy Teddy, who gave me a tape to listen to and they wanted me to join their band. However, at the same time, Ric had also given me a tape and wanted me to join their band. In retrospect, I suppose it should have been obvious, but at the time, I really wasn't sure which one to do. But in the end, I decided on Ric and Ben's band.

"We went to the basement, and of course, Ben really didn't say much through the whole thing. As soon as we began to play a few of the new songs [it was minus a couple of the other Cap'n Swing members and no keyboard player], it was clear to me that this was going to be really good. I really liked the whole vibe and was excited about how good it was, right on the spot . . . like, instantly. Of course, I am also noticing how it wasn't difficult at all for Ben. He wasn't straining to do anything."

Robinson also just happened to have a particular name (for a band) that he always wanted to use, and suggested it to his new bandmates. The moniker was *The Cars*, and the guys loved it, of course! The name somehow fit this new direction the band was going in. Sharp, sleek, and precise, like a brand-new sports car!

"Who can forget the day he got his driver's license? Or his first car or first trip to the drive-in," Ben told the *The Plain Dealer*'s Jane Scott in 1978. Orr also remembered the old Orzechowski family car, a 1949 Buick. "Black and big, I can still see it, with those brownish-gray velvet seats. If I hadn't had a car, I wouldn't have driven over from Parma Heights to Fairview Park to go shopping, and I wouldn't have met my wife, Kris."

With the new lineup and band name cemented, The Cars started rehearsing while Ric began compiling all these ideas and writing the songs that would ultimately create one of the most definitive debut rock albums ever. Obviously inspired by this new band, Ric crafted a collection of tight, hook-laden rock songs he then presented to the band for fine-tuning.

"I didn't think the songs were much different than the old songs I was writing, maybe I was just learning to do it better," Ocasek told *Washington Rock Concert* magazine in 1979. "I remember I wanted to get rid of the jam thing. We got more defined as a band, less loose and more concise."

The Cars finally emerged from Ric's basement with an album's worth of new songs, and there was a feeling of great potential, as if the band had created something truly unique. The songs bridged elements of seventies classic rock with the current punk attitudes and emerging "new wave" rhythms that were about to bubble to the surface.

The guys were excited about their new direction and made a pact that within a year, they were going to record an album. "We knew we were good before we played our first gig," David Robinson once told music journalist and *Crawdaddy* magazine editor, Jon Pareless.

With the band's new musical direction now in place and beginning to flourish, it was David Robinson who set out to refine and perfect a new look and image for The Cars. A former art student, David would assume the role of creative director in modifying the band's appearance in a sleek, pop-art style.

Having learned from their experiences in Cap'n Swing, The Cars were realizing they needed a more consistent visual image. David incorporated a black, white, and red-dominated color scheme into the band's wardrobe, and encouraged the guys to be a bit more demonstrative onstage. In fact, along with each band member's visual image being refined, each was given their own role or persona of sorts to bring to the stage, embellishing their personalities and roles in the band, without it appearing contrived.

The tall, lanky Ric Ocasek would be the mysterious songwriter with the unique voice and dark shades, flanked by Benjamin Orr, the heart-throbbing bass player with stoic stage presence and smooth-cool vocal style. Elliot Steinberg would be "Elliot Easton," the cutting-edge guitarist with the sharp riffs and solos. The multi-tasking keyboardist, Greg Hawkes, who would not officially join the band until after the first couple of shows, was the diminutive, electronics wizard.

Of course, this was all backed by David, the stylish, rock-solid, and visually creative drummer. Robinson would also design the band's logo, create stage backdrops, record concert intro tapes for the live shows, and start working on ideas for what would *almost* become the cover art for the debut album. Onstage, the left-handed Easton always played on the right side of the right-handed Orr, in a visual nod to the Beatles' imagery of the left-handed Paul McCartney and right-handed George Harrison.

AT THE RAT

Although it is widely assumed that The Cars made their official live debut on New Year's Eve in 1976, at Pease Air Force Base in New Hampshire, the fact is, they had already performed a one-off, impromptu show just a few days before that "official" New Year's Eve concert. What's more, Greg Hawkes did not take part in either of the first two shows.

David Robinson: "Music-wise I cannot remember a thing about the New Year's Eve show in New Hampshire, but that was actually our second gig. We played one gig before that, in a motel lounge somewhere on Route 9 [outside of Boston], I believe, but I can't remember the name of the place. It was sort of an experimental gig, just to play out somewhere and not be in the basement. To experience a few people looking at us and to run through the songs before the Pease gig. I believe a roadie got us that New Year's gig, but I really don't remember anything about it."

Greg Hawkes: "I didn't play at the first gig or the New Year's show at Pease Air Force Base because I hadn't officially joined the band yet. I saw The Cars play in January at a place called The Bell Buoy on the South Shore somewhere [Bosco's at Scituate Harbor]. They had already played a couple shows as The Cars before I saw them again in early February of 1977 at The Rat in Boston.

"I wanted to be part of a band that had a shot at success; I had already known Ric for a few years before The Cars formed, and I always liked his songwriting. I had also worked on a few of his early demo tapes, so we had already developed somewhat of a working relationship."

Owned by Jim Harold, who was good friends with Ben over the years, The Rathskeller was affectionately known as "The Rat" and was one of Boston's premiere live-music venues from 1974 through 1997. The Rat hosted countless local bands and many "soon-to-be" legendary acts along with The Cars, including The Ramones, R.E.M., The Police, Talking Heads, Metallica, and Red Hot Chili Peppers, to name but a few. Harold first knew Ric and Ben as Milkwood, and actually booked one Cap'n Swing show at The Rat, before the first Cars showcase gig.

Jim Harold: "Even when it was just Ric and Ben I knew they were going to be good, but when I first saw Cap'n Swing, they didn't really knock me out, and I told them as such. They definitely weren't *The Cars* yet, but one night after a show at the Music Hall, Ric said they had a plan . . . and they cer-

The Cars first appearance at The Rat in Boston, February 1977.
Photo by Robert Post

tainly did. They made some changes and then, just became different. The Cars didn't sound at all like the other bands that were playing around at that time."

That first Cars show at The Rat was on February 7, which prompted subsequent Boston gigs at The Paradise Rock Club (opening for Rick Derringer and enticing an encore from the audience) and Paul's Mall. Before long, the band was creating a buzz around the city and started getting some favorable local press from such newspapers as the *Boston Globe, Boston Herald American,* and *Boston Phoenix.*

"We knew The Rat was a place that we wanted to play," Ocasek stated in the Turner Studio interview of 2000. "A lot of bands around town were playing there, plus the fact that they accepted new bands playing their own material."

Robert Post was the manager at The Deli Restaurant, also in Kenmore Square and not only witnessed that first Cars show at The Rat, but also photographed it.

Robert Post: "The Rat lay beneath a German-named restaurant called The Rathskeller. No German food though. In fact, the kitchen was actually called Voodoo BBQ for a time. The crowd that frequented the place was a mix of punks, musicians, drunks, and students. Downstairs in a large basement was the club. It was dark, dingy, and smelly. The carpets were patched with duct-tape and the tables and chairs were miss-matched junk. I loved it!

"I was introduced to The Rat by my dishwasher, Monoman [a.k.a. Jeff Conolly], who was the lead singer, keyboardist, and creator of the punk band DMZ. Soon after that, I got to know David Robinson when he was drumming with DMZ. He and Ric Ocasek would often meet there along with other band members of The Cars.

"I had recently purchased a camera with the idea of photographing live DMZ shows and became a regular at the place. Well, one thing led to another and I was soon immersed in the booming Rat music scene and photographing every band I could.

"The night of their debut at The Rat, I was waiting outside the club when I saw Ric Ocasek walking up to the place with a blonde on each arm. He was smiling, laughing, and excited. As the show got closer and the crowds began to gather, you could tell something big was about to happen. Inside, the tiny club was packed and set behind the stage hung a satin banner reading 'The Cars.' Unusually, there were no other bands on the bill that night and it was their debut!

"They took the stage, and I knew right away that this band was different. They were polished, tight, and having fun! Their music was a fresh, new, and different rock-and-roll. The tiny dance floor was packed, and I knew I had to capture the event on film. I believe their music inspired me. To this day, it's the best live shoot I have ever done!

"During the set break, I made my way to the green room, which was more like a walk-in closet. They put on no airs, but I could tell they were focused and in the moment. They were like boxers between rounds, with towels and sweat included. Their second set was even better than the first.

They played the entire song list from their upcoming debut album. It was a great night that was incredibly enjoyable as is their legendary music."

Boston-area music journalist Joe Viglione was also at that first Cars show at The Rat and would later become a friend of Ben's. "The first night The Cars performed at The Rat, there were a handful of Boston musicians there," Viglione told The Cars fanzine *Drive* in 2001.

"We had already heard Cap'n Swing on the 'Demi Monde' show on WTBS-Radio [the FM radio station at Massachusetts Institute of Technology or MIT], and taped the songs. This was a fun night; I remember the band playing 'Gimme a Little Sign,' the Brenton Wood song, and 'Don't Worry Baby' by the Beach Boys. We were Cars fans from the start. They just had that something special."

Jim Harold: "The Cars were The Rat's band! Blondie and Talking Heads were Hilly's [Kristal, owner of the famous New York City club, CBGB] bands . . . and The Cars were *our* band!

"Before going onstage, Ben would just flip a switch and become the rock star of the band. Always looking to his left, he knew that he was the one they were all looking at . . . and he would just smile like he could handle it all, no problem. The way he performed, took image-control of the band onstage, being that focal point that would simply take care of itself. It was all so easy for Ben . . . he was just so smooth."

Veteran Boston rocker Robin Lane, of Robin Lane and The Chartbusters, remembered seeing the band around town.

Robin Lane: "I remember a brown-haired, sort of hippie-like Ric and his pretty wife working at Northern Studios. I did a lot of recording at Northern when I first arrived in Boston, and Ric's wife, Suzanne, was the secretary there. I also remember seeing Ric outside the Paradise in Boston when Cheap Trick was playing for three nights. He had long black hair, wore a red leather jacket, and was playing the cool part very well."

The late Richard Nolan was the lead singer of another long-time Boston rock band called Third Rail, and knew the band going back to their days as Cap'n Swing.

Richard Nolan: "I first knew them as Cap'n Swing, as Ric was a fan of Third Rail and came to lots of our shows at The Rat. Ric and I hung out quite a bit back then, but Ben was certainly the funniest member of The Cars.

"I remember one night at the Portland Civic Center in Maine, with The Cars headlining and The Dead Boys [who were from Cleveland] opening. The show had just finished, and The Cars jogged off stage into the dressing room. There were about a dozen people in the room having a drink and eating square slices of this decorated Halloween cake.

"Ric was talking with someone when Ben shouted 'Hey Ric!' from behind him. Ric turned around suddenly and Ben whipped that frosted cake right at Ric's forehead, and then everyone began grabbing and throwing chunks of cake at each other! Yes, Ben was very funny and witty, and just had a great personality. And of course, he had such a great voice too!"

Melanie Ransom worked at The Rat, whose staff has stayed in close contact with Jim Harold over the years, and was a longtime friend of Ben's.

"We used to call him 'Party Boy Ben,' but it wasn't because he was a partier. It was because you could take a room of bored people waiting for their time to go onstage or their transportation home, and insert Ben, with his infectious laugh and sense of humor, and suddenly, the boredom room was a party.

"Ben loved animals and animals loved him. Whether it was the skittish cat that normally hid under the couch when company came, or the friendly family dog, animals all had an affinity for Ben. I remember him telling me about diving in Hawaii and how a group of gigantic sea turtles separated him from the dive group and just circled around him."

Fox Pass singer Jon Macey knew that The Cars were unique and possessed something different than most of the bands around them.

Jon Macey: "The Cars were way more professional than most of The Rat bands at the time. They had tried other styles, were not really a grassroots-punk or new wave band, and they had no real ties to the homegrown 'Boston garage band' scene. They came into their sound a little after the whole scene was already happening, but by doing so, were more polished, refined, and focused. That was very obvious to me from the beginning that they already had an image and they made good tapes.

"It seemed that David Robinson helped bring them to a new image because suddenly, the hippy-ish Cap'n Swing was now the aloof and hip Cars! They were also smart enough to know that the studio recordings are what really mattered, and The Cars quickly took the lead and jumped ahead of everyone else. They also had the business end of it figured out.

"They perhaps never seemed as genuine as some bands on the scene, but that was never the point anyway. The Cars did not have a great club show. Many other bands were more exciting live at The Rat and had bigger followings, but they were smart and cool and sure had the whole concept down."

Mark Cripps worked the back door at The Rat, became good friends with Cars soundman Thom Moore, and also watched The Cars emerge onto the Boston music scene.

Mark Cripps: "I was the 'keeper of the back door' at The Rat from 1977 to 1982, and my acquaintance with a lot of musicians who played The Rat was born out of the convenience of being ten feet from the stage.

"Those days were truly magical, and once The Cars were signed to a record deal, the euphoria that overtook The Rat was indescribable. I wish I still had my collection of Cars shirts from back then, but who could have imagined what a success they would be?

"Ben would hang out at the back door, was always good for a beer and a bit of conversation, and it seemed like he never really understood what all the fuss was about. Ben Orr was just a sweet, down-to-earth man, who just wanted to play his bass and sing.

"Just as The Cars were really starting to take off, in anticipation of the debut release, Thom Moore showed up at my house to pick up enough 'dessert' to keep his lunch box full while out on the road for a few weeks. At the time, he was driving a humongous rental truck with practically everything the band owned in the back, and my parents lived on a little side street.

"And for some reason, known only to us and possibly cannabis, Thom parked in the driveway and upon his departure, I stopped traffic, directed him out of the driveway, and waved good-bye as he took down every low-hanging power line from one end of the street to the other!"

The Cars started hanging posters all over Boston, and played any gig they could get for the next year-plus. Their hard work and tenacity was finally starting to pay off, and all of a sudden, the local press was starting to show up at the clubs, the audiences were growing, and lines started forming down the street to get into a Cars show.

They were labeled as a punk band early on, likely because of the mostly punk band scene surrounding The Rat at the time. However, in reality, The Cars' music was simply hard to label and didn't really sound like anything else at that time.

In early 1977, The Cars went back to New York and played at the famed CBGB club, on the heels of other up-and-coming bands such as Blondie, Talking Heads, and The Ramones, all of whom were now getting radio airplay and appearing on the record charts.

· 9 ·

Revving the Engine

DEMO CARS

In April 1977, the band's first official recording session as *The Cars* took place at Northern Studio, under the direction of Jesse Henderson. The band laid down twelve tracks, and all were recorded live to two-track, with no overdubs. These sessions included the original demo version of "Just What I Needed," the song that would reach the Boston-area radio waves and help land The Cars a record deal.

Other songs recorded during those sessions included "You're All I've Got Tonight," "Don't Cha Stop," and "I'm in Touch with Your World," all of which would appear on the debut album. Two other songs recorded that day, "Leave or Stay" and "Ta Ta Wayo Wayo," would appear on a much later Cars release. At this time, the right-hand man from Richard and The Rabbits and Cap'n Swing, Allan Kaufman, was still working with the band.

Allan Kaufman: "I did a deal with Bill Riseman [owner of Northern Studio] where me, Ben, and Ric wainscoted Bill's office in exchange for the studio time. If you can picture Ric doing manual labor, God love him, and Ben and me, of course. We'd go smoke herb and be like 'doin' this shit sucks!' So, we cut the pieces of wood, applied the glue, and nailed them all in, before realizing we put them in upside down, so we had to take them all out and do it again [laughs]!

"So, we wainscoted and painted Bill's office in exchange for the studio time that produced the demo for 'Just What I Needed,' 'Bye Bye Love,' and 'Best Friend's Girl.' That's the tape, literally *the* analog tape that Maxanne Sartori added into heavy rotation at WBCN."

Music and media entrepreneur Bill "Trip" Wilkins was a Bentley College student in nearby Waltham and a new assistant engineer under Riseman, Jesse Henderson, and David "db" Butler.

Bill Wilkins: "At the time, I was looking to get into the music business, and figured I could get my foot in the door as a recording engineer. I went around to all the local Boston-area studios, most with little interest in bringing me on board.

"However, because Northern Studio had the old Emerson, Lake, and Palmer touring console installed, and it had needed so much maintenance, Bill Riseman brought me in with an eye on using my technical skills. In return, Bill let me assist on sessions at Northern, sitting in and working on recording sessions under David, Jesse, and on very rare occasions Riseman himself. These sessions included such incredible artists as Queen, Tommy Bolin, Talking Heads, and a not-yet-signed band called The Cars.

"I remember they weren't yet polished musicians and [were] still working on capturing what, even at that time, was their extremely unique sound. Ric Ocasek stood out, mainly because of his deep focus and the immense respect he showed to everybody he came into contact with.

"[That was] before The Cars got their record deal; I remember Ben as a happy-go-lucky party kid during the time of those first sessions. He didn't talk a whole lot but was funny, partied and giggled a lot, and liked to pull practical jokes."

Not long after the Northern recording sessions, Maxanne Sartori had begun playing "Just What I Needed" and "You're All I've Got Tonight" from those demo sessions on her WBCN radio show, which began generating interest from the listeners and really started The Cars' engine.

The demo tape, despite not being of the best quality, won a local radio "Super Bowl Battle of the Bands" contest, and all of a sudden, The Cars started appearing on radio station tip sheets, next to other already successful Boston bands such as Aerosmith, Boston, and The J. Geils Band. On said tip sheets, the word "tape" was listed next to their song, for the band didn't have a record label yet.

The fact that an average-sounding demo tape was generating consistent airplay on a major FM station started raising awareness around the city, and when The Cars opened for Rick Derringer at Boston's Paradise Club, the crowd was screaming for "Just What I Needed" from the start of the set. The late Thom Moore recalled the song suddenly gaining momentum in the J. Yuenger website blog.

Thom Moore: "The Cars sent a demo tape of 'Just What I Needed' to Boston radio stations and the DJs started pushing the track big-time. After that, there was a frenzy at The Rat, as record labels were trying to sign the band.

Two weeks later, the band was playing The Rat again, and I drove into Boston to check them out. During a break, I saw Ric at the bar, and introduced myself. He remembered me and asked me how I liked the set.

"I told him the songs were great and the performance was awesome, but the mix wasn't clear and the sound lacked punch. He told me that he'd heard similar comments and asked what I was doing the following weekend, and if I would travel to a gig in New Hampshire so their manager could see what I could do. This is how I became their FOH [front-of-hall] mixer, and a month later, I flew to London to help record the first Cars album. I was an assistant engineer on all of their albums from that day on."

CARS RECORD DEAL

The Cars were now getting more attention from music management circles, which prompted the band to make another change bringing in a more experienced manager in Fred Lewis. A former Boston radio personality and Atlantic Records promotion manager, Lewis had worked alongside fellow WBCN radio personality Peter Wolf, later of J. Geils Band fame, and had also been Geils's road manager.

Allan Kaufman: "My own personal take on it is that we took Ric's music and vision and made it more like Steely Dan-meets-Little Feat-meets-Motown, which he doesn't like. I was still with them when they made the transition to The Cars and Fred Lewis, who had success managing the J. Geils Band.

"Ric called me up one day and said, 'I need to talk to you,' but it was finally Ben who told me, 'Allan, there's nothing I can do here. Ric feels you're too young to be able to take it from here.' Looking back, I *was* only twenty-one years old at the time."

Lewis was already familiar with The Cars from their Cap'n Swing days, having heard their demos on the local radio airwaves. He approached the band with a plan to create a bidding war between major record labels, and subsequently, the Fred Lewis Organization became The Cars' official management.

With more experienced management now in tow, Ocasek and the band went back to his basement. Through the summer months, Ric wrote more songs, which produced even tighter recordings that the band hoped would finally secure a record deal.

"There were three things that had to happen for us," David Robinson told *Trouser Press* in 1978. "We needed airplay from our tapes, people at our gigs, and record company interest; and it all came at once."

Fred Lewis then convinced famed Boston music promoter and club owner Don Law to have The Cars open a show for Bob Seger at the five-thousand-seat Boston Music Hall. This, coupled with increasing local radio exposure, finally cultivated serious interest from the major record labels. Top label executives such as George Daly of Elektra Records, Clive Davis and Bob Feiden of Arista Records, and representatives from Epic Records all went to see the band play live at Worcester Polytechnic Institute (WPI) in Worcester, Massachusetts, in an attempt to sign The Cars to a record deal.

However, as it turned out, the Elektra A&R director, the aforementioned George Daly, had already seen The Cars perform at Harvard University less than a week prior to the WPI show. Daly had heard about The Cars through a couple Boston-area Elektra representatives, including their New England promotional manager, Kurt Nerlinger and the national singles sales manager, the late Lou Maglia. Maglia was also instrumental in the development of reintroducing 45-single "picture sleeves" back into the music marketplace.

Before becoming an Elektra and Columbia Record executive, Daly had played in bands during the sixties as a guitarist and then as a bassist in a band called The Dolphin with legendary guitarist Roy Buchanan, and later, as a bassist with a trio dubbed The Grin with guitar-great, Nils Lofgren. Therefore, Daly had some standards to judge by as a musician, not just as an A&R director.

George Daly: "I had already heard of The Cars through Kurt Nerlinger, our radio promo guy in Boston, and he just *loved* music and bands of that era. All of which made him an enthused and informed radio person back in those 'FM radio' days.

"Kurt had been introduced to me by my best friend at Elektra, a national sales executive, and another Massachusetts guy named Louis Maglia. Lou, being a true Bostonian, also promoted The Cars to me, along with Kurt. They were both acquaintances of Maxanne Sartori at WBCN. She was a strong advocate of the band as well, and I heard that affection loud and clear when we met and she pitched The Cars to me.

"They already had one track on the radio, so between the fans in Boston and these folks promoting them, The Cars had some visibility for me at Elektra out in West Hollywood. I should also note that the cassette demos I got from Kurt and Maxanne where shaky. However, the recordings were totally *not* representative of, as I was later to find out after traveling to Boston, the true sound of The Cars performing live.

"There was an unusual music disparity with those early demos, a sound and feeling 'gulf' [that was] bigger than with almost any band I have ever signed before or since. So, as the responsible head of A&R for Elektra, I filed the name 'Cars' away in the back of my mind, and mostly just waited to hear something better from them."

In June, The Cars recorded more tracks at Music Designers Studio in Boston using a sixteen-track machine, including "My Best Friend's Girl," "All Mixed Up" (which featured Ric on vocals, not Ben), and a more rocking version of "Bye Bye Love," culled from the Cap'n Swing days.

George Daly: "During 1977, there was a big music industry sales conference held in Hollywood, Florida, for all of the Warner Bros., Atlantic, and Elektra-Asylum record labels, and I was invited to attend. However, at the same time, I got a call from my kid sister, Barbara Jeanne, who was studying at Harvard University at the time. She said 'You've got to come see this band The Cars that is playing at a freshman dance at Harvard this weekend, because they're a great live band!' I told her I knew all about them, and if she liked them, I would come up and we'd go see them.

"I really wanted to see my sister, so I booked a flight, and after the conference I went to Beantown. Seeing The Cars live would be a bonus, and a justifiable business rationale for the flight up to Boston. After all, two of my Elektra colleagues from Boston had already pushed me to see them. I recently checked back in with my sister, regarding that week, and she reminded me that we both went to hear them at the freshman dance, but she had to walk home alone since I ended up doing some business with the band after the show.

"So, I went to this not too impressive venue, and I was met by an excited and friendly greeter, the manager of the band, as he described himself, a local guy named Freddie Lewis. We watched the hall fill up from the back wall where we were sitting, and the band started playing to a fairly full house of dancing students, a young, happy crowd where almost any music probably would have been appreciated.

"Several things became apparent to me as they played their first few songs. First, that they were the 'real deal,' with Ric as the writer/band leader, and he was an unusual and creative songwriter and singer. Also, the band really stood out instrumentally in the left-handed Strat player, Elliot Easton, and the melodic and hooky synthesizer player, Greg Hawkes.

"Then, a few songs into the show, Ben is singing, and the only thing I remember thinking is 'Why isn't this guy singing more?' because he had a hit-making voice and a beautiful one at that. Just as appealing, he was instantly recognizable as the great-looking heartthrob every band should have. A few years later, I was watching the movie *Blade Runner* and realized Ben resembled a better-looking Rutger Hauer.

"Later in the set, Elliot did his astounding James Burton–like country solo lead in between his Chet Atkins–like finger picking rhythm parts on 'My Best Friend's Girl,' and I thought to myself; 'great image, fine quirky songs, good rhythm section, and punchy solos with great, fat original keyboard counter melodies. There were also radio hooks and all this, with two truly exceptional singers. I'm signing this band!'"

Before the show was even complete, Daly had decided he was going to go out on a limb and make a push to sign the band *that very night*. It was indeed taking a chance because, after all, he was only seeing the band for the first time, and he hadn't even met them face-to-face yet.

George Daly: "You have to understand that the job of an A&R head, first and foremost, is to find the best talent and hire their services, as in, sign them. Then second, don't get *fired* for doing so!

"Nevertheless, I was sure of this band and was prepared for the risks. I had made up my mind within about twenty-five minutes of hearing them play five or six songs at most. They had also become so much better than the rough cassettes I originally heard.

"So, sitting there at the back table, after the set ended, I said to Freddie 'I'm signing you guys to Elektra,' and the first thing he asked was [paraphrasing] '*Really*! For how much money?' Of course, as any good manager should ask.

"I said, as I recall, something along the lines of 'the band gets [so much money] to sign as a cash advance, up front. Then, if we want them, we need to be able to get at least five years' worth of albums from you.' He agreed instantly and we both wanted to write it out, so I wrote it down in ink on a folded napkin, right there at the table!

"I would later come to understand that Ric was a genius in many ways. Perhaps not blessed with a traditional 'rock' voice, but blessed with multiple strengths to create a vivid and lasting impression with music. He had put quite a group together, and as I said, a group much better-sounding than those original recordings I had heard.

"As for Ben, he had the rock star look, and I could see his bass playing was fine, deeply in time, and musical. On that point, I always expected the rhythm section of any band that I signed to have that kind of solid-feeling beat that Ben and David Robinson had together. But for Ben to have that musical feel *and* that physical look, plus that amazing voice as the counterpoint and adjunct to Ric's quirky and powerful voice. That was special. They had a deep bench, as they say."

This was a pivotal moment for both The Cars and George Daly. Not only was the band about to secure a multi-album record contract, but Daly was taking a huge leap of faith on a band he just saw perform for the first time.

George Daly: "At that point in my early career, five years as a musician and five years as a music executive, this was a serious moment. Clearly, committing a label to an essentially unknown band, as a formal senior executive at a record label, is a powerful moment for all concerned. The A&R signing-average for a medium-sized label in the seventies could have been as few as only one or two new artists a year.

"That little napkin was a momentous signing commitment from me, but I placed my bet because I knew I had to do it. They were a great band; therefore, signing The Cars with Ric and Ben singing those songs, and with that band of great players and counterpointed vocals, it didn't feel like a risk; it really did feel like a necessity.

"I'm a little hazy here, as this all happened over thirty-five years ago, but I don't think they had a lawyer yet, and I remember saying 'Use my pal, Brian Rohan. He's my lawyer and friend, and will make this deal happen fast.'

"I called Brian in San Francisco that same night, and I said to him 'I'm giving this band $30,000 to sign,' plus a few more particulars, and he did the rest."

Daly then reported to Joe Smith, who led the A&R Department at Elektra/Asylum Records and had hired George the previous year. In retrospect, George recalls no resistance from Smith in his decision to sign The Cars. Mel Posner was the president of Elektra Records when The Cars signed to the label, and would later become director of international for Geffen Records.

Mel Posner: "I was president at Elektra when George brought in The Cars and although I did not have an intimate connection with Ben, I remember him as always being a nice guy. He was very professional as a musician and was also interested in the marketing aspect of the record industry, as he would ask intelligent questions about how we were going to promote the band. 'Drive' was a big hit for us, and to this day, I still listen to that song."

George Daly: "Joe Smith was a real music powerhouse, a great manager, and blessed with good ears himself. The artists liked him because he was smart, tough, and personable, as well as being a dyed-in-the-wool sports fan with a near eidetic memory for games and players.

"He also had a sense of me and the level of music quality and the commercial potential I was interested in, so my memory is that everything went smoothly where Joe was concerned and it was 'all systems go' for The Cars to come into Elektra. The dollar figures I offered the band weren't necessarily the biggest for those vinyl sales–rich times and the moderate terms helped expedite the deal as well.

"Since I had come to Boston to see my sister, I took a few days off to stay in town and hang with her, and I remember the band was playing another gig, just a few days later, it seems like. But I did see them a second time, and looking back now, I recall another funny little chapter regarding the 'business side' of The Cars' story.

"After the 'napkin signing,' I had assumed that the band and Freddie Lewis were good for their word and that the deal was done, particularly since I had suggested Brian to represent them; he wasn't one to fool around.

"So, it was with some surprise that while sitting and watching the band at that second gig, I see my old boss from Columbia Records walking by my table, the justifiably renowned record executive, Clive Davis, now working at his own new label, Arista Records.

"Clive and I were both startled to see each other, and after very short and happy pleasantries, where he said he had heard great things about the band, I said something to the effect of 'Clive, they are really good, and I signed them last week.' His eyebrows arched and we both looked surprised that the other was even there, and we said good-bye.

"I didn't hear anything from Clive about The Cars ever again, even to this day, for this may have been one of the few times the rightfully legendary Clive was beaten to a record deal by timing, because he was, and still is, so perceptive and hyper-sensitive to emerging talent.

"I *got* The Cars, right away. And, while their amateur demo, one I heard multiple times in California, was sub-par, just a tiny cassette, poorly recorded and with very little of anything like their final hit songs on it, it still had *something*. As well, I had been pitched on them by people I respected, including my own musical sister, with whom I could conveniently see the band. (And, it turned out later, at Clive's old law school alma mater, no less.)

"But, could The Cars perform live? So, fate was on my side, Kismet as they say. I had gotten there a week ahead of the crowd, and I saw no other label or A&R person but me at that first gig at Harvard. And, most importantly, I stayed with the Kismet/cosmic flow: after finally hearing the band play live, I made the deal, wrote out the basics of the contract there with The Cars that night, right there at the gig. And that was that!"

A few days later, the Cars show at Worcester Polytechnic Institute took place in which a few major labels, again, descended upon the band in an attempt to try and sign them to a record contract, but the deal had already been done.

Allan Kaufman: "I wasn't at the Worcester Polytechnic gig, but Thom Moore mixed the sound and my booking agency with Tim Collins and Steve Berkowitz, Natural Axe, booked the show.

"We were still booking some of the early Cars' dates, even after Fred Lewis became their manager, and literally, as The Cars were driving on the Mass Pike from Boston to Worcester for the show, they noticed one limo with Elektra Records executives in it, another limo with Clive Davis and Bob Feiden from Arista, and a third limo with people from Epic Records. They were all headed to Worcester to give The Cars an offer at that gig.

"I also remember Ben calling me after and saying 'Hey, we've finally made it, man. We got a deal!' Yes, Ben specifically called me to say thank you for my help and for believing they would get a record deal, because you see, that's the kind of person Ben was. He wanted to let me know that they certainly wouldn't have gotten that far without my help. He wanted to give me that. I love Ben, and the memory of him makes me smile in my heart all the time."

A few years later Joe Smith would authorize a bonus payment for Daly, as a "thank you" for signing The Cars and for the overall success of the band. In fact, Daly says he doesn't think he ever really felt "for sure" that everything was going to succeed for them, until Smith gave him that check, proving once and for all that The Cars *were* what George had told himself that first night. A great band that, if recorded properly, would have big hits.

George Daly: "It is here I must say that Ben and I always smiled and chatted. He basically seemed pleased to see me, 'the label guy.' But also, I always felt that, though he actually had the most self-contained, classic vocal talent, which I marveled at, Ben and I didn't ever really get that close, nor did we need to.

"Recorded music was my job, and I wanted Ben to sing, and sing often. That was it, and that was an issue I could deal with the easiest, by working with the record producer that Elektra would pay to record the band. I didn't really need to confer with Ben about the direction of the band, as I did occasionally with Ric. I only needed Ben to keep playing his bass, and to sing as much as he could."

CARS REDEMPTION

After toiling away on the road for many years—from Cleveland to Columbus to East Lansing, to New York and back, then finally Boston—a record contract with a major label had certainly been a long time coming for Ben and Ric. They had been playing together for nearly ten years before finally settling into the right band and situation. True to their word, The Cars had secured a record deal one year after they had played their first gig together.

In a 1979 *Trouser Press* interview, Ben was asked whether he and Ric had ever considered going their separate ways. "No, we never said that. Maybe it was just time to take a break, and we went our own way for a year [referring to Ocasek's original trip to Boston, before Ben followed suit], but Ric kept calling me up and saying, 'Come to Boston.'"

Back in Cleveland, family and friends were truly excited that Ben's persistence to be in a successful band with a record deal was finally paying off. Old friends like original Grasshopper Dante Rossi and bandmate Wayne Weston were thrilled to see their friend finally getting the recognition they felt he deserved.

Dante Rossi: "When The Cars finally got their record deal, I remember being invited to a Christmas party at Benny's mother's house and everyone was just so proud. Benny was thrilled; he just sparkled! All the hard work and fighting though adversity had finally paid off. Think about all the talented musicians out there that never make it, never end up being heard, but Benny had the tenacity and determination to see it through, and I couldn't have been more thrilled for him."

Wayne Weston: "I remember Chris Kamburoff [Ben's Mixed Emotions bandmate], who at the time worked for a record distribution center in Cleveland, called me one day and said, 'Hey, we just received a promo album of this hot new band from Boston, and guess who the singer is?' and I just said, 'Benny.' Chris was quite surprised, and asked me how in the world I knew that, but I didn't have to be told. I figured it was Benny, because I just knew that someday, someway he was going to make it big. He was just *that* talented."

Kris Orr: "I had felt that all of Ben and Ric's bands should have been successful, but the first time that they were played on WRKO radio in Boston, that was when you knew it [the debut album] was going to get national radio play."

The Cars

THE DEBUT ALBUM

*G*eorge Daly: "The rocket had been launched, and after that, my job would be essentially done, but in those early weeks and months after the band signed, the job wasn't completely done, for I still needed to get the label people, as many as possible at Elektra, to believe in The Cars.

"Of course, the original demos [not sounding good] probably contributed to the fears on others' part. Either way, during those early discussions someone suggested to me that perhaps Queen's producer, Roy Thomas Baker, would be a good producer for the band, really, as eccentric as they could be.

"I can't recall, but I'm sure that it was the very savvy Joe Smith that liked that idea and supported it. Also, the great vocal engineer/producer that he was, I felt that Baker was potentially a good match for the band as well, and I got in contact with Roy."

The band wasn't exactly sure Baker was the right fit at first, considering his more polished, vocal-layered style captured with the legendary Queen, but after spending some time with "RTB," they were convinced he *was* the right choice. However, it was not Baker's work with Queen that impressed The Cars, but rather his work with the bands Free and The Zombies.

George Daly: "Roy was a unique person with great instincts, and as talented as he was, he was also quite different from most Los Angeles producers, and a very good fit for a very *different* band. He was very well known for recording Queen's spectacular vocal sound, and Baker would be the guy to get Ben's and Ric's distinctive voices out front on the record.

"So Roy and I had a couple of meetings, and we talked about how the record would be made and how much emphasis would be put onto the vocals.

Over the phone, it became apparent that the actual making of the record would be a carnival of emotions, repetition, and supreme hard work.

"This was a recording project that included such only-in-the-seventies events as me, just for Roy, authorizing a round-trip, Los Angeles–London–Los Angeles ticket in first class on the supersonic Concorde airplane, so that his rare forty-track Stevens tape recorder could be sent to Roy in England, posthaste, to get that inimitable full sound we hear on the first Cars record.

"Yes, I agreed to that multi-thousand-dollar plane ticket for a tape recorder just to make sure the record had those voices on it, great multi-track vocals for which the band will always be remembered. It was Ric's and Ben's voices which had originally induced me to sign the band, with Ben having the most purely impressive, classically warm, and really romantically evocative voice. Ben's sound was unique, as a few years later, the biggest Cars hit, 'Drive' proved beyond a doubt."

In turn, Baker was already confident about what they could create together after seeing the band perform at a local high school on the night of a blizzard at which only a handful of people showed up for the show. However, The Cars played the gig as if the house was full, which impressed Baker.

"I agreed to produce them on the spot," Baker once told *International Musician* after seeing the band perform. "The songs were basically there; they

The Cars perform during their European tour, 1978.
Photo by Ebet Roberts

just needed to be rearranged slightly. A chorus put in here, a verse taken out there, and the speed needed to be adjusted, but apart from that, they were already excellent."

A six-week recording schedule was set up in Studio B of London's Air Studios under the direction of producer Roy Thomas Baker, along with engineers the late Geoff Workman and Nigel Walker.

The recording sessions began in February 1978 and were completed in just twelve days, with another nine days taken for mixing. In fact, much of the recording time was consumed by recording the multiple-layered vocal tracks for which Baker is so well known.

"Roy had a forty-track recording machine back then [in the days of only twenty-four-track], so he had his own special machine," Ocasek stated in the 2000 Turner Studio interview.

"I love segues," Roy Thomas Baker told the *Daily Events Book* website in 2006. "I like records to be continuous. In the beginning, they [radio stations] played the first three or four songs off The Cars' first album, because the disc jockeys kept missing the end of the songs. It worked out well."

There was really no writing or rehearsing to be done in the studio because the band already knew the songs inside and out, with the only difference, of course, being the influence and direction of Baker in the studio.

"He took our three-part harmonies and multilayered them to sound much bigger. I think that was a bit of a Cars' trademark after that," Ocasek told *Only Music* in 1987.

The now-iconic album cover featured a close-up of the late Russian-born model, journalist, and musician Natalya Medvedeva, sitting in a classic car and behind a glowing steering wheel. The concept was developed by Elektra after David Robinson's original cover idea was discouraged. However, David's design was modified and used on the record's inner sleeve.

Renowned award-winning photographer and creative director Elliot Gilbert has photographed musicians, athletes, stage, film, and television stars. Gilbert also photographed the front and back cover images for the debut album.

Elliot Gilbert: "Ben was a very good-looking guy, very kind and easy to be around, and a quiet person. He did not exhibit a 'rock-and-roll' persona at all. I got to spend an afternoon with him at Farmer's Market, a well-known part of Los Angeles. The Cars were not stars yet, but it was still like being out with a friend, low-key, just two guys hanging out.

"Everywhere we went, though, young girls 'circled' him. He was very cool, he ignored all the groupies and concentrated on our time together. Just quiet talk, while these beautiful girls circled close by. I felt great hanging with him . . . it was like, 'Yeah, I'm with him.'

"He hardly said anything during the shoot. He was very self-assured and left it to me to do what I wanted to do. I was sad when I heard he died many years ago, way before his time. Ben was very handsome and very quiet, and he was very easy to be around."

It was also during the album cover photo shoot that Ben met Judith, a beautiful blonde makeup artist, who would much later become his second wife.

Judith Orr: "Ben and I first met when The Cars came to the studio for their photo shoot for the back cover and album inserts for The Cars' first album. Elliot Gilbert and Johnny Lee [the art director] thought it would be interesting if I painted Natalya Medvedeva icy-white for the shot, although when I look at the photo now the whiteness seems much more natural in the final printing. I worked with Natalya on a shoot a few months before and I suggested that the wild Russian singer/model would be perfect for the concept.

"Ben was really hilarious, with a positive, upbeat energy, and we both loved animals and joking around. We also both loved spicy food, and much later, when we were married, I used to carry around a little container of hot sauce for us.

"At the end of the shoot on the last day, Ben invited me to go out with him and Elliot and we all went to the Rainbow Room and a few other places. We talked and laughed a lot, and Ben was great, one of the sweetest people I had ever met. He really touched me as a person, but at that point we were just friends and we didn't start dating until a long time later."

On June 23, 1978, friends were invited (private invitation only, through radio promotions man, Kurt Nerlinger) to "Start your engines with The Cars!" as the band hosted an album release party, complete with buffet and cocktails, and held in the Georgian Room at Boston's Park Plaza Hotel. When the band hit the stage, the audience of over one thousand rose from their adjoining tables and created an impromptu dance floor as the band performed their soon-to-be hit album.

Originally from West Newton, Massachusetts, Tyler Sweet is a longtime musician and recording engineer who currently works with the Brian Setzer Orchestra, among many other music-related projects. Through working with many Boston-area bands over the years, such as Third Rail, Sweet knew Ben, Ric, and The Cars going back to 1978. In fact, Tyler not only remained close friends and worked with him later in his solo band, he even babysat for Ric, who also lived in Newton.

Tyler Sweet: "I first met Ben and The Cars in 1978 at the record release party for the debut album. By the time of *Candy-O*, I felt I had the liberty to go there [Ric's house] when I pleased and play his pink half-moon guitar.

"I loved the first record and told Ben that it inspired me to become a performer, too. He told me to learn the guitar on my own and I'd develop my own style, so I did, and to this day, I think it was the best piece of advice anyone has ever told me in the music business."

STAR CARS

"We're five different personalities and all five come out on the record," Ben told *The Plain Dealer*'s Jane Scott in 1978. "Easton, our lead guitarist, is kind of hilarious, incredibly funny. Robinson is a typical drummer, a little subdued. Hawkes, our keyboard man, is a living cartoon, and Ric can be bouncy onstage sometimes. You have to really know Ric."

Jane Scott: "Ben was always very humble and gracious to his hometown media, even though he could have very well acted like the iconic rock star that he certainly was in Cleveland. It was truly an honor to follow his career, going all the way back to his early days with The Grasshoppers and The Mixed Emotions. I always knew that Ben had something special."

Greg Hawkes: "We wanted the music to fall somewhere between a pop band and an art-rock band, and it sort of developed into more of a straight-up rock band, with an arty edge and interesting arrangements."

Elektra Records released the first single a week before the album came out. "Just What I Needed" hit the airwaves in late May, and climbed to number 27 on the *Billboard* "Hot 100" singles chart. *The Cars* was released in the first week of June, and although the album garnered instant success throughout the Northeast, it took some time for the debut to *really* take off across the country.

All nine tracks were written by Ric Ocasek, except "Moving in Stereo," which is credited to Ocasek and Greg Hawkes. Ric and Ben shared the lead vocal role, with the former singing the lead on five tracks and Ben singing four, including "Just What I Needed," "Bye Bye Love," "Moving in Stereo," and "All Mixed Up." Ben also stood out instrumentally, laying down the heavy "donk-donk-donk-donk" base lines that punctuated tracks like "My Best Friend's Girl," "Just What I Needed," and "Bye Bye Love." Ben was not necessarily a virtuoso bass player, but possessed a rock-solid touch in the pocket, balanced by a rare stage presence that was unmistakable.

David Robinson: "When Ben would work on music in the studio, it was like a 'Frank Sinatra' thing. Ben sort of just standing around, didn't want to run through the songs a lot, he'd just say, 'I'm ready,' and I'd be like, 'You're ready? He's ready? How could you possibly be ready?' [laughs].

"Then he'd go in and do a vocal in *one* take. He'd put his cigarette in the ashtray and sing it, then pick the cigarette back up and walk out, and it would be all done. We actually got *used* to working like this with Ben.

"There was never really a question of him making a mistake. Oh, he might stop *himself* once in a great while, maybe say he wanted to make a subtle change here and there during a recording, but we probably wouldn't have even stopped him if he had just kept going with whatever he was singing. It was always such easy work with Ben, and he never wavered from this ever, ever, ever! He never hit a flat note, never strained or lost his voice, and I also don't remember him getting sick with colds or anything like that. Oh, and he also never complained about anything *ever*.

"And when we would play together as a rhythm section, we would never really have to speak too much about what we were doing at all. If we started working on a new song in the studio, we'd go through it three or four times, then we'd both come to a conclusion about one or two minor details, but they were usually things I sort of knew anyway.

"But honestly, it hardly ever had to happen because Ben always just played exactly what I wished that he would play. I never really played with another bass player like that. We just never had to change anything or go over much.

"Although, I do remember this one time when we were learning 'Just What I Needed.' I really liked the band Roxy Music and there was a song called 'Virginia Plain' where the drummer turned the beat around for part of the song. So I decided to try it and play the song on a different beat, but the kick drum didn't line up anymore.

"So all Ben says about my experiment is, 'Yeah, could you maybe do something different there, like, don't change the kick pattern.' And of course, he was right, because the song sounded much better without changing anything. And that's about the only thing I can remember Ben *ever* saying to me about my drumming. Over the *entire* history of the band!" [laughing].

The music press embraced the album immediately, with favorable reviews coming from major market entities such as the *New York Times, Boston Globe, Village Voice,* and *Los Angeles Times.* Within a few months, *The Cars* had sold over 300,000 copies, and was now climbing the *Billboard* album charts.

Rolling Stone magazine critic Christopher "Kit" Rachlis wrote, "The pop songs are wonderful," and "easy and eccentric at the same time and all are potential hits," while *AllMusic* reviewer Greg Prato said the album was "a genuine rock masterpiece. . . . All nine tracks are new wave/rock classics. Flawless performances, songwriting, and production, The Cars' debut is one of rock's all-time classics."

Coinciding with the increased album sales, the band also started expanding their concert tours beyond the Northeast region.

"I'm anxious to see friends in Cleveland again," Ben told the *The Plain Dealer's* Jane Scott in 1978, the week after The Cars' debut album was released. "I've always dreamed of having a record on the Cleveland radio stations, so this is a dream come true. I have high hopes that our band will really take off.

"We took our live tape to an FM station [WBCN] and it became the station's #1 requested song. Then the song made the top five at another station [WCOZ]. We will soon be touring this summer and should be in Cleveland by August."

The Cars did return to Ben's home turf in July, playing a couple sold-out shows at the now extinct Agora Theatre. The show was broadcast live over the Cleveland airwaves on WMMS-FM, and a longtime Cleveland photographer, Janet Macoska, was at the Agora that night.

Janet Macoska: "There was a promo party before the show, in a club downstairs from The Agora called The Mistake, and I had a chance to snap

Ben and Joe "The Emperor" Mayer at The Cars' promo party, The Agora Ballroom, 1978.
Photo by Janet Macoska

a few photos of the band, including a shot of Ben with 'The Emperor' Joe Mayer, as well as some from the show.

"All the guys in the band were very approachable at that party, and I chatted a bit with Ben, but it was his hometown, so he was surrounded by people! Ben was a really good guy, and folks in Cleveland were obviously very proud of him."

In the fall of 1978, The Cars began opening shows for such national rock acts as The J. Geils Band, The Kinks, Cheap Trick, Foreigner, and Nils Lofgren, which further exposed the band to the rock masses. They also appeared on national television as guests on the popular music program *The Midnight Special* [aired September 15, 1978], looking sophisticated and aloof in their black leather and sunglasses as they performed "Just What I Needed" and "My Best Friend's Girl."

From this time, Ben's image would be strongly associated with the Music Man Stingray bass he played during that show and other performances during 1978–1979, along with a cherry-red Vox Constellation IV. It was now becoming clear that The Cars did not look or sound like any other band of the time, which surely added to their charm and growing mystique.

This is also when local musician and booking agent, Steve Berkowitz, David Robinson's old record store coworker, started working with the band as tour manager.

Steve Berkowitz: "I was seeing The Cars play live around town, and then after they got signed, I was their tour manager during the first tour. They were doing well around Boston and throughout New England, and during the tour, we all traveled around with me and the band in a station wagon, and soundman Thom Moore driving with the band's gear.

"However, early on, the band was hated in some areas of the country, as some looked at them as 'this band with the strange clothes and haircuts.'. . . We would hear things like 'those English fags.' One time the band played a club in Chicago called Park West, opening for Dickey Betts of the Allman Brothers Band. Let's just say the Southern rock crowd didn't like the band too much, as they were getting things thrown at them, and we're not just talking empty beer cans, I mean full beers smashing right next to them onstage.

"I took them off the stage because someone was going to get seriously hurt. However, overall, the reactions around the country were positive, and the band continued to develop a strong following."

All of a sudden, The Cars were becoming a big concert draw around the country. That summer, a Boston radio station sold over seven thousand tickets for a leukemia benefit concert featuring The Cars in Shrewsbury, Massachusetts. Three days before the event, the concert had to be relocated to the

Providence Civic Center in Rhode Island, with the entire twelve-thousand-seat arena selling out in two days.

Elektra released "My Best Friend's Girl" as the album's second single in early October, which climbed to #35 on the *Billboard* "Hot 100" singles chart. The single would also become the first-ever vinyl "picture disc" to become available on a commercial level. "Good Times Roll" was released as the album's third single a few months later (February 1979) and reached #41 on the "Hot 100" chart.

The Cars peaked at #18 on the *Billboard* "Top 200" album chart, while also peaking at #4 on the "Top Pop" albums chart of 1978. The debut album would sell over a million copies by the end of 1978 and ultimately, remained on the "Top 200" album chart for an astounding 139 consecutive weeks. Yes, that's nearly three years, and simply incredible numbers for *any* album, never mind a band's *debut* release. Entering the fortieth anniversary (in 2018) of its release, *The Cars* has sold over six million copies worldwide.

Moreover, The Cars were voted 1978's "Best New Band" in *Rolling Stone* and other music magazines as well, and were nominated for a Grammy Award as "Best New Artist." However, they somehow lost to the disco one-hit wonder band, A Taste of Honey. The Cars were in attendance at the ceremony, and at one point the camera caught a playful Ben pulling a face while country star John Denver was singing in the audience nearby.

Despite not winning a Grammy, the nomination created even more national exposure for the band. What had started a little over a year before as a modest cult following in the basement bars of Boston had now grown into a national following, as The Cars were now returning to theaters performing as the headliner, not the opening act.

FOREIGN CARS

With a solid and growing American following now in place, The Cars embarked on their first European tour in the fall of 1978, a relatively short tour that included stops in London, Paris, Brussels, Hamburg, and Amsterdam. However, the trip did not quite turn out as planned, for as acclaimed as the band had become in the United States, the British music press, for whatever reason, created somewhat of a negative opinion about this new American band, seemingly before they even arrived.

Greg Hawkes: "I am still not quite sure why we were not initially accepted by the British press. We arrived there during the latter stages of the punk era, so perhaps that had something to do with it. . . . Maybe we were just a little too pop-oriented for their tastes at that time."

Interestingly enough, after that brief tour The Cars would not find their way back to London again until the recording of the *Heartbeat City* album six years later. Despite the seemingly negative vibe, however, The Cars planted some seeds of exposure in Britain with appearances on the popular music television shows *Rock Goes to College* (England), *Chorus* (France), and *Musikladen* (Germany).

After she had met the band during a magazine photo shoot, renowned photographer Ebet Roberts was hired to travel with The Cars to document their first and ultimately only, tour through Europe. Roberts would go on to work with The Cars numerous times over the years and in fact, photographed the band on nearly every one of their American tours throughout the next decade.

Ebet Roberts: "I first met The Cars at the Gramercy Park Hotel in New York City in 1978 when I was assigned to photograph them for *Crawdaddy* magazine. Their first album had just been released and was doing really well. I was excited to get to photograph them and had a really great time working with them. They became and still are one of my favorite bands both musically and personally.

"I'll never forget when Ric called me on a Monday or Tuesday, shortly after that *Crawdaddy* shoot, and asked, 'What are you doing on Thursday? Do you want to go to Europe with us?' Of course I wanted to go. I quickly rearranged my schedule and a couple days later I was on my way to Germany with the band.

"The initial [negative] reaction to The Cars in Europe was not particularly noticeable to me, as we were not in any one place for very long. We were constantly moving from one city and country to the next. However, I do remember being surprised they weren't as big in Europe as in the States where they were exploding. They appeared on the cover of *Rolling Stone* magazine just after we returned from the European tour.

"I worked with The Cars many times over a ten-year span, and photographed all of their tours. In Europe I hung out with both Ric and Ben a good bit. They as well as the rest of the band were great fun to be with. Ben seemed to always have a lot of women following him around.

"One of my favorite photographs of Ben was one that I took on the street in Brussels of him hugging the sheepdog that belonged to a writer who had interviewed the band [a photo that would appear in a *People* magazine tribute article after Ben passed away]. I really have nothing but great memories working with The Cars over the years."

Although the band was disappointed about the brief tour overseas, they returned to America and wasted no time in getting back in the studio to begin working on their second album.

"I hated Paris," Ben told the *Boston Globe* in 1978. "Most people knew how to speak English, but they would fall back on their French and it was really hard to communicate. Now I'm looking for my first Frenchman over here so I can get back at them."

They appeared on the *Rolling Stone* magazine cover in January 1979, just a few weeks before going back into the studio to begin recording the follow-up album. Of course, with the huge success of the debut release, there was all of a sudden pressure on the band to produce another hit record that would continue the momentum that the debut release was producing.

The success and pressure that comes along with it created greater expectations, as the national spotlight was already burning bright. Always a social person, Ben was indulging in somewhat of a rock-and-roll lifestyle and certainly enjoyed the nightlife and the sudden fruits of all his labor.

• *11* •

Candy-O

$\mathcal{A}$s The Cars got ready to record the follow-up to the highly successful debut album, Elektra Records was surely counting on the band to duplicate that success. However, the band did not want to produce a facsimile of the debut album simply to appease the record company.

In fact, as he sat in his new top-floor Boston apartment and listened to the disco beats blaring below him, Ben vowed that he would never succumb to playing trendy music just to please the masses.

Ben Orr: "It [the disco music] was the same exact beat for forty-five minutes. It could have been fifteen different songs for all I know. I guess they get machines to play it. I'd saw my fingers off before I'd play that stuff."

It was also around this time the band started expanding upon their live shows and became more interested in creating a production design for the next tour. Enter Stephen Bickford, an experienced show designer including lighting, scenery, and special effects. Bickford had already worked with several national acts throughout the 1970s including Neil Young, Electric Light Orchestra, Hall and Oates, Herbie Hancock, and Pat Benatar.

Stephen Bickford: "The Cars were beginning to work on the release of their second album and wanted a production design for the upcoming tour. I lived in Manhattan at the time and started traveling to Boston to hang out with them, and then to hang out more with Ric. I would end up designing all The Cars lighting, scenery, and production designs, and I traveled with the band and ran shows.

"My thoughts on Ben; Ben, Ben, Ben. Always smiling but stayed to himself a lot. A mysterious smile that made others think he had some sweet secret going on, but not to tell because after all, secrets are secrets. Ben could give you a twinkle with his eye and you'd want to give him anything he wanted, or he could give you a theatrical, withering look that would shrivel you down to a mummy.

"He had an ultra-casual way of handling himself. Entering a room, getting up out of a chair, passing through a doorway; he seemed ever so carefree, yet no question, he was always fully aware of who he was, where he was, and the presence of others around him. Ben could be a buccaneer and could be a dashing thief of hearts. Ben had a way of being very discreet about his activities, his interests, or anything else that might be in his life or on his mind except music, The Cars, and the show that night.

"Ben kept to himself a lot. He was very sociable, sure, very cordial and engaging, very much like a 'well-brought-up young man.' He clearly learned how to be polite and cordial in social situations and one assumes he was raised that way, even though he did cast a 'bad boy' persona at times. However, in my opinion, this was a disguise, because like many of us, he wanted to do what was needed to keep people away from the person he really was, the person he may not have felt free to share with more than a few people."

Bickford had a good relationship with the band, seeing firsthand how they worked and played on the road.

"The Cars had no drug scene. Most, as I recall, smoked cigarettes and pot, which was referred to as 'putting on a hat' or '*le grand chapeau*.' There was minimal drinking, a few beers or perhaps some wine.

"The band was also very aware of fashion and were clothes horses, particularly Ben, Ric, and David, with girlfriends, wives, and fashion consultants helping them find the clothes they wanted. Hip clothes that they saw in magazines and clothing stores.

"Ben and Ric built large, expensive wardrobes of front-line designer and couture clothes that they not only wore onstage, but also on the streets in their personal lives. When we had a day off in a major city, I'd hear them that evening in the dressing room before the show, Ben or David unpacking items they'd scored and deciding which to wear onstage that night.

"Ben had an unfailing sense of style, and during some tours, he wore black jodhpur pants and a black Spanish vaquero hat that had such a wide brim that his face was always in shadow. He would stand there at the center mic with his feet apart, chunking out 'Moving in Stereo' with that big black hat, and he and I both knew that because of the angle of the light, his face was dark, which is what we both wanted. That's great theater, and Ben certainly knew theater!"

Not wanting to go back to London to record the new album after the recent lukewarm tour experience, the band chose Cherokee Studios in Los Angeles, with Roy Thomas Baker and Geoff Workman once again producing and engineering, respectively. However, before commencing at Cherokee, the band returned to Bill Riseman's Northern Studio to rehearse new songs for the upcoming recording sessions.

Bill Wilkins: "The Cars practiced at Northern for the second album to thank Bill Riseman, which gave Riseman the ability to invoice the record company for top dollar against the band's expenses. During those sessions, however, it was very noticeable to me that Ben had changed dramatically from the happy-go-lucky kid [he had been] during the first demo recordings, before they had gotten the record deal.

"It was still Ben, but a much more serious and introverted Ben. Clearly, through the emotional gauntlet of their immediate success, he had experienced certain realizations about fame that, I feel, caused him to retreat emotionally."

Once the band got to work at Cherokee Studios, the entire process of re-cording and mixing the thirteen tracks (eleven of which made it to the album) for the follow-up, *Candy-O*, took less than a month to create.

"We started recording the second album in February, and the recording itself took fourteen days, two more than the first album," Ric Ocasek told *Record Review* in 1979.

Most of the songs for *Candy-O* had already been written by Ric while the band was on the road, which helped eliminate pressure to come up with new material after entering the studio. A couple of the *Candy-O* tracks had actually been written before the debut album and played live on the first tour. Additionally, Baker was now more familiar with the band and vice versa, mak-ing the recording process more comfortable.

For this album, David Robinson would take control of the cover design by recruiting the late Alberto Vargas, famous for his classic illustrations of pinup girls. Robinson loved the fact that the eighty-three-year-old Vargas had never created an album cover design in his career and although retired, the renowned illustrator was persuaded (and not only by Robinson, but Vargas's grand-niece, who loved the band) to create the cover art.

Vargas's painting, which depicts a voluptuous redhead leaning back across the hood of a 1972 Ferrari sports car, was based on a photo shoot that Rob-inson set up at a Beverly Hills Ferrari dealership. Coincidentally, the model's name was Candy.

Before its release, there was an industry rumor that Elektra Records had held back the release of *Candy-O* because the debut album was still riding the charts, a notion that was dismissed by Ric. "We just didn't get around to making it until February because we didn't even come off the road until December," Ocasek told *Record Review* in 1979.

George Daly: "The time between the first two album releases was just about a year, but if The Cars were 'riding' the charts with any kind of real sales, we would not have jumped in with a whole new album on top of already-charting sales.

"There is always some overlap, but the real test would have been, 'are there any singles left on the first album?' So, a review of the singles and how they did on the charts would clue you into the trigger of why and when the second album would be released. As for the band 'touring until February,' a year's spacing was a fairly normal schedule in those days, and it was all about how many singles were left on the previous release."

Candy-O was released in June 1979 and record sales were steady, despite some critics being a little less enthused about the follow-up to the hugely successful debut album. Of course, having to meet those expectations may have influenced the opinions of some critics.

An August review in *Rolling Stone* magazine made conflicting statements such as: "It's almost inevitable that *Candy-O* doesn't seem nearly as exciting as their first" and "the element of surprise is gone," yet also claiming it as "an elaborately constructed, lively, entertaining LP that's packed with good things."

However, one must wonder about the validity of a review that describes the vocals on the opening track, "Let's Go," as Ric's when Ben sang the song. Another question arises when the album is described as "too predictable and relying on established devices," yet praised in the same review for being "lively, having refined techniques, and being full of good things."

Although it certainly did not have the dramatic impact that the debut release created (frankly, how could it?), *Candy–O* featured a collection of tight rock songs, full of concise lyrics and inventive pop-quirkiness. Whereas the debut album was at times quite arty and dreamlike, with songs such as "I'm in Touch with Your World," "Moving in Stereo," and "All Mixed Up," *Candy-O* was more of a straight-up, rock band effort. The material was less heady, featuring tighter song structures.

From radio-friendly tracks such as "Let's Go" and "Since I Held You," to the low-fi rock of "Shoo Be Doo" and "Candy-O," to the punky-attitude of "Night Spots," "Got a Lot on My Head," and "Dangerous Type," *Candy-O* flows as if meant to be, not unlike the debut album in this regard.

Candy-O would ultimately chart higher than the debut release, climbing to #3 on the *Billboard* "Top 200" album chart, and going platinum (one million copies sold) in less than two months. The album remained on the charts for over a year and was also listed in the *Billboard* "Top Pop" albums chart for 1979. All of this was happening, mind you, while the debut album was *still* riding the charts.

Released as the first single in June, "Let's Go" reached #14 on the *Billboard* "Hot 100" chart, followed by "It's All I Can Do," released in September and reaching #41. As 1979 was coming to a close, "Double Life" was also released as a single (in December), but failed to chart.

Ben's lead vocals were once again prominent, including "Let's Go" and "Candy-O," as well as "It's All I Can Do" and "You Can't Hold on Too Long." Yes, Ben was now emerging as the band's heart-throbbing bassist with that crooning, smooth vocal style.

Despite a few quizzical reviews of *Candy-O* from the music press, there were also good reviews and accolades as well. *High Fidelity* called The Cars the "first intellectual garage band," *Rolling Stone* dubbed them "the American Roxy Music," and *Billboard* stated the band had a "punchy pop/rock style accessible enough for AM pop play-lists and eclectic enough for FM-album action."

The Cars' popularity was now clearly hitting overdrive and so were the media demands on the band, as well as some rather "interesting" promotional events. Such as the time in Houston when a record store invited the guys in to promote the new album and sign autographs.

The band arrived at the event to find an old car parked out front, complete with sledge hammers for the kids to wreck the car! Some four thousand fans showed up, got autographs from the band, and then took swings at the car, which was completely flattened by the end of the event.

Despite this sudden burst of fame, the band still managed to stay grounded in their beliefs. The Cars actually turned down television offers to appear on both *American Bandstand* and *Don Kirschner's Rock Concert*, primarily because they believed these shows were narrow-minded in the bands they would book to appear on the show.

However, in the fall of 1979, the band did agree to appear on the music television show *The Midnight Special* (aired September 29, 1979) before heading out on the road, provided that a couple of unique "friends of the band" were also allowed to perform, including the synth-punk duo, Suicide. Other appearances on the show included the British power-pop band The Records, new wave songstress Lene Lovich, as well as music video performances from Iggy Pop and M. The band also demanded that there would be no verbal introductions, no banter, and no Wolfman Jack. It became the first and only 'wordless' episode of *The Midnight Special* to be recorded.

The Cars would tour throughout the Midwest over the next three months, before winding their way back to familiar ground, Cleveland and New York. As the demands of fame increased, so did Ben's partying lifestyle.

The late Murray Saul was a local promotions representative for the Elektra/Asylum label and worked with Ben and The Cars whenever they came to Cleveland.

Murray Saul: "Of course, Ben grew up in Cleveland and his mother still lived here, so he would always visit his mom when the band was in town and bring her and a bunch of his hometown friends to the show, complete with limo rides, backstage passes, you name it!

"Ben was very generous, a great person and a lot of fun. He liked to go out and party a bit and *always* treated his family and friends well whenever he was in town. Yes, the man loved Cleveland, and never-ever forgot where he came from."

Yes, Ben would always reconnect with the people he grew up with, from family members and old friend Diane Kokai from the Grasshopper days, to his old bandmates and even his "band boy" from back in the day, Steve Dudas.

Diane Kokai-Akins: "Whenever Ben played Cleveland, he always rented limousines for his friends and family. When The Cars first toured Japan, he bought my parents gifts, and he would always send us postcards from the road, 45s and albums before they were released. That was just Ben . . . all the time."

Steve Dudas: "I was living in Florida and hadn't seen Ben for many years. I believe [it was] around 1978, I was reading our local newspaper and saw that The Cars and Foreigner were going to be playing locally. There was a picture of The Cars included with the article.

Ben with Diane Kokai-Akins, and his dog, Shauna, at Diane's parents' house, 1979.
Courtesy of Diane Kokai-Akins

"I had gotten away from music for quite a while and didn't know anything about The Cars, but I knew that it was Ben in the picture, even though he had shortened his name to Orr. I took a shot and called a local promoter, who surprisingly gave me the name of the motel where the band was staying.

"So, I called the motel and asked to speak to Ben Orr. And surprise again, they put me through to his room. Ben answered, and I said, 'Hey Ben, it's Steve Dudas.' I could not believe how excited Ben was to hear from me. After all, I was just a band boy [roadie] from the old days, but he was truly excited.

"He said, 'You're coming to the show tonight. How many tickets do you need?' He didn't ask me, he *told* me I was coming and that I would also have backstage passes. But that was Ben.

"We hadn't talked in more than fifteen years, and he acted like his best friend in the world had just contacted him. He was just so genuine for a guy who had made it big in the rock world. He could have easily been full of himself and understandably so, but I never saw him act any different after he became a success than he did when we were together in the early years.

"My wife, a couple of friends, and I went to the show that night. It was the first time I had heard The Cars music, and I was hooked! The song arrangements and lyrics were something that was brand new and totally fresh. After the show, we went back to Ben's room and talked for a couple of hours.

"This became our routine, and whenever The Cars played in Miami or Fort Lauderdale, Ben always had tickets and backstage passes waiting for me. He never had that 'big star' ego and always acted like the same Ben from the old days."

That summer, The Cars also played what was arguably their most significant show to that point, headlining at New York City's Central Park for an estimated half a million fans. Not long after, while touring in Canada, the band connected with music photographer, Philip Kamin, a Toronto native who met The Cars at Maple Leaf Gardens. Kamin would ultimately photograph roughly thirty shows for the band over the next few years.

Philip Kamin: "I got to spend a good amount of time with the band, and especially had some great times with Ben. We would cruise around in his Corvette, did some target shooting together, and I was a guest at his house as well. One moment that really stands out for me, though, was a time when Ben and I were at a mall in Texas, during a tour.

"Well, Ben got noticed at the mall, and some people started to gather around and ask for autographs. I was really impressed with the fact that Ben took time to mingle with the fans and sign some autographs. Yes, he was genuine and appreciative to the fans and it was really nice to see."

David Robinson: "One time I was sitting near a window in a restaurant where I live and all of a sudden, I see Ben walking up the street. He had what looked like a crowd of adoring family members all around him. There were little kids tugging at his sleeve and adults hugging him, it was kind of a funny and bizarre thing to see.

"He comes up to the window and I'm like, 'Ben, what in the world are you doin'?' Of course, he hadn't even told me that he was coming to visit. He had just showed up out of nowhere."

· *12* ·

Panorama

MANAGING CARS

$\mathcal{B}$y the end of the *Candy-O* tour The Cars were fully realizing stardom, which left much less time for privacy and creativity. Whereas in the past Ric could simply "retreat to his basement" and write a batch of new songs, there was now much more of a commitment regarding their time. On top of all this, the band was also ready to make another management change and part ways with Fred Lewis.

Now needing a more experienced manager (among other reasons), music and show business veteran Elliot Roberts of Lookout Management was chosen to handle the band's business moving forward. The Los Angeles–based Roberts had a lot of experience in the music industry and was a former business partner of David Geffen, founder of Geffen Records.

Roberts had helped Geffen create Asylum Records in 1970 (which would merge with Elektra Records in 1972) before he launched Lookout Management. This management shift would not be a smooth transition, however, triggering legal issues between The Cars and their former manager.

The hiring of Roberts caused some friction within the band as well, for Roberts was known more as a "singer/songwriter-oriented" manager, having worked with such legendary artists as Bob Dylan and Joni Mitchell. Therefore, there was some concern about Ocasek being groomed as the leader and star, perhaps moving focus away from the rest of the band. However, Lookout Management also handled the careers of legendary "bands" as well, such as Talking Heads, The Eagles, Tom Petty and The Heartbreakers, and Devo.

Adding to the uneasiness of the time, Ben and Kris ended their decade-long relationship, officially divorcing in 1982. Understandably, Ben's emerging rock-and-roll lifestyle did not sit well with Kris, and as his popularity grew,

115

so did the number of women that surrounded him. However, she was also very proud of Ben and supported him to become the musician he was in his heart and soul.

Steve Berkowitz: "When the band was starting to move away from Fred Lewis, I was acting-manager during the transition to Elliot Roberts and Lookout Management. Ric and I had talked about me becoming the full-time manager, but they were becoming too big by then, so instead, we joined together with Lookout. At first I was tour manager and then also studio manager and band co-manager."

Bill Gerber is an acclaimed film producer and Warner Bros. production executive, whose credits include such major motion pictures as *Gran Torino*, *Grudge Match*, *The In-Laws*, *JFK*, and *The Dukes of Hazzard*, as well as *A Star Is Born* with Bradley Cooper. However, Gerber began his career in the music management business, working under Elliot Roberts of Lookout Management, and has also worked with Lady Gaga.

Bill Gerber: "I had started out as a drummer in several bad rock bands, and had been a music promoter and record company executive before I joined Lookout Management in December 1979. My friend David Geffen introduced me to Elliot Roberts, and Elliot took a flier with me and let me manage Devo. Ironically, Danny Goldberg and I had tried to sign Devo two years before that, after we made them the opening act for a Mink Deville show at Santa Monica Civic Auditorium.

"After managing Devo for a couple years and start[ing] to kind of know what I was doing, I started getting offers to join other management companies and agencies. Elliot wanted me to stay at Lookout, however, and sweetened the deal by making me his co-manager of The Cars.

"I remember when The Cars came to L.A. and met all the big managers and then chose Elliot. These guys were *real* rock stars, and furthermore, one of my favorites. When I first heard them, I thought Roxy Music had finally made a hit record! They were about to put out *Panorama*, which ultimately didn't perform as well as their previous two albums, but was still an awesome record."

Steve Berkowitz: "We had started out doing these small Boston and Cape Cod–area gigs and just one year later, The Cars were headlining arenas like the Spectrum in Philadelphia! We had a lot of great shows, opening for bands such as Fleetwood Mac, Styx, and Bob Seger. We basically stayed on the road and lived in motels for the better part of two years."

The Cars had now been recording and touring nonstop since first securing their record deal, and with two multi-platinum albums under their belts, they were full-fledged rock stars and drawing attention wherever they went. Ben, in fact, was already widely considered a rock-and-roll sex symbol for many female Cars fans.

David Robinson: "After The Cars broke up, it finally gave me a real opportunity to look at the band from the audience's point of view, through watching video footage, because I was so used to looking at the back of their heads all the time. I could see the audience reacting to the other guys in the band, but never really knew what they were doing to get the reaction.

"But then I would watch the footage and think 'Look at him [Ben], he has the audience in the palm of his hand.' Elliot and Ric are trying to add a little movement onstage or whatever, but Ben is acting completely natural, nothing artificial, and it's just so natural that you don't even notice what he is doing. It's a little show business, yes, but still so natural.

"And the poor girls [laughs], they didn't stand a chance! Ben would literally melt them with his eyelids and his 'droopy' expressions. Sometimes we would make fun of it, but actually, a lot of the time, we were just amazed at how well it worked. How good he was at it. That's because he was doing the same thing, and working toward the same goal since he was fifteen years old."

In a 1979 interview for *Trouser Press*, Orr was asked what he noticed when looking into a Cars' audience. He replied, "Women. That's who I see."

David Robinson: "Ben was the consummate ladies' man. Just like he had the 'rock-and-roll thing' down since he was a kid. Well, he had *that* down, too."

SHIFTING GEARS

Entering the 1980s the band took a much-deserved short break from being *The Cars*. During the hiatus, however, tragedy would strike. In early 1980, the Boston apartment building Ben was living in was ravaged by a fire that destroyed everything he owned, including his Music Man Stingray bass, his immaculate Vox teardrop bass, and many other personal treasures, such as his art collection and wardrobe. He literally lost everything in his apartment except the very clothes and jacket on his back.

Steve Berkowitz: "Ben was living in Brighton [a neighborhood of Boston] when in early 1980, the apartment building he was living in burned down. He lost everything. He was only able to grab his new, genuine wolf coat, which he had bought in Canada, as he ran out of the building. Ben literally only had the clothes and coat on his back. He needed to get money out of the bank, but he didn't even have his wallet or any form of ID.

"So, I drove him to the bank, and I showed them my autographed, framed copy of The Cars' *Rolling Stone* magazine cover to prove it was Ben. 'See, look . . . it really is Ben Orr!' Immediately after that, we were on a plane

Ben on tour in Japan, 1980.
Ben Orr Collection

and headed to Los Angeles for recording sessions, and in fact, I proposed to my wife on that plane ride with Ben as our witness."

Bill Gerber: "At one point, Ben was in a serious relationship with a songwriter named Amy [Reichardt] LaTelevision. He asked me to help, and I managed to get her a publishing deal with Kathleen Carey. Ben was so grateful and always remembered that I was able to help Amy out."

Devastated after losing nearly all his equipment, as the band and Roy Thomas Baker entered Cherokee Studios to begin recording sessions, Ben started playing a Fender Precision Active bass and an Alembic amplifier, before discovering a Steinberger bass as well. He also started working with a new Roland guitar synthesizer and bass pedal setup.

Of course, Ben also needed a new place to live, and purchased his first home in the Boston suburb of Weston. He completely remodeled the house, including new exterior siding, white stucco interior walls, an open-concept living room upstairs, and the addition of a recording studio on the ground floor. Ben's old friends Grasshoppers drummer Wayne Weston and Mixed Emotions guitarist Chris Kamburoff paid a visit to Ben during this time.

Wayne Weston: "We went to visit Benny after he bought his house in Weston, while the renovations were still in progress. Weston was a well-off town, and Benny's house sat on top of a big hill. It wasn't an overly big or extravagant house, but it was really cool after the renovations were complete.

"The house was built 'green,' which was a pretty new concept back in the early eighties. All the exterior wood was stripped, and a crew installed this thick, Styrofoam material, and then stucco over it. The interior was set up really cool, with the living room and bedrooms upstairs and the recording studio on the ground floor.

"Something else that stands out is that I remember Benny had all his framed gold records in the living room, but they were all on the floor, just leaning up against the wall. So, when I asked him why they were not all displayed on the wall, because if it were me, those awards would be prominently displayed, Benny simply said, 'I know who I am.'"

Ben quickly settled into his new neighborhood, making friends with the neighbors up and down his street. "I met Ben when I went to high school in Weston, as he lived next door to a good friend of mine," a fan, Lockie McNeish, stated in 2015.

"Ben was always nice to us, and he also had a great relationship with our parents. In the winter, he used to plow most of the driveways on his street just for fun and always refused money.

"One night, when The Cars were playing the Boston Garden, Ben decided to get us girls a limo to go to the show. We were waiting for the limos to show up and one did, but not the second car. So, we all piled into one car, which included Ben's mother. When we got to the Garden, it appeared that Ben's mom didn't realize just how big her son and The Cars had become. She was totally flustered and didn't seem to like all the attention."

Released in August 1980, *Panorama* was easily The Cars' most unorthodox and least understood album, both musically and lyrically. If *Candy-O* was a relative departure from the debut release, then *Panorama* was an even greater departure from both its predecessors, featuring ten songs (all written by Ocasek) full of electronic drones, mechanical beats, cold and sharp guitar riffs, and Ocasek's even darker, but now more personal lyrics.

George Daly: "*Panorama* was aggressive, hard, and not as palatable to the general public or their fans. I didn't need to say this to the band at the time, because it doesn't work like that with bands at the point they were in their career. They were artists, successful ones, and so past the point that Elektra-Asylum could do any real advising or shaping. Sink or swim, the band had to do what they had to do."

Most of the music press was not kind to *Panorama* and adjectives such as "gloomy" and "electronics excessive" were used in the reviews. However, the album was truly misunderstood in that the darker mentality of the songs was indeed orchestrated. Whereas most of the first two albums were full of rock-and-roll songs written in the third person, most of these songs were of a much more personal nature, such as "Gimme Some Slack" and "Misfit Kid."

Indeed, The Cars had now created an image all their own, and even more than before, truly sounded like no other band. "I read in the trades about bands that are 'just another Cars' clone' and it just doesn't wash," Ben told *Musician Magazine* in 1982. "But if you ask me if the band has influence, yeah, I think it does, simply because it's had so much exposure."

Ben would again be prominent vocally, singing lead on the rocking "Down Boys," the hypnotic "Don't Tell Me No," and "You Wear Those Eyes," and the quirky "Running to You."

"Touch and Go" was released as a single in late August, and with its clever interplay between haunting verses and guitar-jangle chorus, was surely an unconventional Cars' pop song, as it only reached #37 on the *Billboard* "Top 100" singles chart. "Don't Tell Me No" (November 1980) and "Give Me Some Slack" (January 1981) were subsequently released as singles, but failed to chart.

Although not released as a single, the band also filmed a promo video for the title track, "Panorama," which featured the band (and Roy Thomas Baker) in a sort of spy-film parody.

Ben onstage. *Panorama* tour, 1980.
Photo by Vernon Gowdy, courtesy of Billie Flory

Bill Gerber: "Elliot and Gerald V. Casale from Devo directed the 'Panorama' video, and that was really my first interaction with Ric, Ben, Greg, David, and Elliot. Steve [Berkowitz] was also around and handled all the logistics perfectly. Steve is an amazing guy, with a true love of music and a seriously competent manager. I have always had a high opinion of Steve."

Gerald Casale would also go on to direct a second video for the band, featuring "Touch and Go," filmed on the rides at Whalom Park in Lunenburg, Massachusetts, in the summer of 1980. The Cars were on the cutting edge of technology and exploring new musical frontiers, as Music Television (aka MTV) wouldn't hit the airwaves for another year.

The lack of high-charting singles mattered little, as *Panorama* climbed to #5 on the *Billboard* "Top 200" album chart, and in four months, sold over a million copies. In just a three-year span, The Cars had now produced three consecutive platinum albums, combining to sell over seven million units—all while the band prepared in their Boston-area rehearsal studio for the biggest Cars tour yet, a five-month journey across America, Canada, and Japan.

Throughout the *Panorama* tour the band headlined the biggest venues available and premiered a new sound stage, which reflected the larger rooms they were now playing. The Cars enjoyed a very successful, sold-out tour to close out 1980.

• *13* •

Shake It Up

CARS CLUBHOUSE

At the start of 1981, The Cars were looking for a fresh approach to their next album project, and what better way to *shake things up* than to buy and renovate your own recording studio. Ric Ocasek had originally contemplated moving to New York or Los Angeles in order to be closer to a quality recording facility such as Electric Lady or Cherokee. However, in the end, he decided to bring a quality recording studio *to* Boston.

The band purchased Intermedia Studio on Newbury Street, in Boston, where Aerosmith had recorded their debut album some eight years prior, and renamed the studio Syncro Sound. The Cars would spend much of the year redesigning the narrow building into a state-of-the-art, thirty-six-track recording facility dubbed "the clubhouse" by David Robinson.

"After the third album went platinum, the band bought the old Intermedia Studio, and I assisted on the recordings, but I was about to get more education," the late engineer and soundman Thom Moore stated in the J. Yuenger website blog.

"It took eight months to renovate the old studio; walls were knocked down, and the control room was completely redesigned. We kept all the old tube compressors and equalizers, bringing the studio up to date in every sense of the word."

The band also brought in Michael Blackmer, their engineering friend from the Cap'n Swing days and now owner of Audio Professionals of Boston. Blackmer was a friend of Thom Moore, had previously worked on the original Intermedia Studio installation with studio designer/architect John Storyk (also the designer of Jimi Hendrix's Electric Lady Studios), and was, arguably,

Boston's top studio technician. Blackmer would help complete all the technical installation for Syncro Sound.

Michael Blackmer: "I was involved with Syncro Sound and The Cars from *Shake It Up*, right through all of their solo albums, including working with Ben at Blue Jay Recording Studio during the recording of *The Lace* and into *Heartbeat City*. I maintained this site [Intermedia Studio] through three changes of ownership. The studio started as Petrucci and Atwell, complete with the third sixteen-track two-inch tape recorder in the world, the Ampex MM-1000 SN-003, a *real* nice piece of history. It is important to note that this is the machine that Aerosmith recorded on [for their debut album in 1973], as well as Patti Smith, Bonnie Raitt, and many others. The name got changed to Intermedia sometime in the late seventies.

"Ross Sabella bought the studio and rebuilt it as simply Intermedia with, I believe, John Storyk doing the design. At this time, operating as Audio Professionals of Boston, I directed a select crew during the installation of a new MCI JH-636 console and MCIJH-24 two-inch tape machine. A few years later, The Cars bought the place and re-named it Syncro Sound. Again, I found myself upgrading this address, this time with Roy Thomas Baker's Stephens forty-track, two-inch machine and a bunch of new, then state-of-the-art, signal processing gear. My company maintained the technical system continuously for the entire time that The Cars owned the studio. I also got to work on many of the other music projects Ric and the boys brought into the studio."

The new studio created a more flexible schedule and relaxed environment for the band to record in, and it wasn't long before Syncro Sound became a hotbed for recording sessions, including many national artists such as J. Geils Band frontman Peter Wolf, punk icons Iggy Pop and Bad Brains, 'Til Tuesday, Bebe Buell, and Romeo Void, as well as local acts such as The New Models, The Dark, Boy's Life, and Vinny and The Dawgs.

Steve Berkowitz: "When the band bought their Boston studio on Newbury Street and rebuilt Syncro Sound, my office was set up in the front part of the studio, with the music coming from the studio piped right in! I really had a lot of fun during my time with The Cars. It was truly a thrill to work with them, and I am happy to say that we remain friends to this day.

"Ben had the ability to play multiple instruments, and everything just seemed to come so easy for him. His vocals were always great and his pitch was incredible. I recall the band recording backup vocals over and over again in the studio with Roy Thomas Baker, harmonizing so well and building up that giant wall of vocals that The Cars became known for.

"However, I also regret not finding out about Ben's illness until just after he passed away. He was a nice and sweet guy and dangerously handsome with those 'Elvis eyes' of his. He was truly a babe magnet!

"I went to Cleveland to celebrate The Cars' induction into the Rock & Roll Hall of Fame. . . . I am so happy and proud of them and wanted to celebrate. They are so deserving of this honor, for not only their hit songs, but continued influence, sound and style. I went to the sound check for old times' sake, and Ben was seriously missed. He would have enjoyed the whole thing, especially in his hometown of Cleveland, and he is deserving of the focus."

RETURN TO FORM

In the fall of 1981, before the construction work at Syncro Sound was even complete, The Cars had begun working on their fourth album with a renewed enthusiasm. They were also recording some tracks at nearby Blue Jay Studio in Carlisle, Massachusetts, with a young engineer named Walter Turbitt.

Walter Turbitt: "I was studying at Berklee College of Music in Boston and working with local bands as engineer and producer. I was working as chief engineer in what was the premier area studio [before Syncro Sound came along], called Blue Jay Studio. One day I got a call from the owners that The Cars wanted to come in with their producer, Roy Thomas Baker, to lay down a few tracks, as their new studio was not yet finished.

"Obviously, this was an exciting opportunity because it was the first time I was going to work with artists and producers of such caliber and worldwide success. Roy Thomas Baker had produced Queen, and was one of the top producers in the world at the time."

A few weeks after those sessions, The Cars contacted Turbitt about actually coming to work at Syncro Sound as a full-time engineer.

Walter Turbitt: "I got a call from, I believe, Steve Berkowitz, saying that Ric was impressed with my 'vibe' and abilities and that they were looking for a chief engineer at Syncro Sound, as the studio was now about ready to open.

"Of course, I jumped at the chance, went to Syncro and was thrown into the world of The Cars and their incredible music, and learned how to *really* make music! I believe the time frame was about 1983 to 1989. I got to work as an assistant on the *Shake It Up* album as Roy already had his own engineer, Ian Taylor.

"As for Ben, he was the quietest of all The Cars, the 'sexy crooner,' and Ric was the 'quirky one.' I distinctly remember recording Ben's vocals and thinking how beautiful and rich-sounding it all was. He seemed to keep his emotions to himself, but seemingly expressed them when he sang. I'd have to say that my favorite Ben vocal was 'Drive.'

"I think his mysteriousness was part of Ben's charm, and he sometimes seemed to be the 'odd man out.' This, of course, was just my impression, as I was new to the cast of characters. I think it took me a little more time to get to know Ben, and I of course, hit it off with the others, as I certainly was not shy.

"I can remember looking at Ben and sometimes wondering, 'What is he thinking?' with all this rock-and-roll craziness going on around him. Yes, I have many great Cars memories that I will always cherish."

Michael Blackmer: "Ric was deep, as was Ben. . . . It wasn't just a paint job. Ric was an intentionally hip character, who wasn't writing songs about his inner struggle, but rather gathering up all these little ideas over time and putting the hooks together in order to create hits! He was very calculated and knew exactly what he needed to get from the people around him in order to create what he wanted. Ric thought in hooks.

"I remember one time, when Ric walked into the studio wearing one of his zoot suit ensembles with the wide shoulders, and his body was entirely covered in those orange city parking tickets. Apparently, he had collected enough of them to cover his entire suit! But the thing was, everyone just acted like nothing unusual was happening; that was just Ric.

"I have only great memories of Ben, and I miss him greatly. He had a fantastic voice and was such a kindhearted, generous person with a great sense of humor. I never once witnessed him being in any way negative, which if you think about it, is *very* hard for any human being to pull off.

"An example of his sense of humor, you may ask? I was also in the core group at Blue Jay Studios in Carlisle during the time that Ben was recording his solo album *The Lace*. One morning I went to open the computer room closet to boot the SSL console, and when I turned the doorknob, a full-featured, plastic inflatable blow-up doll exploded out of the closet and scared the daylights out of me! *This* was Ben at his finest. He was a lot of fun."

After the somewhat negative response surrounding the *Panorama* release, the band was ready to bounce back with a new album. Despite some bad press, however, the popularity of The Cars never wavered as the pressures and demand of their time continued to increase.

There were more promotional projects, radio interviews, and photo shoots than ever before. And, yes, it was about to become even more taxing to concentrate on creating music with the dawning of Music Television, or MTV, in the summer of 1981.

In the 1970s, bands would create short promo films in order to impress record companies, land record deals, or promote a new album, but the arrival of MTV would change the entire visual landscape in music. Fortunately for The Cars, they were on the cusp of this new music-marketing phenomenon and rode the wave to the fullest.

Now firmly established as one of the premiere rock bands in the world, The Cars did not have to answer to anyone, a far cry from the days when

"Benny and Richard" were getting chased out of redneck bars because they wanted to play their own songs.

As the band began recording full-time at Syncro Sound, there were suddenly no more questions about hit singles, because they now had several, and there were no longer "suggestions" about what their album covers should look like. Along with this newfound freedom also came the opportunity for Ben to let loose and really enjoy his success, including doing more traveling and investing in his hobbies.

Roy Thomas Baker returned as producer for *Shake It Up*, with Ian Taylor as engineer. The new studio surroundings created a much lighter atmosphere, compared to the darker vibe of *Panorama*. Along with Ric's new batch of songs, the band recorded two cover songs and although neither would make the cut for the final release, one cover was a rousing rendition of The Stooges' "Funtime," which featured Ben singing a chilling, spot-on Iggy Pop vocal.

In fact, after seeing Iggy Pop perform at the Paradise Club in Boston, the band invited him back to Syncro Sound where Orr performed his vocal impersonation of Iggy. A performance about which Iggy commented, "You sound more like me, than me!" . . . and the partying continued.

Released in November of 1981, *Shake It Up* was just what the doctor ordered for Cars' fans that had, perhaps, not embraced the previous album. After losing some momentum in record sales as a result of the somewhat cold and calculated *Panorama*, *Shake It Up* was essentially the opposite, filled with pop hooks, lighter rock riffs, and a much more positive vibe throughout.

The songs brought melody and brighter production values back to the forefront, while also sounding less individualistic and more like a band effort. Even the cover art was upbeat, a close-up shot of a pretty, smiling woman (model Mary Ann Walsh) holding a cocktail shaker.

Indeed, *Shake It Up* was perhaps The Cars most melodic album to date and definitely their most pop-accessible, exemplified by the one-two vocal punch of Orr and Ocasek. Ben would take the lead vocal on the ballad "This Could Be Love," as well as the low-fi rockers "Think It Over" and "Cruiser."

The title track, "Shake It Up," was released as a single in early November and would become The Cars' first *Billboard* Top-Ten hit, reaching #4 on the "Hot 100" singles chart. The second single, "Since You're Gone," reached #41, before "Victim of Love" was also released as a single. *Shake It Up* would climb to #9 on the "Top 200" album chart, proving once again that The Cars could completely shift gears in their approach to a new record, and the fans would love the results.

The timing of the album's success was perfect, as the MTV video age had by then fully blossomed onto the pop culture landscape and The Cars would indulge full-throttle, filming videos for the singles "Shake It Up" and "Since You're Gone."

The band also appeared on late-night television programs, including the *Tomorrow Show* in New York City, before embarking on another US tour that would take them through the holidays and into 1982. Travel accommodations for the tour also became much more comfortable for the band in a new, custom-designed tour bus.

As the tour ended in April, *Shake It Up* went platinum, making it the fourth consecutive million-selling Cars album as the band took a break for a few months. In September, the band surfaced again at the inaugural US Festival, a three-day concert held on Labor Day weekend at Glenn Helen Regional Park in San Bernardino, California. The crowd was an estimated two hundred thousand, and the festival lineup featured several of the biggest rock bands in the world, including Tom Petty and The Heartbreakers, Santana, Fleetwood Mac, Talking Heads, and The Police.

In the fall of 1982, now officially divorced, Ben would meet Diane Grey Page, a beautiful blonde Boston television personality originally from Virginia and a graduate of Smith College in Northampton, Massachusetts.

Diane Grey Page: "I was hosting a show on the local ABC television affiliate [WCVB-TV in Boston], and one of the directors I worked with lived

The Cars perform on the *Tom Snyder Show* in New York City, 1981.
Photo by Ebet Roberts

across the street from Ben. I was visiting John at his house one day when Ben came over. His hair was dark at that time, and he looked quite ordinary in a hooded sweatshirt. He seemed shy but quite nice. If opposites attract, then this was a case of it, because Ben was all about rock and roll!"

Despite their different backgrounds, Diane, a college graduate from a Southern family, and Ben, with a Midwestern, blue-collar background, connected quickly and developed a strong relationship, with Diane eventually moving in with Ben while he was still remodeling his Weston home.

Diane Grey Page: "I believe we were exotic to one another. There was a strong physical chemistry, and as time went on, we found that we had a lot in common, as we both loved the outdoors and animals. We played a lot of tennis, went cross-country skiing in Stowe [Vermont], and we took lots of walks. Ben also loved scuba diving, and I got certified with him in Hawaii.

"We both loved all kinds of music, and Ben always loved the Beatles, but when we were together, and especially after spending time in London, his music tastes were running toward new or more progressive bands like Yes, The Police, and Eurythmics. He also *really* loved Elvis. You can hear some of Elvis in 'Drive.'

"Ben was also mesmerized by the voice of Roy Orbison, and when we went backstage to meet him once, Ben told Roy that the hairs on the back of his neck stood up with some of his high vocal notes. Ben never thought it was especially cool to get autographs, but he wanted one from Roy.

"I moved into the house in Weston and lived with Ben for eight years, but we were never married. Ben remodeled the house and took out most of the walls to create an open concept. The living room upstairs had a lot of glass and mirrors all along one wall, with a large, red and black Chinese rug in the center of the room. The bedroom was closed off with retractable shoji screens.

"I also love swimming, so we put a pool in the backyard. We had lots of fun, cooking bratwurst on the grill with tiki torches all around the pool. I especially remember one Christmas when Ben grabbed an acoustic guitar and we went to a nursing home and sang carols. No one even knew who we were and it was just the greatest thing!"

• *14* •

Solo Cars and *Heartbeat City*

$\mathcal{A}$fter having produced over a dozen albums and EPs for other artists since the opening of Syncro Sound, Ric worked out a deal with Geffen Records to release his debut solo album.

Recorded at Syncro Sound and released in December 1982, *Beatitude* garnered mild success and spawned a video for the single, "Jimmy Jimmy," a song that The Cars would later include in their live set. Guest appearances on the album included Cars' bandmate Greg Hawkes, Jules Shear, and old friend Fuzzbee Morse on guitar and keyboards.

Fuzzbee Morse: "During the time of Ric's solo project, I also visited Ben at his home in Weston and we rocketed around the Massachusetts countryside in his Stingray. We had a ball and experienced the same easy vibe together as in the Rabbits' days. As ever, I had nothing but good experiences with Ben. We had an easy camaraderie, both in the Rabbits' days and during the Cars era. It remained the same after The Cars broke up, when I'd see him from time to time in Los Angeles."

Greg Hawkes also released his own solo album in April on the Passport label, titled *Niagara Falls*, while Elliot Easton did some studio work for a few artists, including Jules Shear. Also during this time, Ben had begun working on songs at his home studio, beginning the process that would become his first and only solo album.

"Before we recorded *Heartbeat City*, we were off for about a year and a half," Ben told author Peter Goddard in the 1985 book *The Cars*. "And when everyone wanted to get together, we just decided to do it. So, I don't imagine any problems coming from these solo things."

Also around this time, a budding filmmaker, Luis Aira, was producing music videos for various Boston-area bands. He would create a production company and come to work with both The Cars and Ric as a solo artist.

Luis Aira: "I started making music videos in Boston. My first one was for the local rock band The Neighborhoods, and it started getting my name out in the local music scene. I met David Robinson, and we became friends; then, a few weeks later while walking down Newbury Street, there was a man standing at the corner that turned and asked if I was the guy who made music videos. It was Ric Ocasek.

"It was a pivotal moment for me. Ric invited me to go see The Cars' studio down the street and a few weeks later, he was producing a short film of mine that won a few festivals. Two years later, Ric rented us the floor above the studio to have a production company. We produced many music videos for artists like Alan Vega, 'Til Tuesday, and General Public, as well as television commercials in that space.

"Despite being around them every day, I did not work with The Cars very often. I was friends with David and had a close relationship with Ric, and I directed several videos for Ric's solo career, including 'Jimmy Jimmy,' 'Something to Grab For,' 'Hello Darkness,' and 'The Way You Look Tonight.' I also taped a rehearsal that was released as a live version of 'Heartbeat City,' and some footage I created was utilized as video visuals onstage during the *Heartbeat City* tour.

"As for Ben, I remember him as an honest man, a prankster, and sometimes a very funny guy. He was quiet and reserved with most people and always a gentleman with the ladies. Ben loved all the testosterone-induced things like trucks and guns. He was a real man's man.

"I remember at one time Ric had a stalker (and I mean certifiably insane) who kept showing up and banging on Syncro Sound's window. He had thrown a bottle at me one night, threatened to kill Ric another, harassed Julia Channing [Syncro Sound's office person] one morning, and just about spooked out everyone else.

"One day, Ben walked outside and had a little talk with him, and he left. The guy eventually turned back up several months later, but whatever Ben had said to him that day had kept him away for quite a while.

"As a performer, I always saw a bit of Elvis in Ben. He was extremely charismatic and there was no doubt that his presence center stage filled arenas. He also had a beautiful voice, and just a special connection with Ric's songwriting that could bring the compositions further into greatness.

"I remember one night, the band Cheap Trick and a few other musicians showed up at The Cars' studio and jammed all night. I was quite impressed, because Ben's voice really stood out, a powerhouse amidst the sea of rock

Ben tracking vocals for the *Heartbeat City* album. Battery Studios, London, 1983.
Ben Orr Collection

stars. Yes, Ben was a star and meant to be onstage, and I also must say that he always treated me with great respect, and for that, I was always very appreciative of him."

In early 1983, The Cars reconvened to begin recording their fifth studio album, which had the working title of *Who's Gonna Drive You Home?* However, for the first time, the band had to decide on a new producer, as Roy Thomas Baker was now an in-house producer for Elektra Records and had an existing schedule that wouldn't allow him to work with the band.

The Cars ultimately chose renowned producer Robert John "Mutt" Lange, who at the time, was enjoying huge success producing powerhouse bands and artists such as AC/DC, Foreigner, Def Leppard, and Bryan Adams.

Bill Gerber: "When I started working closely with The Cars, Ric had started writing and making demos for *Heartbeat City* and I spent a lot of time in Boston at Ric's house and The Cars' office/studio on Newbury Street.

"Ric was incredibly generous about letting me hear the music and, shockingly, even asked for my opinion. The band went into the studio with Mutt Lange instead of Roy Thomas Baker, which was kind of heavy."

Lange had a reputation for producing pristine recordings and the pursuit of perfect sound quality, a process The Cars would soon learn firsthand. However, in order to work with Lange, the band also had to travel to London, which they hadn't done since that brief, somewhat disappointing tour back in 1978.

That summer, the band set up shop at Chelsea's Priory Mansions in London and began recording sessions at nearby Battery Studios. The different surroundings not only created a renewed excitement for the band, but also produced fewer distractions as The Cars immersed themselves in the studio. What they were not aware of, however, was just *how* deep they would submerge under the direction of their new producer.

In the past, The Cars had gone into the studio with songs that were already rehearsed and ready to record; however, Lange would create a much different process by exploring every avenue and detail of each song in search of that perfect take. Ric described it this way in the liner notes for the 2018 expanded edition of *Heartbeat City*: "Poor Ben—he is a great bass player. But Mutt had him in there for days, weeks. And I don't even want to get into the vocals: 'Let's try that syllable again.' Then Mutt would sit there for two days and edit together—for three days, five days. It was every millisecond."

David Robinson: "*Heartbeat City* was very much influenced by Mutt, and I didn't really have much input on the way it sounds. On our previous albums, I would record drum parts along with everyone else doing their parts, but on this one we did it backwards. I wasn't really involved when the songs were arranged and did all the drum parts last, so my input was very limited."

As a result of the new recording process, what was supposed to have been a two-month stay in London turned into a six-month marathon, before the band finally returned to Electric Lady Studios in New York City to complete the final mixing process. The entire project took over a year to complete, as compared to their previous albums that would only take a month or two.

The close quarters and the long distance from home would start to take a toll as the months passed. Ric admitted to *Music and Sound Output* magazine in 1984: "There were times when we'd fight. There were times when people had their plane tickets, ready to go home. There were screaming arguments. And then there were times we were out to dinner together, having a good time. Everybody had their own little space in the house. There'd be fights if somebody's stereo was too loud, or over the refrigerator. But we didn't have too many problems."

By the time *Heartbeat City* was released in March 1984, it had been nearly two and a half years since the release of *Shake It Up*. Despite the circumstances surrounding the lengthy recording process, the band was nonetheless very pleased with the finished record, as were the fans.

Bill Gerber: "Watching those sessions was inspiring, and the record was a huge hit. Elektra made five videos because they were so blown away with this record. Bob Krasnow [the late chairman and CEO of Elektra Records] was a huge champion of the band and was 100 percent behind them, and of course, Elliot [Roberts] knew how to get the best out of a record company."

Heartbeat City would arguably become the most pop-accessible album in The Cars' catalog, reaching #3 on the *Billboard* "Top 200" album chart while producing four hit songs that year. The first single released in March, "You Might Think," rose to #7 on the "Hot 100" singles chart, followed by "Magic," released in May, which reached #12.

"Drive" was then released in July and climbed all the way to #3, making it the highest-charting single of The Cars' career. It featured a hauntingly memorable lead vocal from Ben and was, arguably, his finest moment as a vocalist. Ric had originally written "Drive" for his *Beatitude* solo album, but it somehow hadn't made it to the final release.

"'Drive' was something I was going to use for a solo album. But Ben and I both sang on demos for that, and I felt that he should sing that for sure," Ric stated in the liner notes from the 2018 *Heartbeat City* expanded edition. "That was perfect for him. I loved his voice so much. He never sang 'off.' He was like Frank Sinatra. He could hold the notes, the vibrato. He had what they called the 'radio' voice."

Bill Gerber: "Ben had a voice that was right up there with [Bad Company vocalist] Paul Rodgers, and his Cars' songs are unmistakable. His charisma was off the charts. He really was the Julius Caesar of rock stars, as women flocked to him and he played it beautifully. Ben really was a spectacular guy and very soulful. I always loved hanging out with him and experiencing his joie de vivre."

"Drive" also cracked the Top 10 in Britain, where huge success had always seemed to elude The Cars. A fourth single from *Heartbeat City*, "Hello Again," was released in October and reached #20. Yes, The Cars' popularity was at its highest, with the new album garnering the best reviews the band had received since their debut release and Ocasek seemingly at his hit songwriting finest.

"Sometimes, the way he writes, you're conscious about doing a lyric in a particular way," Ben told Peter Goddard in *The Cars* book. "At times, it just comes off so naturally you don't have to even think about it; it just sort of comes out of your mouth. 'Drive' was that kind of natural thing."

Ben on set, "Drive" video shoot, 1984.
Ben Orr Collection

The video for "Drive" featured a dramatic, black-and-white opening-shot of Ben, directed by actor Timothy Hutton and starring a young model named Paulina Porizkova, who would later marry Ocasek. Another video from *Heartbeat City*, for "Hello Again," was directed by the legendary artist Andy Warhol (who also made a cameo in the video) and filmed at the famed New York City hot spot, Be Bop Café.

With MTV now a full-blown media power, The Cars took full advantage, releasing videos for six *Heartbeat City* tracks. "Why Can't I Have You" was also released as a single in January 1985 and reached #33 on the *Billboard* "Hot 100" singles chart, giving The Cars an impressive *five* Top 40 singles within a span of ten months.

In fact, The Cars released an official video album, visually documenting the entire recording of *Heartbeat City*. "You Might Think" won the "Video of the Year" award at the inaugural MTV Video Music Awards, as well as at the International Music Video Festival in St. Tropez, the Billboard Music Awards.

It also won the Eastman Kodak Award for excellence in video in 1984 and the "Festival Award" for video album of the year. For a band that was originally not supposed to be about the visual aspects, The Cars certainly developed a knack for producing innovative, award-winning videos. Because of his prominent roles in the music videos, Ric emerged as the "face" of the band. "He's taller and has a funnier haircut, so he attracts more attention, I guess," Ben commented about Ric to the *Detroit Free Press* in 1986. "A lot of people don't know I'm me. I've done half of the songs we recorded. But it's okay—the thrill is being part of The Cars and doing that, which is all I wanted in the first place."

In Rob Tannenbaum's book *I Want My MTV*, David Robinson is quoted as saying, "My own mother saw [the video for] 'Magic' and said I wasn't in it. I had to play it for her, pause the video, and say, 'Look look look, *that's me.*'"

"At this point, a lot of people still don't know who I am or what part I've played in the band," Ben told the *Chicago Tribune* in 1986.

On top of the accolades they were receiving, The Cars also appeared on the season-ending episode (May 12, 1984) of the iconic television comedy series *Saturday Night Live*, their first live public appearance together since the US Festival the previous year, as well as the *Good Morning America* television show. Orr and the band performed a chilling version of "Drive" for a national audience on *Saturday Night Live*, one of Ben's finest moment as an entertainer. These national appearances were a great warm-up before going back on the road and also provided tremendous exposure leading into the tour, which started in the summer of 1984.

The Cars proceeded to sell out arenas across America right through the fall, performing a career-spanning set that included nearly all the songs from the new album, with many of their classic hits mixed throughout. The band would close out the tour and 1984 with five Grammy Award nominations, including "Best Pop Performance for a Group" for "Drive," "Best Engineered Record," "Best Rock Performance," "Best Video Album," and "Producers of the Year" (for their collaboration with Mutt Lange).

With The Cars now at the height of their worldwide popularity and fame, one would think it all couldn't be better, but in fact, all was no longer well within The Cars camp. At this juncture in their careers, fame and royalty checks were now clouding relationships, especially between Ben and Ric.

After the successful *Heartbeat City* tour, the band took a much-needed break. In the spring of 1985, Ben participated in a Cleveland-area charity project organized by hometown rocker Michael Stanley, called *C.A.R.E.* (Cleveland Artists Recording for Ethiopia).

Michael Stanley: "I contacted Ben about the *C.A.R.E* session, which was Cleveland's answer to the 'We Are the World' recording, and he was gracious enough to help us out. Ben was the biggest name that was involved in the project, and it went a long way toward giving the song some gravitas and having people outside of Cleveland give it a listen.

"He showed up at the studio with no more fanfare than any of the others involved and banged out his vocal in no time; no 'star' trips or anything, just another musician lending his talents to a hometown project. We hung out for a bit after he sang and then he was gone."

In July, The Cars appeared at the now legendary Live Aid concert at Philadelphia's JFK Stadium with nearly 100,000 fans attending the event, plus an estimated 1.9 *billion* people in more than 150 countries, viewing around the world via live satellite broadcast.

Other bands appearing at this now iconic event included Joan Baez, Black Sabbath, REO Speedwagon, Pretenders, Madonna, Santana with Pat Metheny, Tom Petty, Crosby, Stills, Nash & Young, Duran Duran, Hall & Oates, Bob Dylan, Robert Plant with Jimmy Page, and Mick Jagger with Keith Richards. The Cars performed a twenty-minute set that included "You Might Think," "Drive," "Just What I Needed," and "Heartbeat City."

Ben recalled to *Goldmine* magazine being a bit nervous before the set, realizing the band was about to perform in front of a worldwide audience. "I normed-out quick when we went into the first song and then, before I knew it, we were finished."

When asked in a 1986 *Line One* radio interview what his most memorable experience was with The Cars, Ben stated, "Oh . . . probably Live Aid I would say. We had a really nice time there and it was great playing for the world."

Another memorable moment from that show was the Canadian Broadcasting Company featuring "Drive" in a video for the Ethiopian famine, which was introduced by David Bowie at the Live Aid concert at Wembley Stadium the same day.

In the fall, Ric began working on his second solo album, titled *This Side of Paradise*, as well as putting together tracks for Elektra's *The Cars Greatest Hits* album. The greatest hits package, which also featured a new song titled "Tonight She Comes," was released in October 1985 and rose to #12 on the *Billboard* "Top 200" album chart. The "Tonight She Comes" single reached #7 on the "Hot 100" chart, while "I'm Not the One" (from *Shake It Up*) was also released as a single and reached #32.

As 1985 came to a close, the *Heartbeat City* album would hit the three million mark in sales, however, by early 1986, more and more friction was building within the band over songwriting, royalties, and touring schedules. Even so, Ben, Greg, and Elliot all contributed to Ric Ocasek's next solo album, with Ben singing backing vocals on multiple tracks.

By this time, Ben was also seriously working on songs with Diane Grey Page for his own solo album.

"I'm optimistic about The Cars," Ben told the *The Plain Dealer*'s Jill St. John in 1985. "I might be wrong, but I think we'll stay together. We all enjoy each other, and a solo album is just an extension. You might as well do as much as you can. If the offer is there, you might as well take advantage of it."

"Being in The Cars makes it a whole lot easier to do any kind of a side project right off the bat," Ben later stated in the official Elektra Records press release announcing his solo album. "But I never really intended to do any kind of songwriting, up until just a few years ago."

· 15 ·

The Lace

$\mathcal{A}$lthough it certainly wasn't Ben's goal to record a solo album over working with The Cars, once the opportunity presented itself, the initial commitment with Elektra was for three solo albums, and he enjoyed the challenge and process of creating his own material.

"Actually, the reason it took me so long to do a solo project is simply because nobody had asked me to do one before," Ben told the *Chicago Tribune* in 1986. "But when Elektra Records asked if I wanted to do an album, I said 'yes,' and then, I kind of went crazy, because I had never really tried to write lyrics before."

Diane had a musical background and enjoyed writing lyrics, which added nicely to Ben's natural skills in writing strong melodies. The couple had been together for over four years and were now working on developing a songwriting chemistry.

Diane Grey Page: "I was a music-major in college, played piano by ear, and was also a singer. I understood the mechanics of music, and I think it portends what came next, the writing of *The Lace*. When you write music together, it is a very strong bond, almost like creating life. The process can be very magical and potent.

"Ben had been writing mostly melodies but was feeling somewhat uncomfortable around the lyrics, so he handed me the music to what turned out to be 'Stay the Night' and said to have a go at it."

Most of the material for the album was written by the couple either at home in Weston or aboard Ben's Chris-Craft speedboat dubbed *The Blue Di*. Some of the lyrics revolved around the couple's own relationship; however, not all the songs are specifically about them. They were written to reflect what any couple might go through in their relationship, both the good and the bad.

141

"I had never written songs before, but we wrote 'Stay the Night' the first time we tried," Diane told the *Chicago Tribune* in 1986. "When Ben and I first got together he was kind of at a stand-still, but once he felt that someone was in there with him working on the lyrical end of the songs, things really started rolling and the rest of the songs came pretty fast."

Diane Grey Page: "The studio on the ground floor of Ben's house was just the coolest thing. It was such a joy to be able to go down any time of the day or night and put an idea down whenever the muse struck. It seems to me the album came together fairly quickly, and I believe we wrote *The Lace* in about a year."

On the business side, Ben would briefly work with Jean Renard, a Canadian fashion and music photographer who assisted during the process of creating *The Lace*, including shooting publicity photos and the album's cover photography, as well as directing two music videos. The video for "Too Hot to Stop" was filmed at Boston Center for the Art's Cyclorama Building on Tremont Street.

The Lace was recorded at The Wool Hall, a converted farmhouse and recording studio in the countryside of Beckington, England, that was co-owned in the 1980s by the band Tears for Fears and the music executive Max Hole. Hole was chairman and CEO of Universal Music Group International and a former manager/label executive who worked with such artists as U2, Bon Jovi, Bryan Adams, Arthur Brown, and Camel. The studio would later be owned by Irish recording artist Van Morrison, who bought the property in 1994 and owned it for nearly a decade.

The Wool Hall was centuries old, allegedly haunted by a child who had died there, and next door there was a castle built by King Henry for Anne Boleyn. There was an eeriness about the place. Ben had to be moved from his room during the recording sessions because of the sounds of moving furniture upstairs, and in fact, old friend Thom Moore was put in the same room after Ben's little incident, and he had to change rooms as well.

The recording sessions took several months, although Ben had already recorded some very good-sounding demos of the songs at his home studio in Weston, parts of which were actually utilized on the final recording. The ten original tracks were produced by Ben, along with the late, Grammy Award–winning producer/engineer Mike Shipley and musician/songwriter and Grammy Award–winning producer Larry Klein. Shipley recorded and engineered the tracks, with additional engineering and mixing assistance from Thom Moore, and programming assistance from Paul Ridout. Additional recording for *The Lace* was also done at Blue Jay Studios in Carlisle, Massachusetts.

Larry Klein: "I was friends and previously worked with Mike Shipley, who was already involved with Ben's solo project when I was invited to participate. I believe a couple of reasons Ben chose The Wool Hall to record was that Mike had already worked at the studio quite a bit and the owner, Max Hole, had been managing Mike and later came to manage me as well. Producer Chris Hughes, who was also managed by Max, had worked at The Wool Hall on Ric Ocasek's solo album (*This Side of Paradise*) on which Ben had done backing vocals.

"When we were working on the record, we had Ben's demos close at hand and in our minds, because they were good and just had this thing about them. They had a signature sensibility about them. The sounds and presets he chose, he really was a stylist in his own right. So, even though we wanted to take those demos to the next level sound-wise, we also didn't want to lose the feeling he had initially captured, because they really had a certain charm and vibe about them."

Ben sang the leads and played bass, guitar, and keyboards on the album, and Diane sang backing vocals. Other musicians to participate included Cars' bandmate Elliot Easton, guitarist Mike Landau, and Larry Klein on keyboards. Most of the sessions were recorded at The Wool Hall, with some final details and vocals finished up at Blue Jay Studios, including Easton's guitar parts.

Larry Klein: "A funny little story about the beginning of that project is when Ben first arrived at customs in England, he didn't have the proper working papers and they wouldn't let him in! I believe he had to fly back out somewhere for a couple days, while Elektra Records took care of the paperwork so he could

Ben and Diane Grey Page. Portrait by John Dalphe.
Courtesy of Diane Grey Page

reenter the country. I was also a little late, having to deal with a personal issue, but once we all got settled in, everything worked out great."

During the recording of *The Lace*, Ben also did some session work for the legendary artist Joni Mitchell, who was married to Larry Klein. Ben sang backing vocals on the songs "Number One" and "The Beat of Black Wings" from Mitchell's 1988 album *Chalk Mark in a Rainstorm*.

Larry Klein: "During the recording sessions, Joni came over to England and we rented a cottage in the village of Frome, near Beckington. During this time, I had also been playing on Peter Gabriel's solo album, *So*. When I told Peter that Joni was coming, he had already finished up recording and his studio was idle, so he let us work on her stuff there. Joni finished up writing three or four of her songs that ended up going toward *Chalk Mark in a Rainstorm*.

"So, Joni would be working on her stuff at Peter's studio during the day, while I was working at The Wool Hall, and then I'd drive over there after to work with her. As was often the case with Joni, she was fond of utilizing the talent around her, and after hearing some of the stuff we were working on for *The Lace*, she said 'Oh, I love Ben's voice! Let's bring him in to record some background vocals.' So, Ben ended up on a couple songs, and I remember he was very excited about doing it, and we all had a lot of fun."

As Ben was finishing up the recording of *The Lace*, he was also contemplating putting his own band together for some shows and possibly recruiting a couple of his old bandmates from Cleveland to participate, including his longtime friend and drummer, Wayne Weston.

Wayne Weston: "Before the release of *The Lace*, Benny was telling me that when the solo album came out, we'd put a band together and that we would book three jobs: *The Tonight Show*, *Late Night with David Letterman*, and *Saturday Night Live*. I was thinking 'Oh boy, here we go!' But the idea ultimately faded away when The Cars ended up getting back together to record what would be their final album."

Released in October 1986, *The Lace* would peak at #86 on the *Billboard* "Top 200" album chart and produced a Top 40 single, as "Stay the Night" climbed to #24 on the "Hot 100" singles chart. "Too Hot to Stop" would also be released as a single and did get some radio airplay, but failed to chart.

Filmed in Toronto, the video for "Stay the Night" went to #1 on both MTV and VH-1, earning Ben an ASCAP Award (American Society of Composers, Authors and Publishers). After going out of print, in 2006 the Wounded Bird music label released *The Lace* on CD format.

Diane Grey Page: "I remember one of the happiest days of my life was when we did our first promotional tour for the album. We were in Cleveland

and riding in the backseat of the promoter's car when 'Stay the Night' came on the radio for the first time. We were so excited and yelling like kids!"

Ben hosted an album release party for *The Lace* at The Cars' recording studio, which included a few friends, guests from Elektra Records, and a couple WBCN radio personalities, including DJ Carter Alan.

Carter Alan: "I do remember when 'Stay the Night' became a hit and Ben had an album release party at The Cars' studio. We had a great time that day, and Elektra Records took a fabulous photo of Ben, his fiancée, and some WBCN folks."

During this exciting time, Ben had also purchased a condo in Kauai, Hawaii; however, despite the sudden success as a solo artist, Ben and Diane's relationship would start to become strained over personal issues.

Diane Grey Page: "As a result of the success of *The Lace*, we got a contract from Warner-Chappell/Intersong Publishing to write twenty songs for other artists, and after Ben had bought a condo in Hawaii, we started to do some writing there, but unfortunately, the songwriting deal with Warner was never completed."

· *16* ·

Door to Door

RUNNING ON EMPTY

"*Y*eah, it's real important just to have fun," Ben told *Musician Magazine* in 1987. "I can't sit around and wait for The Cars. I just try to amuse myself."

Despite the growing tensions within the band, The Cars reconvened in early 1987 to record their sixth, and what would turn out to be final, album featuring the original lineup. The recording process for *Door to Door* began at New York City's Electric Lady Studios, with Ric taking over the role as producer. Greg Hawkes was credited with "additional production," while engineer Joe Barbaria recorded and mixed the sessions. Electric Lady employee, Jamie Chaleff, was credited as a "second engineer," and old friend Andy Topeka was also credited with "technical assistance."

Joe Barbaria: "We started the recording process for *Door to Door* in late February 1987 at Electric Lady Studios, and for the time, it was a huge setup in the studio, so everyone was anxious to get working. However, Ben was nowhere to be found . . . showing up a week late for the sessions and really taking his time about it. So now I'm thinking that we have to deal with some super-ego rock god?

"But I was wrong. However, I will also say that first impressions are not always what they appear to be, because after that Ben acted very professional, was easy to work with, and I found him to be a very nice and pleasant person. He was a very talented musician, as all The Cars were, and Ben was a huge part of the band's vocal sound. His voice had very good range with a rich tonal quality, and on the group vocals, he performed all the bass parts alone.

"As an engineer during the tracking and overdubbing process there isn't as much time to hang out with the artists, so consequently, our time together was short and sweet. However, I do remember there was a 'one-armed bandit' in the studio [a slot machine that took quarters], which rarely paid to anyone, but was friendly to Ben on a daily basis. But he was also generous enough to buy everyone lunch with his winnings."

Make no mistake about it; Ric had always been the songwriter and leader of The Cars. However, with previous albums, his grip on the reins was also a loose one, allowing room for his bandmates to participate in the evolution of the songs. The one modification for the *Door to Door* sessions was that instead of having an outside producer on hand [Roy Thomas Baker, Mutt Lange], Ric became producer. Consequently, this did not leave as much room for input from the rest of the band.

Released in August 1987, *Door to Door* certainly has its moments, despite stalling at #26 on the *Billboard* "Top 200" album chart, a position many bands would *love* their new album to be in. "You Are the Girl" was released as the first single in late August and reached #17 on the *Billboard* "Hot 100" singles chart, while subsequent singles, "Strap Me In" (released in October) and "Coming Up You" (January 1988) reached #85 and #74, respectively.

The album also featured two songs going back to The Cars' earliest days, "Ta Ta Wayo Wayo," and "Leave or Stay," and in fact, the latter song was the opening number at every club date the band did in 1977, the year before they even scored a record deal. Playing these old songs again during rehearsals spurred the band to properly record them after all those years.

Ben took the lead vocal on several tracks, including "Double Trouble," "Everything You Say," "Go Away," and "Coming Up You," however, as he revealed much later, he was apparently not pleased with the amount of input the band actually had as a whole.

Joe Barbaria: "Ben played his bass parts and sang his lead and background vocals all during the tracking sessions, and since he had no other instrumental parts to my recollection, he was the first band member to leave the remaining recording sessions."

"*Door to Door* was in a separate area," Ben told *Goldmine* magazine in 1995. "It wasn't what the entire band had envisioned it to be. . . . [I felt] it wasn't a group effort." At one point, Ben had also proposed contributing songs for the new Cars album, with Diane contributing lyrics to the mix.

"I said, 'That's not gonna happen,'" Ric Ocasek told *Rolling Stone* magazine in 2011. "We were best friends forever and sometimes [back in the early days], we played his songs. But dear Ben—I could never get into the lyrics. . . . Maybe it was just [my having to be] controlling."

CAR DOORS CLOSE

For Ben, the growing negative vibes carried onto the tour. What used to be a fun and exciting time was seemingly not so much fun anymore, so much so that Ben made his own travel arrangements rather than fly and arrive at gigs with the rest of the band.

"I was really tired of the airlines and getting up at ridiculous hours," Ben told *Goldmine*. "I'm not too big a fan of flying anyway and I wanted to bring down the odds a bit. If I could go in my mode of comfort, give me a 20-ton bus and I'm a happy guy!"

Despite Ben's preference for riding a tour bus, it had also become clear that there was more to the problem than simply travel arrangements, as he essentially only saw the band at sound checks and onstage. It got to the point where band members were doing separate press interviews, and what had once been a partnership with Ric now appeared to be more like a chore for Ben.

"I've always been for the band continuing," Ben told *Goldmine* in 1995. "You live for ten years with a whole bunch of great guys and yeah, I've thought about it, but things just got out of hand towards the end."

Ben messin' around with the local authorities, 1989.
Ben Orr Collection

Diane Grey Page: "There was such a complex relationship between Ben and Ric. They were so close for so long, but it ended up turning into something very intense. We were in Kauai in 1988 when Ric made the phone call to tell Ben that the band was over. It seemed that Ben went into somewhat of a downward spiral for a while after that."

"Life changes, the band attitude, and not having a break for all those years, that was all part of it," Ric Ocasek told *Rolling Stone* magazine in 2011. "It became a big dark thing and I noticed it on the *Door to Door* tour. It was the first tour we did that wasn't fun. Some people took buses, some people took planes . . . nobody talked."

Fuzzbee Morse: "Toward the end of The Cars' days, Ben seemed pretty exhausted and perhaps a bit burned out. Of course, the band wasn't getting along too well by then, and when I had seen him during the recording of *The Lace*, he seemed a good deal lower in energy then he'd been previously."

Along with this sudden and devastating change in his professional life, Ben's personal life would also be greatly altered when his longtime relationship with Diane would dissolve. Ben and Diane had shared a loving relationship for eight years; however, as with all relationships, they also had their ups and downs, which ultimately led to their never being married.

Diane Grey Page: "Ben was a loving man with a very big heart, but his increased drinking had started long before the end of the band, and another concern I had, I must say, was his increased paranoid behavior and obsession with firearms. I didn't enjoy walking around with him when he was strapped with a loaded weapon.

"Ben could also suffer from mood swings that would appear out of nowhere, which could make things difficult. Soon after we broke up, Ben would reconnect with, and ultimately marry, Judith, a very nice girl whom I like, and she was an old friend of his."

Judith was the makeup artist who worked with Ben during those heady days of The Cars' debut album shoot. She was still living in Los Angeles and hadn't heard from him in a while when Ben reached out to rekindle their relationship.

Judith Orr: "In late 1990, there was a phone message from what I initially thought was a doctor with a clinic I had gone to. I guess I didn't erase the message, and when I heard it again a couple weeks later I noticed that the doctor had a very sexy voice for an old man; then it dawned on me that the voice was actually saying, 'It's Ben Orr.'

"I hadn't seen Ben since 1985, when he was in town making a video for 'Magic.' I wondered why he was calling me years later, and I had to think about whether I wanted to call him back . . . but I did.

"As we talked on the phone over the next couple of months, our intense connection resurfaced. My birthday was a few weeks later, Ben sent me a plane ticket to Boston for that weekend, so I finally agreed to fly to Boston for my birthday.

"The day after I arrived Ben had a surprise romantic dinner and production all planned out for me. He told me not to look outside until he came for me, and he came in to escort me outside. Ben had circled the area around his black pool with lit tiki torches, and made a roaring fire in the stone barbeque. He made my favorite lobster dinner and chilling in an ice barrel was Cristal champagne, the best. Was this for real? Here was this incredible man I loved saying the most romantic words. He bent down on one knee and pulled out a stunning diamond ring. He brought me to Weston to propose on my birthday. . . . Who could say no to that?

"At the time, I was working on the television show *Into the Night* with Rick Dees and didn't want to leave Los Angeles, but the pull to be with Ben was strong, and I couldn't resist. We were only engaged for a month and we had the most spectacular tropical island wedding in the Fern Grotto in Kauai,

Ben and Judith at Ben's Hawaii condo.
Courtesy of Judith Orr

Hawaii. Ben planned it all himself while I was working. It couldn't have been more perfect.

"Ben was also very generous and kind; however, at the beginning of our marriage Ben was basically the only friend I had in Boston. We were with each other 24/7, and that's never a good idea. I loved his company, and we would have a great time for months, but then something trivial would upset him and he could go silent for a week or longer. Being such a 'people person' as I am, it was unbearable.

"Although I briefly sang in the choir when I was younger, and I love to sing along to songs on the radio, I don't think I have a very good voice and somewhere along the line I lost my confidence. However, Ben made me feel surprisingly comfortable to sing in front of him and when I apologized once that I couldn't carry a tune, he said that I had a good voice and just needed to learn how to breathe.

"One year, he suggested that we do a Christmas album together for our families. I kind of passed it off because of my shyness, but I desperately wish we had done it, because I would just love to have that Christmas album now!

"Ben also taught me how to scuba dive in our pool and got me a full-out, custom diving suit complete with shocking pink tank and matching fins. Ben was an amazing teacher, very detail-oriented, caring, and patient. I knew he would be a fantastic father, and although his son was young when he died, I pray that he has wonderful memories of that beautiful part of him.

"We would live at his house in Weston, but Ben and I also loved Vermont and went there often. I had gone to school for a year at Dartmouth College [in nearby Hanover, New Hampshire] and we really grew to love Vermont and New Hampshire. I wanted to move there for a long time and I got Ben into it also, so we had looked at land several times.

"We loved to take road trips and stop in all the little stores in Vermont and New Hampshire, and we especially loved French Canada. Once we got snowed in while in Quebec City, one of the most romantic cities in the world. We thought Quebec City and Montreal were pure magic, and went there a few times at Christmas.

"At one point, my dear friend Stacy Gilbert married Rick Allen, the drummer from Def Leppard. She called to tell me they were touring through Rhode Island and she wanted us to meet Rick, and I wanted her to meet Ben, so we drove to Providence and had a blast together. We couldn't stay for the concert, but Rick gave us a CD, saying it was something he never expected to see . . . it was an eighties compilation that had both The Cars and Def Leppard on the same CD. We all had a big laugh over that."

The couple would experience many great times together over about a four-year period, going out to concerts together and enjoying weekend skiing trips to Vermont. Bill Salom, a contributing writer to the Todd Rundgren fanzine *Utopia Times*, remembered meeting Ben and Judith at a Rundgren show in Providence, Rhode Island.

Bill Salom: "Ben and his beautiful wife showed up at The Living Room on his motorcycle and we invited him in to see the sound check. He was gracious and friendly, but then got asked to leave because he didn't have a pass.

"We protested and said, 'Really? This is Ben Orr!' But Ben just said, 'That's okay, I understand' and left. He didn't get mad or play the 'I'm a star' card, and later, I saw him in the parking lot chatting with fans and signing autographs. We did manage to get him a backstage pass, and after the show I saw him having a private conversation with Todd. Then he smiled, thanked us, and rode off."

However, despite having some great times together, and perhaps having moved too quickly in the relationship, Ben and Judith's marriage ultimately did not last long.

Judith Orr: "Continually through our marriage Ben would be a dream husband for months; then, out of the blue, he would get mad and go completely silent for weeks, leading into depression. It was excruciating for me, and no matter what I tried, nothing I would do could change it at all."

$$\cdot \ 17 \ \cdot$$

River of Fire

NEW START

In late 1992, Ben started collaborating with a couple of area musicians and began the process of fleshing out new songs for a follow-up album to *The Lace*. It was also around this time that Ben was looking to sell his house in Weston and move to the Green Mountain State, as he and Judith were looking at properties in Southern Vermont.

The late John Kalishes, a Boston-area guitarist and songwriter for many years, and who passed away in 2006, was brought in to write lyrics with Ben. Cutting his teeth at The Rat as guitarist for, most notably, a band called Susan, John also assisted on the recording of a *Live at The Rat* album release.

One of the first songs Ben worked on was a hauntingly beautiful track titled "Send Me," written by Kalishes and another veteran Boston-area musician, the late Adrian Medeiros. Kalishes and Medeiros had previously been in a popular Boston band called Riser and had also formed a new group called Blackout, which "Send Me" had originally been intended for.

Adrian Medeiros: "Through John, I met Ben during a Christmas party at The Rat and he really liked our song and wanted to record it. So, I went and listened to all of the Cars albums, and listening to Ben's vocals, I changed the chords in the song. As soon as I heard one vocal of 'Send Me' from Ben, I knew he was perfect for the song.

"Ben and I really got along great, and while most rock stars have big egos, Ben had no ego whatsoever and was really just a regular guy. He was even a bit isolated and pretty much kept to himself. Musically, Ben was very serious and all business in the studio and, as everyone knows, simply had an amazing voice and vocal inflection. My music experience with Ben was very enjoyable, and he really made you feel like he was your peer, and not some opinionated 'rock star' looking down at you."

"Send Me" was recorded and engineered at three Massachusetts studios (Tranquility Base, Prophet, and Long View Farm) over about a two-month span, and the song did receive some local radio airplay in Boston.

Ben did the lead vocals, bass, and co-production, while several other musicians contributed to the song, including Medeiros on keyboards and backing vocals, Cars' bandmate Greg Hawkes and David Stefanelli (Peter Wolf, RTZ) on backing vocals, Kalishes on rhythm guitar, and Barry Goudreau (of the band Boston) on slide guitar. The original recording of the song was engineered by Chris Lannon and old friend Jesse Henderson.

Other songs Ben worked on during these early sessions included "Do You Know What It Feels Like (Without You)," "Even Angels Fall," "I'm Watching You," "I'm Coming Home Tonight," "I Am the Man," and a song co-written by Glen Burtnik and Stan Meissner called "River of Fire." Burtnik has recorded and toured with Styx and written for other artists, including Don Henley, Patty Smyth, and Travis Tritt, as well as written music for television and films.

Glen Burtnik: "I honestly cannot recall how Ben was originally exposed to 'River of Fire,' and I only heard one rough, early demo of Ben's version of the song. I remember some of the lyrics had been slightly changed, but I didn't care, I was just thrilled to have *Ben Orr* singing one of my songs.

"I did meet Ben years later when I was touring with Styx and we were doing shows with Big People, a band that Ben was a member of after The Cars. I had a couple opportunities to have a conversation with him, which was a big deal for me because I always thought he was very cool."

Chris Lannon: "I had met Ben through John Kalishes and Adrian Medeiros, and I was Adrian's engineer on the initial project, recording Ben's vocals and bass parts. I remember Ben taking me aside after the mixes and saying that he thought it was just about the best his vocals had sounded, and needless to say, that was quite a compliment for me."

Jean Renard briefly assisted Ben in setting up studio time in Boston and recommended recording engineer and producer David Frangioni to assist Ben in further working up the songs. Frangioni is founder of a music production company based in Florida called Audio One and has worked with such renowned artists as The Rolling Stones, Aerosmith, Ozzy Osbourne, Joe Perry, Chick Corea, and—ironically—The Cars.

David Frangioni: "I worked with The Cars a little when they were doing their thing in the eighties, as I was good friends with the late Andy Topeka, who was The Cars' lead studio tech. Then, after The Cars broke up, I made the additional connection with Ben through Jean Renard.

"I worked closely with Ben for well over a year on those songs, co-producing and engineering what was to be his second solo album, which had the working title of *River of Fire*. Soundtrack Recording Studio in Boston was the main studio where Ben and I worked together, and we also did some work at my home studio.

"Starting out, it was going to be a five-song EP with Brad Delp of Boston fame, singing backing vocals. The songs we were working on included the title track, 'Send Me,' 'Do You Know What It Feels Like (Without You),' 'I'm Watching You,' and 'I'm Coming Home Tonight.'"

Another local guitarist, Charlie O'Neal, had also been recommended by Renard to work with Ben on his new material. Now a member of a blues band, The Delta Generators, O'Neal's previous band was called MUST, which toured nationally with Aerosmith, Def Leppard, Stone Temple Pilots, and Kid Rock.

Charlie O'Neal: "I was only eighteen and in my senior year of high school at the time, and Jean Renard, who was the manager of my band, Tizzy, indicated that Ben was interested in recording more guitar-orientated songs and Renard had recommended my services.

"After I graduated in the spring of 1993, I started working on songs every week with Ben and John Kalishes in Ben's Weston home studio. Then we started working with David Frangioni at Soundtrack Studio in Boston, who then brought in this crazy, but incredibly talented, keyboard player named Igor Khoroshev.

"Igor was in the studio at the time, participating on a song featuring Eric Clapton and Nathan East. John Kalishes and myself also played on a song in which Clapton participated. Igor started programming all the instruments on the Ben songs. Everything but the live guitars were programmed, including the drums and bass.

"Having worked with the likes of Roy Thomas Baker and Mutt Lange, I remember Ben being very mechanical, if not anal, in the studio, with lots of eight- and sixteen-track recordings of guitar and vocals. Being so young, it was a very different way of recording for me, but I also learned a great deal. Looking back now, though, it seems like there might have been 'too many cooks in the kitchen,' if you will."

Kalishes also brought in another friend and Boston-area studio engineer, Cn Fletcher (known as "Fletcher"), to assist on the tracks. Kalishes and Fletcher were, at the time, also working on the debut album of a band called Black Number Nine.

Fletcher: "The first time I met Ben on a professional level was after The Cars disbanded. I had spent some time with John on the production of Black Number Nine's debut release, and John had been working with Ben on some preproduction for his upcoming solo album. John invited me to sit in on the sessions, which were being produced by Ben and engineered by David Frangioni."

Boston-area solo artist, Charlie Farren, of the bands FARRENHEIT, The Joe Perry Project, and Balloon, also sang some backup vocals on the project.

Charlie Farren: "I knew Ben and was able to work with him in the studio, as Brad Delp and I sang backup on one of his last recordings. Ben also introduced me to Igor Khoroshev, who would play keys in my post-FARRENHEIT band in the early nineties. A little later on, Muzz [John Muzzy, FARRENHEIT drummer] also played drums in Ben's solo band.

"Ben was just a terrific singer . . . he reminded me of Rutger Hauer, but with a great voice! I didn't know The Cars well in the early days, but got to know Ben a little bit in his post-Cars days. He was a great guy, very talented, and a real pro in the studio."

John Muzzy: "During the recording of the *River of Fire* songs, both Charlie and Brad Delp were asked to sing some background vocals. I was playing with Charlie in a band we put together after FARRENHEIT called Farren, and was also working with Brad in our Beatles band, Beatlejuice, which continues to perform to this day.

"The orchestrations, drum machines, and bass were helmed by this amazing keyboard player, [Igor] Khoroshev. Charlie was so taken by him that we invited him to play and record with our band. Later on, when it came time to put a live band together for ORR, I was checked out and got the gig."

Fletcher: "After the basic tracks were cut at Soundtrack Recording, they brought the songs back to me so Ben and I could cut some vocal tracks at the warehouse of Mercenary Audio in Foxboro, Massachusetts. One of the offices in the warehouse was used as a vocal booth which pleased Ben, as he said he felt very relaxed there. Ben was also about testing a bunch of the microphones to find the one that suited him best.

"Ben also had a rather unique way of tracking vocals that he'd picked up from working with producer Mutt Lange when recording The Cars' *Heartbeat City* album.

"Ben's method required four tracks, as he would sing the song through one track so we had a reasonable idea of how the vocals were going to sit. Then he would record three more tracks of the same vocal and we would create a 'compilation vocal,' taking the best parts from the four tracks to create one 'lead vocal' track.

"He would then record three more tracks and we'd determine if any of the subsequent recorded lines beat out any of the lines that already existed in the compilation track, and usually a few did. Then we would repeat the process until we had compiled a performance where none of the additionally recorded tracks could beat any of the compiled performance. Then, we would move on to the next song.

"It was a good method that worked well, and I have used it with a few artists since, but not a lot of singers can handle that kind of rigorous recording program, but Ben sure could do it, and do it very well.

"What stood out to me most about Ben was that he was amazingly humble about being *Ben Orr*. When I was hanging out with him, it could have been that I was hanging with any of my friends, as opposed to a millionaire rock star who wanted me to be impressed (or even worse, grateful) that I was in his presence. He and I both loved to party, but when the rubber hit the road and it was time to work in the studio, he was *right* there, 100 percent and serious as a heart attack."

Despite all the work that was put into the songs, however, a record deal was never put in place and to this day the songs remain officially unreleased. There also seems to be a bit of question, if not mystery, as to why these tracks have never seen the light of day. Perhaps it was a case of timing, as the more aggressive genres of grunge and alternative rock had by then hit full stride.

David Frangioni: "The songs were finished, but I don't know for certain why the EP was never released. The songs are incredible, in my humble opinion and Ben's singing was better than ever. Perhaps it never got picked up by a record label and then shelved altogether, in part, because Ben was also going through some personal stuff at the time.

"He was dealing with marriage problems, changing management, and he was smoking and partying a lot. Then, after we had worked on these songs together for about a year, Ben simply disappeared and moved to Vermont. I had no idea he was planning on moving, it just kind of dropped out of the blue sky. I was even out of the recording project altogether at the very end, without explanation.

"Ben and I had a really good relationship throughout the recording sessions, but it somehow faded over time. I sort of got the impression that Ben was listening to the advice of the loudest, most recent voice around him. I can't tell you that is exactly what happened, but it *seemed* like that's what was going on.

"Our personal relationship had its ups and downs, as Ben was a very complex person and could be moody. Plus, I was only in my twenties, but fortunately we did remain friends through it all. Ben was somewhat intense and seemed introverted, but he was really just taking time to get to know you, then he would open up a little more. He was quite a character once I got to know him, and he always had something fun or creative going on. The man never sat still!"

However, despite having done all that work in the studio, Ben was indeed becoming more withdrawn, and in fact, Judith had already gone back to Los Angeles for a work assignment and eventually, decided not to return.

Judith Orr: "In the end, I would have never left Ben in a million years if it were not for some of the behaviors. I was from Los Angeles, and leaving Ben was the hardest thing I ever did in my life, harder than leaving my entire life behind to marry him. I left Weston in May 1994, with Ben's blessing, when I had been invited to finish the last few weeks of *The Arsenio Hall Show* in Los Angeles and to work on another show for a few days.

"I was planning to return for our third anniversary in late May, but Ben was working on the new album and was in one of his silent modes, so I ultimately canceled my flight and stayed in Los Angeles to finish the *Arsenio* shows.

"We had many phone calls over the next few months, some very loving and some very hard, but in my heart, I knew things weren't going to get better. It was months later that both Ben and I realized I wasn't going back, but neither one of us filed for divorce for a long time.

"Ben was the gentlest person I ever knew, but he was also the toughest person I ever knew. I have loved Ben for most of my life and I still do today. Our divorce would become final in 1997. Even though I left Ben, my love for him is as powerful today as the first day I fell in love with him. Sometimes love is just not enough."

THE GREEN MOUNTAIN STATE

By the end of 1994, Ben would put his home in Weston up for sale and buy a house in the small, southern Vermont town of Reading. He had plans to completely transform the property, which included building a half-mile-long driveway and remodeling the main house and upstairs apartment. He would also install a recording studio so he could continue to work on music.

His new Vermont property needed a lot of work, but Ben had always wanted to live closer to nature and was excited about his new surroundings. However, he also remained very low-key about his transition to Vermont, as well as his separation from Judith, and in fact, he made it known to very few people early on.

Once relocated in Vermont, Ben continued working on the songs he had been recording in Boston, while also deciding that he wanted to put a touring band together and play live again. Ben contacted the late David Tedeschi, an associate he knew through John Kalishes and then owner of a stage-lighting and sound company called Top Watt Productions.

David Tedeschi: "I had first met Ben in the late seventies, backstage at The Rat and in the early eighties at The Channel, where my company owned the lighting and PA systems. Boston is a pretty small city in the music business, so it gives you the opportunity to get to know a lot of different people around town.

"Ben told me about the place in Vermont, and talked about the plans he had, building the long driveway on the property and installing a studio so he could continue working on his music. He still had a plan in place to release the songs he was working on, which is why I couldn't really understand why he wanted to move so far north of Boston, but he loved Vermont and the outdoors, and was really excited about his new plans."

Tedeschi introduced Ben to a musician named Kevin McCarty, who would also assist on Ben's ongoing music project. At the time, Tedeschi and McCarty were in the studio working on a couple songs with the late Brad Delp, singer of the legendary band Boston and also RTZ.

Kevin McCarty: "David Tedeschi had sort of taken me under his wing and introduced me to RTZ and John Kalishes; this was before I had met Ben. They had already been writing songs for Ben's next album and John had also played me a few tracks they were working on. Not long after that, I went with John to Ben's house in Vermont, as they were working on some of the material."

David Tedeschi: "Despite Ben having been the bassist and co–lead singer in a famous rock band, I still don't think the masses fully understand just how amazing a musician he was. Ben's talents as a performer were so effortless that even after taking a long hiatus after The Cars ended, when he did get back into performing, it was almost like he had never stopped in the first place. He just seemed to do everything with such style and grace. He just picked it all right back up like it was nothing for him to do."

• 18 •

Traveling Solo

BACK TO THE RAT

The first incarnation of the ORR band consisted of Ben on rhythm guitar and lead vocals, John Kalishes on guitar, Charlie O'Neal on guitar and vocals, Rick O'Neal on bass and vocals, John Muzzy on drums, and Igor Khoroshev on keyboards.

After those earlier recording sessions with Ben, Charlie O'Neal became a highly regarded Boston guitar player and has toured with the band MUST, who've opened for such legendary bands as Aerosmith, Def Leppard, and Stone Temple Pilots.

Rick O'Neal, Charlie's brother, would go on to work with Boston-area guitarist Johnny A. and has opened shows for the likes of the late B. B. King, George Thorogood, Peter Frampton, and the late Etta James.

Ben's new band would rehearse and develop chemistry leading up to their first show, which took place at The Cars' original home turf, The Rat.

Rick O'Neal: "My brother Charlie played guitar on Ben's studio tracks, and because they had used synth bass for those recordings, they now needed a bass player for the live shows. Charlie, Igor, and I were already writing and recording together, so they both recommended me for the bass position.

"This was the first ORR lineup, and our first show was at The Rat in Boston, I believe in December. I remember the band having epic, all-day rehearsals leading up to the show, eight straight hours or more in the beginning, to get the show together.

"We would run through the whole show over and over, with Ben, John Kalishes, Igor, Muzz, Charlie, me, and at times [the late] Brad Delp, of Boston fame, singing backup vocals. The show slowly come together, until it was second nature to everyone in the room. Brad would later do a show with us at the Pickle Barrel nightclub in Killington, Vermont."

Fletcher: "Not long after the vocal sessions that we recorded in Foxboro, I was at Ben's house for a rehearsal of his new band. A bunch of rather good-looking young men who could play well and featuring this insane Russian keyboard player [Khoroshev], a monster player who seemed to be certifiably insane, but somehow in a good way.

"Ben asked me to do the monitors for some local shows that he and John were putting together, and I was happy to do the gigs. We had some rehearsals, followed by a show at The Rat in Boston."

David Frangioni: "After we recorded the unreleased tracks, and then Ben moved to Vermont, he finally reappeared and did a solo show at The Rat. His set included all the songs we had recorded and he let me go backstage, but wouldn't see me.

"After the Rat show, I had very little communication with Ben, but I do know he flew to Los Angeles to meet with record executives about releasing the solo album because it was self-made, so he wanted to sign a deal I believe, through CBS Records, because he knew some people there. Obviously, it did not happen.

"To this day, I remain friends with Judith, and she knows that I always had Ben's best interests at heart. It was truly an honor to meet, work with, and get to know him. I always felt that he was a huge talent. I wish things had gone a little differently, but I really enjoyed my time with Ben and making a great album with him."

RETURN TO THE STAGE

In 1995, now settled into his Vermont surroundings, Ben was told about a local benefit show, the Riverweed Music Festival, created to raise money for David's House, a social services organization dedicated to supporting cancer patients and their families during their stay at Dartmouth-Hitchcock Medical Center in nearby Lebanon, New Hampshire.

Kevin McCarty: "I had been visiting Ben and John when I told him about the Riverweed Music Festival, a local charity event I was involved with, and he really wanted to be a part of it. He had heard of the benefit show, liked what I was up to musically at the time, and offered to play with me at the festival."

The cancer benefit was to be held at the nearby Hawk Mountain Inn & Resort in Plymouth, Vermont. However, Ben first put together a trio with Kalishes and McCarty for a one-night-only performance as The Beacon Hillbillies, which was also held at the Hawk Mountain Inn, prior to the benefit show.

Kevin McCarty: "Ben, John, and I became The Beacon Hillbillies for one night and I can tell you that it was simply an amazing experience. I was just twenty-three years old when we did that show, the place was packed, and Ben insisted that together we all walk from the back of the crowd to the front of the stage. He wanted to purposely give me the experience of a lifetime.

"Heads were turning, and I felt like a million bucks walking onstage with someone I had looked up to since I was a kid. It was quite a moment for me. We mixed up the set list, playing some Cars songs, some Ben solo songs, and some of my original music to create this one-time show."

The benefit performance was a few days after, billed as the 9th Annual Riverweed Music & Outdoor Adventure Festival, held on August 19 and 20, 1995, and it featured Ben's second show as the ORR band. The festival lineup also included a Kevin McCarty solo performance and Brown Trout and The Lunkers, a band that included Davey Davis, who would also become Ben's good friend.

Kevin McCarty: "After the Riverweed show, Ben and I spent some time together. He was a very down-to-earth guy and had a voice of confidence and caring in every song he sang. The material didn't matter, really. Ben never left anything on the table and his kindness in giving others' confidence in their own abilities was second to none.

"I am so honored to say that I am certain that Ben cared about me and was interested in what I was up to musically. I remember one time he complimented me on my vocals, and when I attempted to downplay it, he said with such clarity and force that I will never forget it: 'I never say what I don't mean.' I still feel Ben's presence today, and I can't tell you the number of times when I am stretching, or floundering, and he comes on the radio and reminds me he's there. To this day, that is what keeps me going in music. Ben was truly a great friend."

A local Vermont musician and now the owner of an outdoor clothing line, Davey Davis, spent a lot of time with Ben, not only in his home studio but also on hunting and fishing trips.

Davey Davis: "I became friends with Ben after he had come to Vermont. I got to spend some time with him at his home and in his studio, which was in an outside building near the main house on his property. The studio contained minimum equipment, but it was all first-class stuff. I was thrilled to be able to spend time with such a great musician in this intimate studio setting. I got to spend a lot of time with Ben outside of the studio as well.

"I attended Ben's show at Hawk Mountain Inn when he was on the bill at the Riverweed Festival. I also saw the ORR band's first Boston performance at The Rat, and despite having not been in the public eye for quite some time, I was impressed at how easy and effortless everything seemed to be for Ben onstage even though he was actually quite shy and reserved most of the time.

"Ben also accompanied me and my father on a couple hunting and camping trips to the Diamond Peaks in New Hampshire's Dartmouth College Grant, and we stayed at a cabin where Dwight D. Eisenhower had once stayed. For years after our trip, the folks at camp still remembered Ben's 'pumpkin suit' [a bright orange, one-piece hunting outfit], and his cool, antique rifle.

"When I started hanging out with Ben, I was just getting into learning guitar and writing songs, and yet, he was very supportive and really taught me a lot about music and singing. Ben told me there were five things I needed to remember about singing and performing [holding his fingers up, one at a time]: 'timing, enunciation, singing with pitch, singing with feeling, and eliminating string noise.' Yes, I certainly learned a great deal about music and recording thanks to Ben's guidance."

Leading up to that first show at Hawk Mountain Resort, Ben hadn't been performing much and was also a little self-conscious at the time, as partying had contributed to a gain in weight. However, those first two performances went off without a hitch, and Ben had a great time performing in front of an audience once again. So much so, in fact, that he wanted to perform more.

Jim Nielsen is the owner of Hawk Mountain Resort, which hosted the show that brought Ben back to the stage.

Jim Nielsen: "One thing I do remember is that when the trucks arrived with the equipment, I was amazed at how much was being brought in. I can remember thinking, 'this is going to be a *real* rock concert.' I don't remember much about the warm-up show, but I remember when they played the song 'Drive.' It took me back to some old memories and I was just mesmerized during the performance."

David Tedeschi: "It had been a few years since Ben had hit the stage, and I don't think he realized just how much he missed it, because a couple of nights later, he told me he wanted to get back into music *for real*. Not just doing an appearance here and there, but he wanted his own touring band. So, I put my road crew together, who all had 'world tour' experience, and Ben was off and running."

Old friend, Tyler Sweet, was approached by Tedeschi to take part in the new ORR band road crew he was assembling.

Tyler Sweet: "In the early nineties my friend David Tedeschi started road-managing for Ben and asked if I was interested in becoming the tech for him and the band. Ben had told him he remembered me from the early days and brought me onboard. I worked with Ben on and off until around 1996, and I ended up sitting in on a couple gigs, with Ben handing off his guitar to me . . . but that stopped when I moved around too much onstage and the band felt like I was upstaging them.

"Ben liked having me around because I knew all the words to the songs he sang over the years, right off the top of my head, and he necessarily didn't. I had to occasionally remind Ben about the words, and we would do reviews of them by two-way radios we had in our vehicles, on the way to gigs. 'Hey Ty, you there? What are the words for "Cruiser"'. . . and I'd tell him. I even offered to get him a teleprompter, and he laughed.

"My other job was holding his towel and beer while Ben ate hot wings that were so spicy he had to sign releases, so the restaurants wouldn't be responsible if he injured himself. The sauces were so hot they'd probably kill most people, and I believe it contributed to his pancreatic cancer. It was an everyday affair, and he always carried a bottle of 'ass in the tub' sauce around with him.

"I miss Ben and all the people that have passed that were a part of his solo career . . . and oh yes, the pig roasts."

It was also during this time that Ben met Edita, a pretty blonde of Swedish descent who worked at the Hawk Mountain Resort. The couple would have a nearly four-year relationship, which created Ben's only child, a son

Ben and his son in Vermont.
Courtesy of Julie Snider-Mennie

named Benjamin Charles Joseph. Young Benjamin's name honors two men that Ben loved very much: his half brother, Charles, and his early band manager and "adopted" father, Joseph "The Emperor" Mayer.

Ben (who is not named a junior) attended high school in Southern Vermont and college in the Boston area, where he studied graphic design. He is both athletic and musical, just like his father. He played soccer, lacrosse, and ice hockey in high school and played on his college lacrosse team. Although Ben never formally joined a band in his youth, he took piano lessons, has always enjoyed music, and picks up an instrument from time to time, even his father's bass.

Edita Hartig: "Ben is musical, but I believe it isn't his passion. One time, though, Ben entered a school talent show with his friends and they performed 'Just What I Needed.' Ben played his father's bass during the performance, and it was a really fun moment."

ORR BAND

The ORR band mostly toured throughout the New England area, but also did one-off shows around the country, performing a set of select songs from *The Lace* and his new solo tracks, as well as Cars' hits, in which Ben had performed the lead vocal. This original lineup stayed together for about a year and a half, before Charlie, Rick, and Igor moved on to other music endeavors.

Fletcher: "At the time, I also remember there was talk of doing a short tour of the 'Pac Rim' [Japan, China, Korea, Taiwan]; however, the tour was canceled shortly after Ric Ocasek sent out a press release stating that a 'Cars reunion tour' was imminent."

Rod McCarthy is a longtime musician, concert promoter, and founder of Castle Gate Entertainment, and once booked a Ben Orr show at The Roxy in Boston.

Rod McCarthy: "I met Ben through my friend Muzzy [FARRENHEIT drummer, John Muzzy], who was Ben's drummer at the time. I planned a very cool show at The Roxy, which featured Ben, Missing Persons, and Avatar Blue.

"We took Ben and Dale Bozzio [Missing Persons singer] to WZLX radio for a live, on-air interview with DJ Charles Laquidara. Matty from Kiss 108 called and harassed Ben on the air about 'still being around?' But Ben was very cool about it and did not react, he just chuckled and said that 'Matty will never change.'

"Ben came down from Vermont for the show, and part of booking a rock star is taking care of the rider. So, I put Ben and his dog up in a hotel

next to The Roxy . . . two rooms, one for him and one for his dog [smiling].
I remember speaking to Ben just before he hit the stage and he said, 'What
do you want me to do here?' and I just said, 'Rock this place!'. . . And it was
a great concert, one of the best shows I ever put on. When he sang 'Drive'
there was not a dry eye in the house.

"After the show, we all had a great time hanging out, and Ben was a true
gentleman, telling us stories about his days with The Cars. I am glad that I got
to meet and know him."

Rick O'Neal: "I remember being with the band on an East Coast run one
night, sitting in my hotel room after that night's show and watching television
with some of the guys in the band and crew. Now, you have to remember that I
and others in the group grew up in the 1980s when The Cars were at their peak.

"So, sitting there, we flipped to a channel that was showing the 1982
classic movie *Fast Times at Ridgemont High*. We all started laughing at the scene
in the film that plays The Cars song 'Moving in Stereo,' which not only did
Ben sing, but we had just finished playing to an enthusiastic audience with
him that same night *and* he was now in the room right next to us! It was a
moment that really reminded us just how popular The Cars' music was and
how embedded it was into the pop culture of that time!"

In fact, Cars' fans everywhere were given a special treat in 1995 when
Rhino Records released *Just What I Needed: The Cars Anthology*, a two-CD
retrospective that reminded everyone just how popular and influential this band
was for a decade. The forty-track set not only offered up the hit singles, but also
included several B-sides, unreleased songs, demo versions, and deep album cuts.

Of course, the hits on the two-disc set featuring Ben on lead vocals are
distinct; "Let's Go," "Just What I Needed," "Moving in Stereo," "Candy-O,"
"It's All I Can Do," "Don't Tell Me No," and of course, "Drive." The Cars
truly left an unmistakable impression on music and pop culture for a decade
strong, and Ben's vocal prowess and presence played a key role.

ORR ON TOUR

In 1996, a second incarnation of ORR included Kalishes and Muzzy, with
Muzzy recruiting a couple of his Beatlejuice bandmates in guitarist Bob
Squires and bassist Joe Holiday, as well as Stephen Baker on keyboards. This
lineup toured until the middle of 1996 when Muzzy left the band over management differences. Tommy West would also contribute on keyboards.

Joe Holiday: "I joined the ORR band when Muzz, who had been with
the band for a couple years with a different lineup, asked the members of
Beatlejuice to audition for Ben's band. After rigorous and detailed audition

sessions, Steve, Bobby, Muzz, and I headed up to Ben's home in Vermont to meet him and hopefully gain his acceptance. Ben seemed impressed with our attention to detail and especially our vocal abilities.

"We played a number of shows together over the next two years; most were successful and well received and a lot of fun. Yet for some others, not as much. Ben was still enmeshed in the rock-and-roll 'lifestyle' and would arrive at some gigs on the tail end of a partying day, and not in the best physical condition.

"After Muzz, Bob, and Steve left the band, I stayed on for another two years and played with Richie Bartlett (also my Fools bandmate), Tommy Hambridge, and John Kalishes. Later, Tommy was replaced by Liberty De-Vitto (of Billy Joel's band). It was certainly an honor and pleasure playing with those two storied and talented drummers."

John Muzzy: "Of course, there are 'stories' [revolving around his departure from the band], but mainly, I regret that lineup never reaching its potential, because it was a great band. There were just too many contributing factors. I think the most enjoyable time I had with Ben was meeting his mom at one of the shows when we traveled to near where he grew up. I enjoyed that and really wanted (as always) to do our best.

"I wish I had met Ben in earlier times, because when I see footage of his days with The Cars, I see a really consistent performer. When I played with him, however, it seemed like that commitment and drive was not coming from within him as much. He had a beautiful son and woman and to my thinking, he had every opportunity to do wonderful things, yet somehow, it eluded him. He almost seemed withdrawn from it."

Joe Holiday: "We are all human with human failings. I loved Ben . . . he was quiet, funny, insightful, and one hell of a songwriter. He was meticulous in his writing and never settled on even the smallest part of his compositions. The song 'Do You Know What It Feels Like' still gives me chills, as does the Cars' hit 'Drive.'

"While in Ben's band, I had one of the funniest, weirdest weekends of my career. We flew out to San Francisco to play a few shows, one being an 'eighties festival' at the Santa Rosa Racetrack, and we were on the bill with such acts as Sammy Hagar, Missing Persons, and Flock of Seagulls. All the bands were staying at an area hotel at the same time a Star Trek convention was being held. As you can imagine, the hotel was filled with Trekkies and old eighties rockers, and it was otherworldly! Late nights at the hotel bar left you wondering what planet you were on, it was something to behold. . . . The word Bacchanalia comes to mind.

"I am honored and proud to have been included in Ben's life, and I hope we, as a band, gave Ben some happiness and satisfaction in the competent, respectful way we approached his music."

Auditions were then held to find a new drummer, which included amazing players such as the aforementioned David Stefanelli (Peter Wolf, RTZ), Mike Mangoni (Dream Theatre, Steve Vai), and Dave Danza (Eddie Money, Greg Kihn Band); however, Berklee graduate Tom Hambridge ultimately got the gig. Now a Grammy Award–winning producer, singer, songwriter, and drummer, Hambridge has worked with such artists as ZZ Top, Buddy Guy, B.B. King, Lynyrd Skynyrd, Johnny Winter, George Thorogood, Delbery McClinton, Meat Loaf, and Walt Disney Pictures, to name but a few.

Tom Hambridge: "I started playing with Ben in 1996 and was also playing with him in 1999. I received a call from John Kalishes saying that Ben Orr was putting together a new band and asking if I would be interested in playing drums. I was so busy with gigs and recording sessions that there was no way I could fit in another project. Being that it was *Ben Orr*, though . . . I said yes, anyway."

Also brought into this lineup was Rich Bartlett, longtime guitarist with The Fools, veteran Boston bassist Brad Hallen, formerly of the band Ministry, and Berklee graduate Ross Ramsay on keyboards. Hambridge had recommended both Bartlett and Hallen.

Brad Hallen: "I had played with Tom Hambridge previously, and he recommended me for Ben's band, but ironically, I already had a connection to Ben and The Cars many years earlier. I had worked with Ric Ocasek and Elliot Easton at Syncro Sound back in the early eighties, during my days with Ministry.

"I did some session work for Ric and also played on Elliot Easton's solo album. I remember one time, I was in the studio with Ric and the bass I was using just wasn't cutting it, so he had me use one of Ben's basses. So, in walks Ben and says, 'Hey, you're using my bass!' But he was really cool about it and only messing around with me.

"I worked with the ORR band for basically two summers. Not really touring, but mostly flying out to do a one-off show and fly back. We'd do festival shows with other bands from the eighties such as Missing Persons and The Fixx.

"Ben truly had one of the great rock voices of all time and for me, his voice ranks right there with Paul McCartney and David Bowie. The whole time I worked with his band, and those guys liked to party a little bit, I can honestly say I never once heard Ben sing a bad note!

"Yes, Ben truly had a gift, and even though he was a celebrity—and I mean whenever he walked through airports with that blond hair, heads would turn—he really was a sweet guy, very reserved, down to earth, and always cool."

Ross Ramsay: "I always liked Ben very much, and really enjoyed my time in ORR. I had previously known John Kalishes while gigging with my original band called Absolute, and I started with the ORR band at the same time as Brad and Rich.

"It was always great to hear Ben sing at the shows, as he had an iconic rock voice that was truly unique and enjoyable. I think of Ben all the time and certainly wish he didn't leave us at such a young age and that we could have had more musical experiences together."

Tom Hambridge: "When I joined we would rehearse without Ben, and I actually met him for the first time at Logan Airport as we were boarding a plane for the first show. I would sing the songs during sound check and Ben would just come on out at show time and we would rock . . . and he always delivered! It was after my first show that he nicknamed me 'The Hammer.' I think I was hitting especially hard that night!

"I recently found a great review from one of our shows that someone sent to me. I believe it was his last ever in Boston, at The Paradise (Rock Club) and it was dated March 30, 1999. Greg Hawkes, David Robinson, Brad Delp, Barry Goodreau . . . everybody was there, and I remember that Beatlejuice was the opening band that night.

"Ben also asked me to produce a couple songs that I had written for a potential solo Ben Orr album, so I went up to his house in Vermont and we started recording. I'd stay at Ben's place while we were recording, and those were also good times. However, I then got busy working and producing other artists and Ben and I never did get back to those tracks. I stayed with the ORR band until I moved to Nashville in 1999.

"Ben was truly a rock star but never acted like one. We would go out somewhere and he would get recognized, but he wasn't looking for it. Many times, we would be driving down the road in his car, a Cars' song would come on the radio and he would just keep talking, almost like he didn't even notice. He really was just a regular guy, who just so happened to be a famous rock star.

"Ben was a great singer and musician, nobody sounded like him. He invented a style; the way he sang certain syllables was totally unique. Also, we only did an ORR band show if it was going to be fun. Ben would always say, 'If it's not going to be fun for all of us, then we don't take the gig.' So, all the shows ended up being fun!

"One show that stands out for me was when we played at Denver's Fiddler's Green in August 1997. We had a killer set that night; the crowd went crazy, and I have a vivid memory of what seemed like a million lighters in the audience during 'Drive.' It was like time had stopped. The power and emotion of Ben's voice was really connecting with everyone. It was beautiful, and you could just feel it. It started to rain and the audience was not covered, but nobody moved. We went into 'Moving in Stereo' and finished with 'Bye Bye Love' and the place went crazy."

Brad Hallen: "That Fiddler's Green outdoor show was simply a great night! Ben's vocals were just incredible and he stole the show. It started to rain, but the audience didn't care. Seeing all those lighters go up during 'Drive' was just magical, and I get goose bumps now just thinking about it."

Renowned soundman Tony Lentini, who has worked with such legendary bands as Aerosmith and Van Halen, was also involved with the ORR band early on.

Tony Lentini: "I first met Ben in 1998, when asked to mix his band. I was always a fan of some of The Cars' music, so I thought it would be fun. The lineup I worked with included Tom Hambridge, Richie Bartlett, John Kalishes (rest in peace), and Tom West on keys. It was really a great bunch of musicians.

"Ben was an avid Harley Davidson enthusiast, as am I, so we shared the love of riding and talked bikes all the time. He went to Norway once and brought me back a Harley flask from the dealership there. It was such a very kind and thoughtful gesture.

"As a musician, Ben was a great vocalist and of course, great on the bass and guitar. I was very sad when he passed, and felt the loss of a friend. Whenever we went on the road there was never a dull moment. It was always a great time."

Chris Lannon: "Eventually, I replaced Brad Hallen and toured with the band for a summer, after getting a call from John Kalishes out of the blue. I've had the chance to work with a few 'A-list' musicians, and Ben never let it go to his head like I've seen with others. In fact, he talked a few times about how he saw some of that happen with others. He certainly enjoyed his success, but he didn't rub it in your face."

Yes, the ORR band had become a tremendous musical outlet for Ben after his days with The Cars, allowing him to continue doing what he loved most: playing live and interacting with his fans. However, he had now changed the band lineup several times in a relatively short period of time, and it was becoming increasingly difficult to coordinate everyone's schedules and maintain a consistent band to bring out on the road for mostly sporadic, one-off appearances. Ben needed to find another musical platform to complement the occasional ORR band show.

VOICES OF CLASSIC ROCK

In 1998, Ben connected with Voices of Classic Rock, singing and playing guitar in this unique traveling music show, which featured musicians and

Ben onstage with the ORR Band, Anaheim, California, 1999.
Dana Mennie Collection

singers from various 1970s and 1980s rock and pop bands. The ensemble was originally formed simply as a one-time, special performance for the Twenty-Fifth Anniversary of the PGA Tour's Players Golf Championships. However, the night went off so well that the Voices of Classic Rock would continue, becoming a popular choice for corporate and special event entertainment, performing over 125 shows on four continents over a seven-year span.

A few Voices of Classic Rock musicians included singers (and Voices creator) Mickey Thomas (Jefferson Starship, Elvin Bishop), Bobby Kimball

(Toto), Mike Reno (Loverboy), Jimi Jamison (Survivor), Gary U.S. Bonds, Nick Gilder, and John Cafferty, as well as musicians Pat Travers, Spencer Davis, Leslie West (Mountain), and Glenn Hughes of Deep Purple and Black Sabbath fame.

Mickey Thomas: "I first met Ben through my former agent, who had gotten Ben involved with the Voices shows that I put together. Before I had met Ben, the agent informed me to only introduce him onstage as *Benjamin Orr*, per his wishes. The first few shows we did together, I made sure that's the way I introduced him.

"A short time later, we're having a drink together and I asked Ben if he was happy with the way the shows were going and he said yes, except for one thing: 'Please don't introduce me as Benjamin . . . it's just Ben.' We had a good laugh over that one, and from then on, he was simply *Ben*.

"I remember that the first show we did with Ben was an outdoor event in Maui, and it was your typical tropical paradise setting. There were many singers on the show that night, and of course, we all showed up wearing our finest colorful island wear and sporting fragrant leis.

"Well, Ben shows up with freshly dyed, stark-white hair, skin that looks like it hasn't seen the light of day, black Edwardian coat, and not a speck of color on him. He looked straight out of *Dark Shadows*. It was Ben at his finest, the consummate rock star!

"Ben had an amazing voice, was very serious, and always professional. He had that true, *rock star* aura, and he walked on the stage as if he owned it . . . and he did.

"Ben was rather quiet and could be hard to get to know, but once you did get to know him, you had a friend for life. He had a strong sense of brotherhood and real love of family. In fact, Ben got to be very close with my family, as well as the Starship band. We all loved him very much and miss him greatly."

Bobby Kimball is the original singer of Toto, and a touring solo artist. He worked with Ben during their time with Voices of Classic Rock.

Bobby Kimball: "Benjamin Orr was a very nice person and a wonderful musician. He was not only a fantastic singer, but also a great bass player. The last concert that I sang with him was at a hotel in Hawaii, and Mickey Thomas and Mike Reno were also with us. This was not too long before Benjamin passed away. It was very sad to learn that he had died from cancer, and he was taken from us much too young."

In the fall of 1998, the city of Cleveland was ready to get an expansion NFL football franchise after Cleveland Browns' owner, Art Modell, had moved the original Cleveland football franchise to Baltimore in 1996. Ben contributed to another Cleveland-area music project called the Cleveland Browns All-Star Band and again, in conjunction with Michael Stanley, for a song Stanley wrote called "Here We Go Again."

Michael Stanley: "The Browns' project went down in much the same way as the *C.A.R.E. Session* "Eyes of the Children" song. Bob Pelander (Michael Stanley Band keyboard player) and I were in charge of writing and recording a song for The Browns' Trust, which was an organization trying to get the NFL to award Cleveland a new franchise after Art Modell had taken our Browns to Baltimore.

"This project, however, had far more 'star power' included than the *C.A.R.E.* project. Along with Ben, we were joined by Joe Walsh, Clarence Clemons of Bruce Springsteen's E Street Band, [soul singer] Gerald Levert, members of the Temptations, actor Drew Carey, Browns' football legend, Jim Brown, and more.

"Once again, Ben had generously agreed to help out, sang great, took part in the video, and it ended up being one of my favorite records I've ever been involved with."

Ben with Voices of Classic Rock. With Mike Reno, Joe Lynn Turner, Bobby Kimball.
Ben Orr Collection

• *19* •

Big People

GATHERING A SUPERGROUP

*I*n March 1999, Ben received a call from guitarist Derek St. Holmes of Ted Nugent band fame, asking if he wanted to be a part of a new Atlanta-based group he was putting together.

Big People performed songs from its members' previous bands, which included the aforementioned St. Holmes, Jeff Carlisi (.38 Special) on guitar, Liberty DeVitto (Billy Joel) on drums, and Pat Travers (Pat Travers Band) on guitar. Michael Cartellone (Lynyrd Skynyrd, Damn Yankees, Accept) was originally set to be the drummer but after rehearsals started, he auditioned for, and was then offered a touring gig with Lynyrd Skynyrd.

There was already some familiarity among the guys as Carlisi and St. Holmes previously knew Cartellone, and St. Holmes also knew Travers from their days touring with Ted Nugent and The Pat Travers Band. The Big People name came about after Travers was talking on the phone about the new band and its members, and the person on the other end stated that Travers was sure working in a band with some "big people" in it.

The original trio, Carlisi, St. Holmes, and Cartellone, had gotten together and begun talking about the idea of putting some kind of band together and doing some local gigs.

Michael Cartellone: "I was hanging out with Jeff in Atlanta, and one night, he and I sat in with a local band and played a few blues tunes. A week or so later, we were out to dinner and joined by Derek and a friend of ours, David Preschel, who was prominent in the Atlanta music scene. Jeff and I were telling them how we had sat in with that band and were thinking it would be fun to put together a little blues band and do some gigs. At which point, Derek raised his hand and said 'I'm in.'

"Then David said, 'Well, if you guys are going to do that, don't stop there. Get a few other known guys like yourselves and start one of those all-star bands, like Ringo Starr. You could each play some of your tunes.' So, it was David Preschel who actually came up with the idea, to give credit where credit is due.

"So, the first thing that happened was Jeff, Derek, and I getting together in an Atlanta rehearsal room to jam. It sounded fantastic, and the chemistry was wonderful! Once we knew this was going to work, we started moving toward the next step in completing the band. It was several weeks before anything happened, and during that interim, I was asked to audition for Lynyrd Skynyrd by their manager, Charlie Brusco."

Well established in the Atlanta music scene, Charlie would also go on to manage Big People. "I would land the Skynyrd gig, but it was going to be a few months before the tour started, so I was available to continue helping Jeff and Derek build the new band."

Jeff Carlisi: "Originally, we were just going to put a little band together and do some weekend club dates, but the next thing you know, then there were three (Carlisi, Cartellone, and St. Holmes). Then, I was talking with another promoter friend, who said that we should seriously consider creating a full-time band from this. So then we thought, 'who will play bass?'"

Derek St. Holmes: "The next day I was talking to a promoter friend of mine and he mentioned having just seen Ben Orr performing with the Voices of Classic Rock and that he had been the shining star of the show. He also thought that Ben just might be interested in the Big People project.

"I didn't know him at all, but I was always a huge fan of Ben, so I got his phone number through a connection I had to Elliot Easton and gave him a call. When he answered and I told him that this was Derek St. Holmes from the Ted Nugent band, he just started laughing . . . maybe as if it was a joke.

"So, when I ask him why he's laughing he said, 'Because I can't believe Derek from Ted Nugent's band is calling me!' I just said back to him that I couldn't believe I was actually talking to Ben Orr! We were both Midwestern guys, so Ben and I hit it off.

"After telling him about the band and who would be involved, Ben really didn't think about it very long and I will never forget how he told me. 'Count me in, pardner.' That is what he called all of us, his pardner."

Jeff Carlisi: "I had always been a big Cars fan, and in fact, I still remember first hearing 'Just What I Needed' way back when and they were a big influence on me.

"Derek picked Ben up at the airport, and I was in awe of this guy. I'll never forget the first time he walked through the door for rehearsal and I said 'Hey, you're Ben Orr!' and he just said with a smile, 'So, that's what I've been told.' Ben was somewhat quiet, didn't really say too much, but seemed like a really nice guy."

St. Holmes had also initiated the connection with Pat Travers, having known the veteran guitarist since the days of touring with Ted Nugent, to see if he was interested in coming to Atlanta and checking out the project.

Pat Travers: "I first met Derek in 1980 when I toured with Ted Nugent in Canada, and when he told me that he and Jeff were putting a new band together in Atlanta, I was listening!

"They had this idea to feature two guitars and really wanted to track down Ben Orr and ask if he might be interested in having a play with us. At this point, Michael Cartellone, one of my favorite drummers, was also on-board. Derek had managed to find Ben and he [Ben] accepted the offer to come down to Atlanta. I was also invited to meet with Jeff, Derek, Michael, and Ben.

"Our first get-together happened at a Thai restaurant and we were sort of nervous with anticipation because we were all huge Cars fans. My image of Ben had always been of this cool, aloof 'fashion plate,' but the dude that walked into the restaurant that day was tall, wearing a leather jacket and a scowl on his face.

"To be honest, he did not look like a very happy fellow. A Zippo-lighting, flask-toting tough guy from Vermont, seemingly with a chip on his shoulder. Honestly, at first I was having a hard time trying to separate the Ben Orr in reality from the Ben Orr image I had in my mind for so many years."

However, the meeting went well, and after Ben and Pat agreed to join Big People, Ben started commuting back and forth from Vermont to Atlanta to rehearse with his new band. Also during this time, Ben met Julie Snider-Mennie at a March of Dimes event in which Big People had been booked to play. Julie was the event organizer and immediately hit it off well with Ben.

At age fifty-two, Ben made some changes in his life. He dramatically cut back on drinking alcohol and lost some weight, while also finding a new life partner in Julie. He was now feeling healthier than he had in a long time and was ready and excited to get to work with his new bandmates.

Michael Cartellone: "When Ben and Pat came to Atlanta and joined Derek, Jeff, and myself, we rehearsed for a few days and worked up a half-dozen songs. Those were fun rehearsals, and it was clear that the chemistry was right and this was going to work.

"I remember telling Ben how I was a huge Cars fan and that I had been in a cover band back in our hometown of Cleveland [Cartellone is from Solon, on Cleveland's East side] that played a lot of Cars songs. So, just for fun, I started to play a drumbeat and Ben yelled out 'You're All I've Got Tonight!' Then, I kept playing different beats and he kept yelling out the correct Cars' songs. It was a really fun exchange, and I'm glad I have that cool memory of Ben."

Pat Travers: "At the rehearsal studio for our first play together, I suggested playing 'Just What I Needed,' and when Derek, Ben, and I sang together for the first time, wow! What a blend. Our three voices, with myself on the bottom, Derek on top and Ben singing the lead, had this amazing sound to me that was tight and sweet."

Michael Cartellone: "When the rehearsals were finished, we had a meeting with Charlie [Brusco] and talked about the plans for the band and how to proceed with booking shows, but then Charlie said, 'The first thing you will need to do is find another drummer because Michael's joining Lynyrd Skynyrd.' Then, Ben immediately said, 'That's his problem!' I just thought that was just hilarious and loved Ben for saying it!"

Jeff Carlisi: "So, after it was announced that Michael would be joining Lynyrd Skynyrd, Pat made a phone call to his friend, Liberty DeVitto, the longtime drummer in Billy Joel's band."

Pat Travers: "Liberty had moved to Winter Park, Florida, a couple years earlier, and we had bumped into each other at a local studio and ended up working on some songs together. I suggested Lib to the other guys, and they thought I was bullshitting them at first, but Lib was interested, and we drove up to Atlanta together a couple times to rehearse with the new band. It all just seemed to fall into place, just like that."

Liberty DeVitto: "I had just gotten back to my hotel room after playing Madison Square Garden with Billy Joel when my phone rang, and it was Pat Travers, who I had worked with before and was a neighbor of mine when I lived in Florida. He asked if I wanted to be in this band; he mentioned who was already in and I told him that I had two more shows to do with Billy and after that, I was good to go!"

Jeff Carlisi: "We started rehearsing, with each of us contributing a few songs to the mix. Derek and Pat each had a few of their own songs; Lib had a few Billy Joel songs; I had a few .38 Special songs and of course, Ben contributed a few Cars' songs. We got out and played a few local shows to gel as a band, and then we toured with Styx for some shows. It was sort of a building-up process."

Big People would be managed by Billy Johnson and the Atlanta-based company Crossover Entertainment. An artist management company launched in the late 1980s, Johnson joined the company in 1992, and also had previously been associated with Jeff Carlisi.

Billy Johnson: "I've had a long relationship with Jeff Carlisi, going all the way back to the early nineties. I also manage a tour rehearsal studio, and when this project was being discussed and put together, Jeff and Derek St.

Big People at Atlanta's Crossover Entertainment, 1999. Pat Travers, Billy John-son's son Jamie Johnson, Ben, Jeff Carlisi, Derek St. Holmes, and Liberty DeVitto.
Ben Orr Collection

Holmes visited Crossover to discuss getting started and rehearsing the band at my studio.

"From the first time Ben came to the studio, in April 1999, to begin rehearsals on the Big People project, the second he walked into the lobby you could just feel an aura of star power. It's something that not all stars possess, but that man definitely had it."

Music and entertainment manager Charlie Brusco is president [Atlanta office] of the artist management company Red Light Management and presently manages Styx, Ann Wilson, Don Felder, Poison, The Outlaws, Marshall Tucker Band, and Collective Soul. He was also a concert promoter for Voices of Classic Rock and Big People.

Charlie Brusco: "Ben was a wonderful person to be around and was truly a powerhouse addition to the Big People lineup. He played a solid bass, had one of the sweetest high vocals in all of rock-and-roll, and really added that *something special* to the band. Yes, Ben had a certain aura about him that was felt by all involved.

"From my managerial standpoint, Ben was easy to deal with but also asked very intelligent questions. He brought several great songs he performed in The Cars to the already formidable Big People repertoire."

Joe Dlearo, who has worked with such bands as the Atlanta Rhythm Section and Brother Cane, became Big People's tour manager.

Joe Dlearo: "I first met Ben when we started the rehearsals for Big People and that first day I met him, I just knew he was a star as he carried himself with such grace. I felt so lucky to be working with a guy who I grew up listening to and watching on MTV throughout my teenage years.

"As the tour manager, I was fortunate to communicate with him a lot and I can tell you that Ben and the guys were really on to something 'big' with this band. They had a set list of hit songs, had plans to write new material, and the audiences loved them from the get-go."

Big People's first show was in August 1999, a four-day festival (featuring some forty bands) in Manchester, Tennessee, called the Itchycoo Park '99 Music Festival and Camping Experience and now known as the Bonoroo Music Festival. Big People performed in between the sets of legendary Paul Rodgers of Bad Company fame and John Entwistle of The Who. Others appearing on the festival bill included Styx, Blue Oyster Cult, Steppenwolf, Sammy Hagar, Joan Jett, Dave Mason, Leon Russell, Starship, and Marshall Tucker Band.

Following that festival, Big People played another festival in Nova Scotia that included Nazareth, ZZ Top, and several other bands, before going on tour as the opening act for Styx in the fall.

Big People then started booking some of their own shows as a headliner for the following spring, with a plan to start writing and recording original songs for a new album. Though Pat Travers had already opted to leave the band, Big People was certainly starting to build some momentum.

Billy Johnson: "The concert bookings for Big People were picking up in numbers, and the momentum was definitely in their favor. The advent of 'classic rock' radio was in full force at the time because there were a lot of baby boomers that felt they were displaced from music and what was coming out in the early nineties, especially in the genre of rock. Therefore, bands from the eighties were becoming popular again."

Also during this time, Ben was approached by the US Army about the ORR band booking a USO (United Services Organizations) tour of Scandinavia. Ben was very excited about the prospect of participating in this tour, for he very much believed in supporting America's troops, but unfortunately, the trip would never come to fruition.

Charlie Brusco: "We would have parties at my house for the band, and I can remember that we'd be downstairs having a drink, and when I would come upstairs, there would be my wife, Cindy, among a number of other

Ben with Peter Fonda and Jeff Carlisi, March of Dimes event in Atlanta, 1999.
Courtesy of Julie Snider-Mennie

female guests, and there in the middle would be Ben Orr, dressed like a rock star and holding court. It was during one of those parties that he casually mentioned to everyone that he was not feeling well."

EVERYTHING CHANGES, AGAIN

By early 2000, Ben's weight loss had increased and he wasn't feeling very well, so in April he went to a hospital for tests. Unfortunately for Ben, his family, his friends, and his fans, the prognosis was not good. In a shocking twist of fate, all of Ben's new plans in music and his personal life would be tragically derailed when he was diagnosed with pancreatic cancer, an incurable disease. All of this was happening with Big People already being scheduled to continue touring.

Julie Snider-Mennie had initially noticed that something was not quite right with Ben, so Jeff Carlisi made a phone call and arranged for him to visit Dr. William Mayfield, a top doctor at Piedmont Hospital in Atlanta, for tests.

Derek St. Holmes: "We were in Augusta, Georgia, and opening a show for Delbert McClinton, when Ben showed up not feeling very well. His complexion was off, but we didn't know what to think. Maybe he had hepatitis?

"We were all at the hospital with Ben and Julie and were stunned when we heard the news. . . . My wife had also recently beaten cancer. After Ben was diagnosed, we were all over at Julie's house, helping them as much as we could."

When the news got back to Ben's family and friends in Cleveland that he had been diagnosed with incurable cancer, some had a hard time believing what they were hearing.

Dante Rossi: "When I was told by Ginny Mayer before a gig that Benny had terminal cancer, I just couldn't believe it. In fact, it took a while for me to be able to even comprehend it. Benny left us way too soon, but I will tell you this right now, he loved life and lived every single day to the fullest."

Wayne Weston: "I can honestly say that growing up, I don't remember Benny ever getting sick. He never once missed a gig because of a cold or anything. Not once. This is why I was *even more* shocked when I learned about Benny being terminally ill. I can remember thinking, 'There's *no way* this can be true, because Benny is *never* sick.'"

After coming to terms with his fate, Ben decided he wanted to just keep doing what they were doing and carry on with the plan. The bottom line was that he wanted to continue playing with Big People until he could no longer remain onstage and doing what he was born to do and loved the most, playing music for as long as he could do it.

"Ben said, 'Just book it, [the tour] I'm there,'" Jeff Carlisi told *Rolling Stone* magazine in 2000.

Joe Dlearo: "Ben opted for chemotherapy in hopes of beating the cancer, but we watched as the chemo and cancer took the life out of his body. But also, let me tell you that Ben was one tough cat, as he insisted that we continue doing shows, and we made sure that Julie was with us at all times. Julie was the best I've ever seen in dealing with such a situation, taking everything she could on her shoulders, and we made sure that Ben could be as comfortable as possible on the road.

"Ben would literally be rolled onto the stage by wheelchair, head straight to a stool next to his bass rig, take a big hit off the oxygen mask, then walk up to the mic and totally kill it! It was magic for sure. Then, he would walk back to the stool and repeat for the next ninety minutes, singing hit after hit. He would smile at his bandmates, and I knew that he was really digging it.

"As time went on, we all got concerned that being out on the road was really not the place for Ben to be anymore, but he would quickly tell us that the tour would continue, and when he could not get up anymore, we were to prop him up in front of the mic!"

Jeff Carlisi: "Ben wanted us to book as many gigs as we could, and we became a tight family on the road, as Julie traveled with us on the tour bus. I remember we were doing a festival in Minot, North Dakota, with a bunch of other bands, including Quiet Riot, Huey Lewis and The News, Gary Puckett

Ben and Julie before a Big People concert opening for Styx, 1999.
Courtesy of Julie Snider-Mennie

and The Union Gap, and John Cafferty and The Beaver Brown Band. I was talking with Quiet Riot's Rudy Sarzo after the show and he said what a cool band he thought we were.

"Then I told him about the difficult hand Ben had been dealt and that he probably had only a few months to live. Rudy then mentioned how he had just been bitching about something meaningless that happened onstage. He just put his head down and said, 'The man knows he is going die and he's still out there playing . . . that's it!' As if to say that he really had nothing to be complaining about at all."

Despite the difficult situation, however, Ben and his bandmates created some wonderful memories in the limited time they shared together onstage and in life.

Julie recalled a time, after Ben had brought his motorcycle from Vermont down to Atlanta, the couple riding to a Derek St. Holmes solo show and Ben sitting in with the band that night. However, Ben didn't play the bass, instead he played his first instrument, the drums! Once again, and like he had done his whole life, Ben was just playing whatever instrument the gig might call for.

Liberty Devitto: "I can remember one time, Ben, Derek, and I going into a dive blues club in Atlanta and the band asked us if we wanted to sit in. When we asked Ben if he wanted to do it he just said 'I'm a bass player, not just that guy in The Cars!' So, we went up there and played and Ben was fantastic!"

Jeff Carlisi: "Ben and I loved ethnic and hot food. We just loved hot sauce or 'gasoline' as we often called it. I remember one time I got this hot sauce from New Orleans called *Pure Gold* that was really hot, and I mean it was lethal stuff. We were at an airport getting ready to fly somewhere and Ben was going off to eat at a sandwich shop and said to me 'Hey pardner, got any of that hot sauce?'

"So, he goes off to eat and soon after, Liberty calls me over to the shop window and there's Ben eating his sandwich, and he just looked up at us with a big smile as the sweat is just pouring off his face!

"Ben also loved to cook. I remember towards the end, he invited my wife and me over to Julie's house so he could make his Polish golumpkis [stuffed cabbage], and he was really into showing us how he prepared them. I also remember another time when we went out to dinner and didn't talk about music once, we just talked about our love of kids and how important Ben's son was to him."

Pat Travers: "When I found out that Ben had pancreatic cancer and was given maybe a few months to live, we were all devastated. I had been away from Big People for several months at that point and wasn't sure if I should try and call Ben. Honestly, at that point in my life, I did not know what I could possibly say that would have been any help to him.

"Since Ben's passing, however, I resolved that if I were ever in that situation again with someone I knew, I would not be afraid to try to reach out and say good-bye. I found out that Ben had died when I read the newspaper one morning, and I regret not making that phone call to him. It's good and right to say good-bye to your friends when you know they are going to be gone soon.

"However, I also have a really nice memory of Ben, from when Big People once played a show at Ruth Eckard Hall in Clearwater, Florida. My wife and our two kids, Amanda and Elijah, were also there. Elijah was the same age as his son and Ben just beamed when he saw him.

"I remember there was a portable wardrobe on wheels for hanging clothes, and Ben was pushing Elijah and Amanda around on it, and he had this big smile on his face that was competing with the sun for brightness! At that moment, Ben seemed truly happy and it was awesome to see."

From the end of June through August, Big People continued to travel and played a dozen shows in eight cities, before Ben flew back to Atlanta in September to finally reunite with his Cars bandmates one last time for The Cars' concert DVD release and Turner Studios interview.

· 20 ·

Cars' Last Drive

RECONCILIATION

$\mathcal{T}$he final interview with all five original members of The Cars was included in Rhino Home Video's live DVD release titled *The Cars Live, Recorded Live on Musikladen 1979*. The night before the interview, his bandmates got together with Ben for dinner, along with Julie Snider-Mennie, Ben's son, and a few folks from Rhino, at Ruth's Chris Steak House in downtown Atlanta.

Rhino had taken care of all the details, with a private area set up in the restaurant. And the room, of course, was full of love for Ben. His bandmates were very supportive but also understandably devastated over the sudden fate of their friend. Amazingly, Ben and Ric had not spoken in nearly a decade before that day.

Julie Snider-Mennie: "The restaurant was right down the road from my house, and Rhino was great about setting everything up for us. We all arrived at the restaurant at the same time, and Ben was so excited to see his 'band brothers' once again."

"Things happen and people get side-tracked and stubborn," Ric Ocasek told *Rolling Stone* in 2000. "But he [Ben] was my best friend. The longest and closest friend I ever had, for sure. He was just a model of strength."

David Robinson: "We pretty much knew what Ben's fate was, and we thought the interview would be a good opportunity to make sure he was included. To give him some space to talk a little bit during the interview and not just let everyone else do the talking. Of course, I hadn't seen Ben in a while, and the other guys in the band, I don't think they had realized just how sick he was. We were all pretty shocked about his condition."

Greg Hawkes, Ric Ocasek, Brett Milano, Ben, and David Robinson at the final Cars' press conference, Atlanta's Turner Studios, 2000.
Photo by Jeff Carlisi

"But then, when you looked at him and you started thinking about things like him not being there anymore, you just wanted everything to be as positive as possible and as much about Ben as you could.

"Along with the fact we were recording the interview for the fans to see, it was also an opportunity to get him on tape one more time, because sometimes Ben wouldn't say anything through an entire Cars' interview. So we tried to direct some comments his way. Of course, the interview was also very important because it finally got Ben and Ric back together again."

Ben's final good-bye with his bandmates was extremely difficult for everyone involved, as it marked the end of an era for one of America's most successful rock bands of the late 1970s and decadent 1980s.

CURTAIN CALL

Ben's final public appearance was on September 27, 2000, a Big People concert at the Alaska State Fair, in the city of Palmer. He had flown cross-country directly from The Cars' Atlanta interview in order to be there, and his strength was deteriorating.

Julie Snider-Mennie: "I was sitting behind Ben's bass rig at the Alaska show and just remember the stunning mountain range behind the crowd. What a perfect setting for Ben's final show. It looked like heaven on earth."

His Big People bandmates knew the time was drawing near, as Ben's always-pristine voice was beginning to waiver, and he told the band during the show to skip his signature song, "Drive," because he didn't feel strong enough to perform it.

Liberty DeVitto: "Ben had made it clear that he wanted to keep playing music until he couldn't anymore, but he was growing very weak when we were in Alaska. I can remember during the show, he turned to me and said 'Don't do "Drive."' I looked at Jeff [Carlisi] and said 'It's over.'"

Joe Dlearo: "Ben had lost a lot of weight and didn't look well, so the decision was made that Ben [would] fly back to Atlanta and have hospice take over. We were very fortunate to have had a great friend, Dr. Mayfield, become his consulting physician during Ben's difficult time."

Liberty DeVitto: "We all took it very hard. Derek [St. Holmes] didn't know what to do with himself. I can remember him sitting down and eating an entire pie, because he just didn't know what to do.

"When we flew back to the Atlanta airport, Ben was in a wheelchair and I had to go on to Florida where I lived. I shook his hand, hugged him, and said good-bye. I knew it was the last time I would ever see him, and it was really a tough thing to deal with."

Ben would have to miss the last scheduled Big People show in Texas, and still had aspirations of returning home to Cleveland and Boston for one last visit. Unfortunately, there was not enough time to make it happen because of his declining health.

Julie Snider-Mennie: "If it weren't for all of the guys, Jeff Carlisi, Liberty DeVitto, Rob Wilson, Derek St. Holmes, Joe Dlearo, Billy Johnson, and Dr. Bill Mayfield, we would have been at a real loss. They helped Ben so much with easing his journey into heaven. They helped keep Ben motivated to continue touring right up to his last show, and treated him no differently than they did before he was ill. They were 'brothers' and still are.

"Ben told me that during his career he *never* missed a single show and the only one he did miss was the last Big People date in Texas. I can tell you that he was none too happy about that! As soon as the guys got home from that show, though, they came right over to tell Ben all about it and had a great time enjoying each other's company. Our Big People family was always there whenever we needed them, and were invaluable in so many ways."

Two of Ben's old Cleveland bandmates growing up, Wayne Weston and Chris Kamburoff, were ready to fly to Atlanta to visit their friend one last time, but they had to cancel the trip because Ben's situation had severely deteriorated.

Chris Kamburoff: "I had bought the plane tickets to Atlanta for Wayne and me, but Julie said that it was going to be too late."

His longtime Cleveland friend, Diane Kokai-Akins, and many others from Ohio, Boston, and Vermont, were heartbroken that they could not see Ben during his last days. However, several friends and family members did get to talk to Ben on the phone, to offer their love and support.

Benjamin Orr passed away on October 3, 2000, at the Atlanta home of Julie Snider-Mennie, with his Big People family there to comfort him over those last few days.

Three days later, on October 6, Big People played a March of Dimes benefit show at The Tabernacle in Atlanta, with the show being dedicated to the life of Ben Orr. Jeff Carlisi dedicated a .38 Special song to his friend and the event also featured a PowerPoint presentation with photos of Ben and selected songs that he had sung with The Cars playing over the PA. A private funeral service was then held in Atlanta on Friday, October 13, so that Ben's Big People and Crossover Entertainment friends could pay their respects.

Julie Snider-Mennie: "The time with Ben before and while he was ill were some of the most important, exciting, life- and spiritual-expanding moments I've ever shared with anyone. Ben taught us so much about life, in the way he went through the process of cancer treatment and in day-to-day life. He was also an absolutely fantastic father to his son, and loved him more than he ever loved anyone."

There would be one final version of Big People, including original members Jeff Carlisi, Derek St. Holmes, and Liberty DeVitto, along with Rob Wilson on guitar and then vocalist/bassist Kyle Henderson (formerly of the band The Producers). However, neither lineup lasted long.

Liberty DeVitto: "Ben's loss was too great a void to fill, for as good as this new lineup was, Big People had lost their 'rock star' when they lost Ben."

MEMORIAL SERVICE AT CLEVELAND'S
ROCK & ROLL HALL OF FAME

On November 10, a private memorial service was held in Ben's honor at the Rock & Roll Hall of Fame in Cleveland, a truly fitting venue to honor a son of nearby Parma Heights.

The service was organized by Julie and emceed by Ben's friend and fellow Cleveland musician, Michael Stanley. With some one hundred fifty friends and relatives in attendance, the Benjamin Orr Memorial event was the first memorial service ever held at the Hall of Fame. The private service was held at the Hall's fourth-floor theater, with a live-feed broadcast in the main lobby for museum visitors to observe.

In an opening statement, Michael Stanley referred to Ben as "a cross between Elvis and Paul McCartney," and introduced the various guest speakers throughout the event. Ben's Mixed Emotions bandmate, Chris Kamburoff, was the first speaker, and after stating that Ben "will live on," led the audience in "The Lord's Prayer," before Diane Kokai-Akins spoke of Ben being like a brother to her.

Michael Stanley: "I actually never met Ben until I had asked him to contribute to the 1985 C.A.R.E. session charity project song, 'Eyes of the Children.'

"It was an honor to participate in the memorial service and it was a beautiful remembrance of a special guy, who left us far too soon. I was really looking forward to what his collaboration with Jeff Carlisi, Liberty DeVitto, and Derek St. Holmes was going to produce; those are four seriously talented dudes, and I think that Big People would have been a killer band!

"When I had said that Ben was a cross between Elvis and Paul McCartney, I meant that he had that very rare combination of 'bad boy' and 'charmer' that's hard to come by. I also truly felt that he never got the credit he deserved as a singer, songwriter, and overall musician. The man had serious chops in all those departments!

"For me, The Cars were a far more influential band than they've gotten credit for, and even this far down the line, it only takes about a measure-and-a-half of any of their records to know who you're listening to. I could roll out my laundry list of current members of the Rock & Roll Hall of Fame who have no business being there in front of The Cars.

"They were talented, successful, and innovative. That should be what the criteria for enshrinement is based on. And for 'Benny Eleven Letters,' a kid from Parma Heights who gave the rest of us Cleveland musicians a whole lot of inspiration and hope that we might follow in his footsteps, that [being enshrined in the Hall] would have been really cool!" [The Cars have since been inducted into the Rock & Roll Hall of Fame.]

During the service, the former Grasshoppers' Dante Rossi and (the late) John Matuska spoke of their love for Ben, with Rossi dedicating a poem from his mother to him, while Matuska spoke of Orr as being like a brother.

John Matuska: "In all the time I knew Ben, I don't remember an angry word between us. Ben really was a 'feel-good' guy because when you were around him, you couldn't help but feel good!"

The Grasshoppers' "band-boy," Steve Dudas: "Ben was extremely talented, often funny, and sometimes serious and introspective. Ben seemed very much at peace with the world when I last talked to him."

Cars' bandmates Greg Hawkes and David Robinson also attended the memorial service and reception.

"Ben was the *real* rock star of the band," Hawkes had stated during the event. "He had 'the look' and he had 'the attitude.' On the morning that I heard Ben died, I put on a couple of Cars albums, which I hadn't done in some time, just to hear his voice again."

David Robinson: "I actually didn't find out a lot about Ben's life until after he was gone, and that's kind of the way Ben was. Not really hiding anything, but not really sharing a lot either. You know, all the good stuff he did that anyone else would have put in their bio. He was always loyal as a friend, and did so much for everyone he knew.

"Turns out, I ended up only knowing a tiny fraction about how good Ben was to his friends. People were coming up to us at the memorial, one after another, with their 'Ben' stories. People who were both happy and sad at the same time, but they were *really* excited to talk about Ben. In fact, it was really hard to wrap my head around it, while it was all happening.

"It was just one person and story after another, and these were things that, if it were me, I would have been telling people about all along. I mean, it's only human nature to tell someone when you have done something good to help another, right?

"Ben wouldn't say anything about these things, and some of these gestures were not minor. Some were expensive things that he really had to follow through on for years and years with people, and really invest his time in.

"At that memorial service, I learned more about Ben in one day than in all the time I knew him. I really had no idea of the extent of his generosity and kindness. Both at the memorial service and the reception afterward, we were just barraged with people. Some people I'd heard of, but mostly strangers, who all had stories about Ben.

"People saying things like 'Ben did this for me and my family when I was down and out,' and another person said, 'Ben flew me up to Boston when I was out of work and bought me a new car.'

"Literally, my jaw dropped over it all!

"I swear, Ben was like Elvis Presley in that he was a guy who stayed connected with all of his neighborhood friends, didn't have much interest in getting outside of those people, and he wanted them around. If that meant giving them a flight to Boston, then that's what he did. He'd just pick them up, wherever they were."

Tom Hambridge: "I was asked to speak at Ben's memorial service at the Rock & Roll Hall of Fame and it was a very sad day. He touched my life, and I spoke about how I knew him. The world knew him as a 'golden boy' rock star, but the Ben I knew was just a nice, down-to-earth guy, who just so happened to be loaded with talent. I really loved Ben and it was an honor to make music with him. I miss him very much."

At the memorial service, Hambridge stated, "He had the gift of not saying too much, and he also didn't talk about himself at all. If you were his friend, you were a friend for life. He met Julie and started spending time in Atlanta, and he always carried himself with dignity."

David Robinson: "Mostly, I think about how much more I would have enjoyed Ben now. There were lots of times when I wouldn't see him for a long time, and I didn't really know what he was doing or how he felt.

"You know, there's all these great things we're saying about how nice a person Ben was to his friends, but, on top of all that, he was truly one of the best singers I ever heard in my life. That ever lived, practically!"

At the end of the memorial service, Julie Snider-Mennie was the last to speak.

"When I think of Ben, and all that he meant to me, language is just inadequate. Ben, I wanted you to 'stay the night,' but that wasn't God's plan. We had each other for one glorious year. Thank you and Ben, I love you."

Julie Snider-Mennie: "Ben had a great big loving heart and he wanted to share it with everyone who came into his life. Everyone who knew Ben loved him, and I did too. A lifetime for one person is different for everyone, and it seemed that he left us much too soon. Luckily, I was able to spend an unbelievably beautiful year with Ben, and for that, I will always be very thankful."

In a tribute, his close friend and music partner Ric Ocasek wrote a song for Ben. Titled "Silver," the song appeared on his 2005 solo release, *Nexterday*. Greg Hawkes also played keyboards on the song. Almost melancholy in its approach, the low-tone track has a cerebral, psychedelic feel to it.

• 21 •

Move Like This

Early in 2010, Ric Ocasek, Greg Hawkes, David Robinson, and Elliot Easton decided to get together and make music once again. After twenty-four years, Ric wrote some songs and they recorded the first Cars album of new material since *Door to Door* was released in 1987.

Out of respect for Ben, The Cars did not attempt to bring in a bass player as a "replacement" for their late bandmate, for they and Cars fans already knew there was no replacing such a unique and enigmatic figure as Orr. Instead, Hawkes and the project's co-producer, Jack Knife Lee, shared bass duties in the studio. Hawkes also used one of Ben's bass guitars during the recording sessions.

"It seemed strange when Ben wasn't there for rehearsals," Ric Ocasek told *Rolling Stone* in February 2011. "I'm kinda used to the fact that he passed away a while ago, but when we first got together, it was like 'oh yeah, it's just the four of us here. Whoever wants to play bass, just play.'"

"Ben sort of caught on a little late about the real dynamics of the band, but we needed him," David Robinson told *Rolling Stone* in June 2011. "He was the guy who could go in and sing every song on the first take, with a cigarette dangling out of his mouth, and a cup of coffee in his hand, like it was nothing for him to do."

Ocasek sang lead vocals on all ten tracks; however, in the same 2011 interview with *Rolling Stone*, and just after *Move Like This* was released, he proclaimed, "I was aware that on half of the new songs, Ben would have done better than I did. But we never wanted [to bring in] anybody from the outside. I miss his singing, being thrilled by it."

Released in May, *Move Like This* debuted at #7 on the *Billboard* album chart (#2 on the *Billboard* "Top Rock Albums" chart), while the single, "Sad

Song," reached #33 on the *Billboard* "Rock Songs" chart. Although it wasn't a huge-selling CD, Cars fans were thrilled to see the band together again.

David Robinson: "Ric wrote some great songs, and we really loved how the album turned out, but I still have to wonder how good it all could have been if Ben had sung and played on it."

"Now it's different," Ocasek said in the 2011 *Rolling Stone* interview. "I can hear the Cars' harmonies in Greg's and Elliot's voices, but it is missing that 'Ben' thing, I can easily hear the three voices that should be there."

David Robinson: "Ben's voice was so incredible. It was just so natural and his timing and inflection was so unbelievable to me. All the personality that he could inject into a song, when he was just standing there in the studio smoking cigarettes and saying nothing. Then, to go out there and deliver something like 'Drive,' then he'd just shut it off and go back and sit in a chair and smoke. I'd just think, 'What is he doing and how the fuck did he learn to do that? And how does it sound so damn good?' He was just unbelievable in that way."

The Cars completed a brief eleven-city tour, which started in Seattle on the very day the CD was released, and ended some two weeks later at the House of Blues in the band's hometown of Boston. In a heart-warming gesture, the band invited Ben's son to the Boston concert, and he was able to hang out with his father's bandmates before they went onstage that night.

The last sentence of the *Move Like This* CD liner notes simply states: "Ben, your spirit was with us on this one." His bandmates' statement proves to this day the positive impact Benjamin Orr left on not only his "band brothers," but also his family, friends, and so many Cars' fans around the world. This is truly a sign of a rock-and-roll life lived to the fullest.

Ben in New York City, *Heartbeat City* photo shoot, 1984.
Ben Orr Collection

Afterword

$\mathscr{I}$n the spring of 2018, and on the cusp of the fortieth anniversary of their iconic debut album, the remarkable careers of Benjamin Orr and The Cars culminated with the ultimate recognition for any musician: induction into Cleveland's Rock & Roll Hall of Fame. How fitting that the native son, Benjamin Orr, from the suburb of Parma Heights, posthumously returns home to immortalize his legacy as the "Clevelander" who would stop at nothing to live out his rock-and-roll dream.

Cleveland is a damn proud city that takes its rock and roll very seriously. Therefore, this particular induction into the Rock Hall for "one of their own" is truly a meaningful and monumental event for many in the city, especially those who personally knew and rocked with "Benny Eleven Letters" back in the day!

A common thread (among many) often expressed about Ben throughout the interview process was his generosity and fierce loyalty to his family, friends, and the city of Cleveland. Ben was described as respectful, even-keeled, thoughtful, friendly, and a "feel-good" person, all traits that can surely be traced back to his upbringing, traits that this author experienced firsthand when I visited Cleveland to witness The Cars get inducted. The people I encountered were gracious, kind, and so appreciative of my upcoming book about the "native son."

I was lucky enough to not only witness The Cars induction ceremony but also enjoy the city for six days, checking out the scene and promoting my book about the late, great Benjamin Orr with my public relations coordinator and editorial assistant, Donna Neale. The reception that I received in Cleveland was more than I could have hoped for. The feelings of respect, pride, and joy regarding Orr's induction into the sacred Rock Hall were obvious.

The last day of my adventure in Cleveland was a heady and emotional one. I paid a visit to two of Ben's longtime friends and bandmates, Wayne Weston and Chris Kamburoff, gentlemen I now call friends, who helped me tremendously throughout the process of writing about Ben's early days. They gave me gifts, we had a great time, and they expressed happiness and respect for my book about their "band brother," just what you would expect from a couple of Benny's old friends from Cleveland, right?

I also made the forty-five-minute drive on that cool and gray day to visit Ben's resting place on the outskirts of Cleveland. I spent eleven years of my life writing the story of this man, and although I never had the privilege of meeting him in person, I know *so* much about him now that in a way, I feel like I did know him personally. Therefore, it only seemed fitting to visit Ben's resting place, along with Donna, who has as much (perhaps even more) respect and admiration for Ben as yours truly.

As I stood in front of the gravestone, it was a very emotional moment and hard to put into words, but it sure felt right. Some sort of culmination for me, with finally finishing the book, coming to Ben's hometown of Cleveland to see his band *finally* get inducted, and now visiting his resting place before heading back home to Vermont . . . where Ben once resided himself, I am proud to say. While trying to process it afterward with Donna I was a little tongue-tied, so I asked her to share her impressions of what I had experienced. Here is what she wrote:

> I sit in the rental car near the entrance to the cemetery, giving my friend Joe a moment of privacy at Benjamin's grave. The rain has stopped, and though it is still pretty cold, the birds chirp and sing and the trees sway a little in the wind. I can see from my position behind him that Joe's shoulders are hunched a little, head bowed, hands in his pockets, and I wonder what all he must be feeling . . . what thoughts fill his mind.
>
> The fast-paced celebrations of the weekend have quieted and time has slowed down a bit. Joe is alone with his reflections.
>
> Eleven years. Eleven years he's worked to tell this story. I know that during that time Joe has felt the highest highs and the lowest lows. Elation and despair, triumph and loss, staunch support and violent opposition. I know that no one has had higher expectations of himself, no one has had greater doubts than he has had. As a writer myself and as a devoted fan of Benjamin Orr, I can see how that would be: it is a serious responsibility to narrate the life story of another person, especially one so loved and sought after.
>
> This is a "mountain top" moment for Joe, and yet the pressures continue. He desires for the fans to be pleased. He wants to shed light on a piece of rock history. He hopes to make his loved ones proud. But above all, he wants Benjamin Orr to be known and honored. I'm not sure if Joe

is at peace with it; if he believes he has done that for Ben. For my part, I am convinced no one could have done it better.

When it was time to leave, I looked around for some kind of sign, something to tell me that somehow Ben knew that I was there. Not just at his resting place, but that I had come to Cleveland to promote my upcoming book about his amazing life and to see his band enter the Hall of Fame. I looked up at the tops of the trees and as a slight breeze appeared at that moment, I thought, "Okay, Ben . . . I'll take that as your sign."

But then, as I got back in the car and we were driving off, I turned on the radio (WMMS in Cleveland, of course) and what did we hear, perfectly on cue?

"I don't mind you coming here . . . and wasting all my time . . ." Yes, it was Ben, right there in all his glory singing the timeless Cars classic "Just What I Needed"! I looked at Donna in disbelief—it literally gave me goose bumps—and all I could do was start laughing in amazement as we drove down the road. Ben had surprised me like this before, appearing out of nowhere in song at just the opportune time, but this was different. He was telling me that he was happy that we came to Cleveland to celebrate. I will never forget the feeling of pride and accomplishment I felt at that moment.

Acknowledgments

$\mathscr{F}$irst and foremost, I would like to thank my family: my wife, Kelly; my son, Nate; and daughter, Erin, who have always encouraged my writing endeavors, no matter how many countless hours I spend in front of the computer. I also want to thank my parents, my brothers and their families, and my wife's family for their support.

I want to give special thanks to David Robinson and Greg Hawkes of The Cars, who graciously provided memories about their bandmate for this book. Ric Ocasek and Elliot Easton of The Cars, and record producer Roy Thomas Baker, declined to be interviewed.

I also want to give big thanks to my "Cleveland Connection." I cannot thank Wayne Weston, Chris Kamburoff, Joe Kurilec, Bob Paris, Diane Kokai-Akins, Neil Akins, David Spero, Michael Stanley, and Deanna Adams enough for all their generosity, gifts, kindness, insights, photos, and direction. Without you, this book could never have painted as clear a picture of Benny's early life.

Also, special thanks to Kristina Orr, Diane Grey Page, Judith Orr, Edita Hartig, and Julie Snider-Mennie for their contributions and kindness.

Special thanks to Leanne Jewett for all her editorial and publishing guidance, and Donna Neale for her endless editorial, proofing, and book-promotional contributions.

I would also like to thank (in alphabetical order) the many people who assisted and supported me or consented to be interviewed, contributed photos, or provided insight for this book: Luis Aira, Carter Alan, John Aleksic, Joe Barbaria, Boby Bear, Mark Bell, Steve Berkowitz, Stephen Bickford, Michael Blackmer, Charlie Brusco, Wally and Kay Bryson, Don Burge, Glen Burtnik, Chris Butler, Jeff Carlisi, Michael Cartellone, Mark Cripps, George Daly, Davey Davis, Joan Dempsey, Liberty DeVitto, Joe Dlearo,

Stephen Dodge, Patrick Donahue, Steve Dudas, Glenn Evans, Charlie Farren, Lou Fazio, Alex Finley, Cn Fletcher, Billie Flory, David Frangioni, Kurt and Natalie Gaber, Irene Gaffigan, Tom Gahan, George Gell, Bill Gerber, Elliot Gilbert, Marco Glaviano, Peter Goddard, Jim Goodkind, John Gorman, Brad Hallen, Tom Hambridge, Jim Harold, Harry Harwat, Robert "Jesse" Henderson, Joe Holaday, Brian Jewett, Billy Johnson, Kevin Johnson, Philip Kamin, Allan Kaufman, Bobby Kimball, Dan Klawon, Cyndy Lea Klawon, Larry Klein, Nick Koumoutseas, Robin Lane, Chris Lannon, John Laurenti, Jeff Lock, Bill Louis, Danny Louis, Robin Lull, Jon Macey, Janet Macoska, Carl Maduri, Carl Maduri Jr., Natalie Mandziuk, Walt Masky, (the late) John Matuska, Jimmy McCarthy, Rod McCarthy, Kevin McCarty, Dan "Peanuts" McGinty, Sharon McGuire, Lockie McNeish, (the late) Adrian Medeiros, Andy Mendelson, Brent Milano, (the late) Thom Moore, Fuzzbee Morse, John Muzzy, Jim Nielsen, (the late) Richard Nolan, Pamela Olson, Charlie O'Neal, Rick O'Neal, Benjamin Orr (Ben's son), Cathy Perez, Frank Perry, Andrei Cristian Petrescu, Mel Posner, Robert Post, Louis Pratile, Andy Pratt, Ross Ramsay, Melanie Ransom, Barbara Rhind, Ron Riddle, Bill Riseman, Todd Roberto, Ebet Roberts, Dante and (the late) Maria Rossi, Bill Salom, (the late) Jane Scott, Victoria Simon, Marshall Simpkins, Roland Solomon, (the late) Murray Soull, Derek St. Holmes, Marilyn Dudas-Stolz, Charlotte Tharp-Streeter, Tyler and Carolee Sweet, (the late) David Tedeschi, Mickey Thomas, Pat Travers, (the late) Robert Tuozzo, Walter Turbitt, Mark Turner, Margie van Lierop, Joe Viglione, Don Webster, Nancy Bryson-Western, John Wiley, Bill "Trip" Wilkins, Tom Yates, J. Yuenger, and Jerry Zadar.

Last, but certainly not least, I would like to thank all of the Benjamin and Cars fans from all over the world (there are just too many to list) who contacted me along the way and remained interested, supportive, and patient throughout the long process of writing this book. There were many times when the fans' support and encouragement surely kept me going, and you all know who you are!

In the end, thank you, Ben. Your music, energy, and loyalty to others (and also from time to time, your magical appearance on the radio when I *really* needed it) inspired me through this process, and I hope the results help paint the clearest picture of your unique life, talent, and true greatness. "Let's Go!"

Bibliography

Sources are arranged under the subject of the article, book, or person quoted in order by date.

BAKER, ROY THOMAS

Clark, Rick. "Roy Thomas Baker: Taking Chances and Making Hits." *Mix: Professional Audio & Music Production*, April 1, 1999, https://www.mixonline.com/record ing/roy-thomas-baker-taking-chances-and-making-hits-373531.

"Roy Thomas Baker Speaks About The Cars Debut." *Daily Events Book*, http://daily eventsbookpagethree.blogspot.com/2006/01/roy-thomas-baker-speaks-about-cars .html?m=0 January 17, 2006.

CARLISI, JEFF

Colapinto, John. "Benjamin Orr: A Life in Rock & Roll." *Rolling Stone*, November 23, 2000.

THE CARS

Milano, Brett. *The Sound of Our Town: A History of Boston Rock & Roll*. Boston: Commonwealth Editions, 2007.

HAWKES, GREG

Colapinto, John. "Benjamin Orr: A Life in Rock & Roll." *Rolling Stone*, November 23, 2000.

MAYER, GINNY

Colapinto, John. "Benjamin Orr: A Life in Rock & Roll." *Rolling Stone*, November 23, 2000.

MILKWOOD

Levitt, Howard. *Record World.*

MOORE, THOM

"Just What I Needed." J. Yuenger website, http://www.jyuenger.com/. October 11, 2011.

OCASEK, RIC

Pareles, Jon. "Power Steering." *Rolling Stone*, January 25, 1979.
"The Cars: Second Time Lucky; Product Report." *Trouser Press*, August 1979.
"The Cars, Designed for Platinum MPG." *Washington Rock Concert*, August/September 1979.
"Innerview—The Cars." *Record Review*, October 1979.
Flannigan, Bill. "The Cars." *Music and Sound Output*, February 1984.
Laskosky, Lance and Fred Rogers. "Driving His Point Across," *Only Music*, November 1987.
The Cars: Recorded Live on Musikladen 1979. Los Angeles: Rhino Home Video, 2000.
Colapinto, John. "Benjamin Orr: A Life in Rock & Roll." *Rolling Stone*, November 23, 2000.
"Ric Ocasek Nexterday in Stores September 27th" *Girlposse.com*, August 2005. https://web.archive.org/web/20051027045929/http://www.girlposse.com:80/re views/music/ric_ocasek_0805.html.
Fricke, David. "Out of The Garage: Ric Ocasek on Reuniting The Cars." *Rolling Stone*, February 17, 2011.

Fricke, David. "The Return of The Cars." *Rolling Stone*, June 9, 2011.
Amorosi, A. D. "A Conversation with The Cars' Rick Ocasek," *Magnet*, May 2016.
Fricke, David. Liner notes. *Heartbeat City* (expanded edition). Rhino Records, 2018.

ORR, BENJAMIN

Scott, Jane. "The Cars Take Off Fast in the Record Derby," *The Plain Dealer*, June 9, 1978.
Morse, Steve. "The Cars Spin Home." *Boston Globe*, December 7, 1978.
Pareles, Jon. "Power Steering," *Rolling Stone*, January 25, 1979.
"The Cars: Second Time Lucky, Product Report." *Trouser Press*, August 1979.
Candy-O press kit. Elektra Records, 1979.
Dagnal, Cynthia. *Super Groups*. N.p.: Tempo Books, 1981.
Considine, J. D. "The Cars," *Musician*, January 1982.
"Ben Orr Is Still in the Driver's Seat with The Cars," *The Plain Dealer*, November 1, 1985.
"Benjamin Orr." Elektra Records biography, 1985.
Goddard, Peter, and Philip Kamin. *The Cars*. New York: McGraw-Hill, 1986.
Graff, Gary. "A Few Words with . . . Benjamin Orr." *Detroit Free Press*, November 21, 1986.
Van Matre, Lynn. "Another Solo Act for Cars." *Chicago Tribune*, December 30, 1986.
Muni, Scott. *Line One* radio interview, November 1986.
Tannenbaum, Rob. "Mr. Casual Steps Out" *Musician*, March 1987.
Hot Rocks radio interview with Steve O'Brien, October 1987.
"Take Another Look." *Goldmine Magazine*, August 1, 1997.

PAGE, DIANE GREY

Van Matre, Lynn. "Another Solo Act for Cars." *Chicago Tribune*, December 30, 1986.

ROBINSON, DAVID

"The Cars: Second Time Lucky; Product Report." *Trouser Press*, August 1979.
Pareles, Jon. "Power Steering." *Rolling Stone Magazine*, January 25, 1979.
Tannenbaum, Rob. *I Want My MTV: The Uncensored Story of the Music Video Revolution*. New York: Dutton, 2011.
Fricke, David. "The Return of The Cars." *Rolling Stone*, June 9, 2011.

SARTORI, MAXANNE

Pareles, Jon. "Power Steering." *Rolling Stone*, January 25, 1979.

VIGLIONE, JOE

Drive: The Cars Fanzine, January 2001.

WEBSTER, DON

"Don Webster: Upbeat Nice Guy, Forecasted Music Stars and Weather." *Cleveland Seniors.com*, 2007. http://www.clevelandseniors.com/people/donwebster.htm.

Interviews

Aira, Luis. Email interviews, 2015, 2018
Akins, Diane Kokai. Phone and letter interviews, 2011–2016, 2018
Aleksic, John. Email interview, 2010
Alan, Carter. Email interview, 2015
Barbaria, Joe. Email interview, 2016
Bear, Boby. Email interview, 2017
Bell, Mark. Email interview, 2015
Berkowitz, Steve. Email interviews, 2014, 2018
Bickford, Stephen. Phone and email interviews, 2015, 2018
Blackmer, Michael. Phone and email interviews, 2015, 2018
Brusco, Charlie. Email interview, 2013
Burge, Don. Email interview, 2016
Burtnik, Glenn. Email interview, 2014
Butler, Chris. Email interviews, 2015, 2018
Carlisi, Jeff. Phone and email interviews, 2013, 2018
Cartellone, Michael. Email interview, 2016
Cripps, Mark. Email interview, 2015
Daly, George. Phone and email interviews, 2015, 2018
Davis, Davey. In person and email interviews, 2015
DeVitto, Liberty. Email interviews, 2013, 2018
Dickson, Jeff. Email interviews, 2016–2017
Dlearo, Joe. Email interviews, 2013, 2018
Dodge, Stephen. Email interview, 2014
Dudas, Steve. Email interviews, 2015–2017, 2018
Evans, Glenn. Email interviews, 2014–2016, 2018
Farren, Charlie. Email interviews, 2012, 2018

Fazio, Lou. Email interviews, 2016–2017

Fletcher, Cn. Email interview, 2014

Frangioni, David. Phone and email interviews, 2013–2015, 2018

Gahan, Tom. Email interview, 2016

Gerber, Bill. Email interviews, 2017, 2018

Gilbert, Elliot. Email interview, 2017

Goodkind, Jim ("Jas"). Email interviews, 2012, 2018

Gorman, John. Email interviews, 2008, 2018

Hallen, Brad. Email interviews, 2013, 2017

Hambridge, Tom. Email interviews, 2009, 2018

Harold, Jim. Phone and email interviews, 2018

Hartig, Edita. Phone and email interviews, 2015, 2018

Hawkes, Greg. In person and email interviews, 2009, 2013

Henderson, Robert "Jesse." Email interview, 2008

Holiday, Joe. Email and phone interviews, 2018

Johnson, Billy. Email interviews, 2013, 2018

Johnson, Peter C. Email interview, 2018

Kamburoff, Chris. Phone and email interviews, 2008–2017, 2018

Kamin, Philip. Phone and email interviews, 2010, 2018

Kaufman, Allan. Phone and email interviews, 2015, 2018

Kimball, Bobby. Email interview, 2017

Klawon, Dan. Phone and email interviews, 2015, 2018

Klein, Larry. Phone and email interviews, 2016, 2018

Koumoutseas, John. Email interview, 2017

Koumoutseas, Nick. Phone and email interviews, 2015–2016

Kurilec, Joe. Email interviews, 2010, 2017–2018

Lane, Robin. Email interviews, 2010, 2018

Lannon, Chris. Email interview, 2013

Lentini, Tony. Email interviews, 2010, 2018

Lock, Jeff. Email interview, 2009

Louis, Danny. Email interviews, 2015, 2018

Macey, Jon. Email interview, 2009

Macoska, Janet. Email interviews, 2015, 2018

Maduri, Carl. Email interviews, 2016–2017

Masky, Walt. Email interviews, 2008, 2018

Matuska, John. Email interviews, 2013, 2018

McCarthy, Jimmy. Email interview, 2015

McCarthy, Rod. Email interview, 2018

McCarty, Kevin. Email interviews, 2015, 2018

McGinty, Dan "Peanuts." Phone and email interviews, 2008

McNeish, Lockie. Email interview, 2017

Medeiros, Adrian. Phone and email interviews, 2012
Mendelson, Andy. Email interview, 2016
Mennie, Julie Snider. Phone and email interviews, 2012–2018
Milano, Brett. Email interviews, 2008–2009, 2018
Morse, Fuzzbee. Email interviews, 2015, 2018
Muzzy, John. Email interviews, 2015, 2018
Nielsen, Jim. Email interview, 2015
Nolan, Richard. Email interview, 2009
O'Neal, Charlie. Phone and email interviews, 2015–2016, 2018
O'Neal, Rick. Email interviews, 2015, 2018
Orr, Judith. Email interviews, 2010–2016, 2018
Orr, Kristina. Email interviews, 2015–2017
Page, Diane Grey. Email interviews, 2010–2015
Paris, Bob. Phone and Email interviews, 2016–2017
Perry, Frank. Email interviews, 2016–2017
Posner, Mel. Email interview, 2016
Post, Robert. Email interviews, 2015, 2018
Pratile, Louis. Email interview, 2012
Pratt, Andy. Email interviews, 2014, 2018
Ramsay, Ross. Email interview, 2013
Ransom, Melanie. Email interviews, 2016–2018
Rhind, Barbara. Email interviews, 2016, 2018
Riddle, Ron. Email interview, 2015
Roberts, Ebet. Phone and email interviews, 2012–2016, 2018
Robinson, David. Phone and email interviews, 2009, 2013
Rossi, Dante. Phone interviews, 2012–2013
Salom, Bill. Email interview, 2015
Saul, Murray. Email interview, 2008
Scott, Jane. Phone and email interviews, 2009
Simon, Victoria. Email and letter interviews, 2009, 2018
Simpkins, Marshall. Phone and email interviews, 2018
Solomon, Roland. Email interviews, 2010–2012
Spero, David. Email interviews, 2010, 2018
St. Holmes, Derek. Phone and email interviews, 2013
Stanley, Michael. Email interviews, 2014, 2018
Stolz, Marilyn Dudas. Phone and email interviews, 2018
Sweet, Tyler. Phone and email interviews, 2018
Tedeschi, David. Phone and email interviews, 2010, 2012
Thomas, Mickey. Email interview, 2013
Travers, Pat. Email interview, 2013
Turbitt, Walter. Email interview, 2015

van Lierop, Margie. Phone and email interviews, 2015–2016
Viglione, Joe. Email interview, 2008
Webster, Don. Email interviews, 2008
Western, Nancy Bryson. Email interview, 2013
Weston, Wayne. Phone interviews, 2008–2017, 2018
Wiley, John. Email interviews, 2009–2010
Wilkins, Bill "Trip." Email interview, 2007
Yates, Tom. Email interview, 2010
Zadar, Jerry. Phone and email interviews, 2012

Selected Index

About the Author

Joe Milliken has been a music journalist, freelance writer, editor, and website publisher for over twenty years. A die-hard music fan with a degree in visual arts, Joe would ultimately turn to writing about music and the arts as his creative outlet. He first wrote as a local reporter and then sports/arts and entertainment editor, before moving into independent freelance and public relations writing for various local and national newspapers, magazines, and businesses.

In 2014, Joe launched *Standing Room Only*, a website dedicated to music and the arts on a local (New England area) and national level, with a concentration on promoting not only nationally recognized bands, musicians, and artists, but also those artists and performers who might not always receive the attention they deserve.

Let's Go! Benjamin Orr and The Cars is Milliken's first book, a labor of love written in his spare time and spanning over a decade in the making. Originally from Boston, Joe now resides in peaceful southern Vermont with his wife, Kelly; son, Nate; and daughter, Erin. To learn more about Joe's writing activities, visit his website at www.standing-room-only.info, and follow his Benjamin Orr book activity at www.facebook.com/BenOrrBook/ and on Twitter: @benorrbook.

Lightning Source UK Ltd.
Milton Keynes UK
UKHW041037141218
333811UK00021B/373/P